PACHI TANGLANG CHUAN

EIGHT ULTIMATE PRAYING MANTIS FIST

八極矇昭拳

PACHI TANGLANG CHUAN
EIGHT ULTIMATE PRAYING MANTIS FIST

Master Su Yu-Chang
蘇昱彰

Translated from the Spanish by
Juan Acevedo and Cristóbal Rodríguez
衛安皇　　　　李德寶

八極螳螂國際武藝協會
Pachi Tanglang International Martial Arts Institute
Cambridge · Kristiansand · Taipei

Title of the original edition:
Pachi Tanglang Chuan
Editorial Visión Net
San Benito 21, local
28029 Madrid, Spain

Original transcription in Spanish by Francisco Orejudo
Photographs by Su Yu-Chang and Marit Ramberg

In the photographs appear:

José Antonio Bonilla	Izuru Kawai
Guillermo Arroyo	Wei-Jen Su
Iraima Orejudo	Carlos Alonso
Hisakata Noda	Chikai Shum
Yasuhiro Suzuki	Tetsuya Yamochi

Special thanks to Daniel Collins and Bernhard Strauss
for their help in the revision of the final English version

Copyright © Su Yu-Chang 2014

This first edition published in 2014 by
Pachi Tanglang International Martial Arts Institute
Cambridge · Kristiansand · Taipei

ISBN: 978 82 303 2650 3

*All rights reserved. No part of this publication
may be reproduced, stored in a retrieval system,
or transmitted in any form or by any means, electronic,
mechanical, photocopying, recording, or otherwise,
without the prior written permission of the Publisher.*

Pachi Tanglang International Martial Arts Institute is a cultural association for the dissemination and teaching of the traditional aspects of Chinese culture, including philosophy, martial arts, acupuncture and meditation. Its founder and president is Master Su Yu-Chang. Its head office is in Taipei, Taiwan, with branches in several countries.
For more information, see contact details at the end of the book.
Taiwan Tatungshan Pachimen International Martial Arts Institute
5th Floor, No. 26, Section 4, Xinyi Road, Da'an District
Taipei City 106
Taiwan – Republic of China
Tel: +886-2-27000787 | Fax: +886-2-27000331

Contents

再版自序		xi
Author's Preface		xiii
Translators' Preface		xv
1	Chinese Martial Arts	1
	1.1 Northern and southern styles	4
	1.2 Internal and external styles	5
	1.3 Names and forms	9
	1.4 Historical review	13
	1.5 Martial Arts today	21
2	History and Masters of *Pachi Chuan*	23
	2.1 The origins	23
	2.2 Historical *Pachi Chuan*	26
	2.3 Li Shu-Wen	29
	2.4 Li Shu-Wen's successors	32
	2.5 Liu Yun-Chiao	34
	2.6 Su Yu-Chang	41
3	*Pachi Chuan*	46
	3.1 Simplicity and effectiveness	46
	3.2 Studying *Pachi Chuan*	49
4	Learning *Pachi Chuan*	53
	4.1 *Pachi*: Eight extremes	53
	4.2 Learning stages of *Pachi Chuan*	55
	4.2.1 Natural relaxation	56
	4.2.2 Stretching the tendons and separating the joints	58

	4.2.3	Energy of the Five Elements	62
	4.2.4	Energy in any point of the body	63
	4.2.5	Cleansing the marrow	64
4.3	*Pachi Chuan* and *Pikua Chuan* forms		65
4.4	Traditional transmission in Kung Fu		66
4.5	The essential forms		67
	4.5.1	*Ting Tzu Pa Pu Suh*	67
	4.5.2	*Chinkan Pa Suh*	69
	4.5.3	*Hsiao Pachi Chuan*	71
4.6	Detailed description of two forms		72
	4.6.1	*Ting Tzu Pa Pu Suh*	72
	4.6.2	*Kaimen Chuan* two-man form	94

5 *Pachi Chuan* Techniques — 113

- 5.1 Fists . . . 114
- 5.2 Stances . . . 116
  - 5.2.1 The twelve methods of stance training . . . 117
- 5.3 Applying the different parts of the body . . . 122
  - 5.3.1 The head . . . 122
  - 5.3.2 Basic *Pachi Chuan* elbows . . . 124
  - 5.3.3 Three basic *Kao* ("leaning") techniques . . . 125
  - 5.3.4 Feet . . . 126
  - 5.3.5 Palms . . . 130
  - 5.3.6 Sacrum-Coccyx . . . 131
  - 5.3.7 The back . . . 132
  - 5.3.8 The hips . . . 133
  - 5.3.9 The knees . . . 134

6 Power and Energy in *Pachi Chuan* — 135

- 6.1 Character of the energy in *Pachi Chuan* . . . 136
- 6.2 Ways of projecting energy in *Pachi Chuan* . . . 137
  - 6.2.1 Sinking energy projection . . . 138
  - 6.2.2 Cross energy projection . . . 140
  - 6.2.3 Spiraling energy projection . . . 141
  - 6.2.4 Explosive energy projection . . . 142
  - 6.2.5 Infiltrating energy projection . . . 143
- 6.3 Energy and its flow . . . 145
  - 6.3.1 The energy of the Five Elements . . . 146

	6.3.2 The energy of the Three Sages	148
	6.3.3 *Wei Chi* and *Ying Chi*	149
6.4	Applying energy in *Pachi Chuan*	150
6.5	"Doors" in *Pachi Chuan*	154
6.6	Energy and technique in Martial Arts	155
6.7	Effects of energy in Martial Arts	157
6.8	*Chi Kung* of *Pachi Chuan*	158

7 Philosophy of *Pachi Tanglang Chuan* — 161

- 7.1 Energy, essence, spirit . . . 161
- 7.2 Internal energy . . . 165
- 7.3 Natural energy . . . 166
- 7.4 Great Circle and Small Circle . . . 168
- 7.5 Spirit, thoughts . . . 169
- 7.6 The ultimate purpose of Kung Fu . . . 172

8 Pikua Chuan — 175

- 8.1 *Pikua Chuan*. Chopping and hanging . . . 175
- 8.2 Techniques and study . . . 177
- 8.3 *Chang*. The palm . . . 178
- 8.4 Twelve characteristic movements . . . 179
- 8.5 Stances . . . 181
- 8.6 Basic *Pikua* steps . . . 181
- 8.7 *Pai Ta Kung* . . . 182
- 8.8 The practice of *Pikua* . . . 183
- 8.9 *Chi Kung* . . . 185
- 8.10 Basic movements of *Pikua Chuan* . . . 188

9 Tanglang Chuan — 200

- 9.1 Praying Mantis: variety, speed, and change . . . 201
- 9.2 Origins of *Tanglang Chuan*. Wang Lang . . . 202
- 9.3 Modern Masters . . . 206
- 9.4 The *Tanglang Chuan* of Master Su Yu-Chang. His masters . . . 208

10 *Tanglang Chuan* Styles — 213

- 10.1 *Ing Tanglang*. Hard Praying Mantis . . . 214
  - 10.1.1 Seven Star Praying Mantis . . . 214

10.1.2 Plum Flower Praying Mantis	215
10.1.3 Secret Door Praying Manis	216
10.1.4 Shake-off Hand Praying Mantis	217
10.1.5 Eight Step Praying Mantis	217
10.2 *Rou Tanglang*. Soft Praying Mantis	219
10.2.1 Six Harmonies Praying Mantis	219
10.2.2 Shining Board Praying Mantis	220
10.3 Praying Mantis of the 21st century. *Pachi Tanglang Chuan*	220

11 *Tanglang Chuan* Techniques — 221

11.1 *Kou Shou*: Praying Mantis hook	221
11.2 Chia Suh 架式. Stances	222
11.3 Basic leg techniques	225
11.3.1 Kicks	225
11.3.2 Steps	228
11.3.3 Knees	229
11.4 Basic arm techniques	230
11.4.1 Shoulders	230
11.4.2 Elbows	230
11.4.3 Wrists	233
11.4.4 Fists	234
11.4.5 Palms	235
11.4.6 Fingers	236
11.5 Combat: energy, force and speed	236
11.5.1 Phases of combat	238
11.6 Basic combat applications	240
11.7 Special techniques	247
11.7.1 *Ti Kung*. Ground combat	247
11.7.2 *Chie Mo Tsu* 截脉穴. Steel tooth	247

12 Praying Mantis Techniques and Forms — 249

12.1 Characteristic techniques	249
12.2 The forms	264
12.2.1 *Hsiao Huyuan Chuan*	264
12.2.2 *Hsiao Huyuan Chuan* two man form	265

Pachi-Pikua Curriculum — 301

Genealogy of *Pachi-Pikua Chuan*   308

Praying Mantis Curriculum   310

Genealogy of *Tanglang Chuan*   319

Glossary   321

再版自序

八極螳螂拳之西班牙文，一九九一年由巴塞隆納市撒拉出版社出版，迄今也經過十年時間了，早前幾年社辰荷西.撒拉(José Salas)託我再出再版，因爲許多愛武術的同好讀者喜歡，但是十年來我的生活變化很多，常常世界各地奔波傳教，最近在吧爾馬馬右卡市住一段長時間，由西班牙分館長法蘭西斯哥.歐雷佛羅(Francisco Orejudo)，同武館學生，我們一同再校訂再從新編寫，改正不適當內容，這再版版本希望更充實真正技術及歷史，獻給愛好武術者。

記得前版我將所有原槁，交達比.貢杰斯(David Conches)先生校對西班牙文文法，能比較通順流利交章，結果他放進人他資料及他的見解，使內容含人不實在事，不關我門派的事情，情多未經考証，或亂抄錄別人騙人資料都加進人，等書成印出版，我發現錯錯誤也就無法改正,達比.貢杰斯(David Conches)先生是一位爱好武術的人，但不是真正有學習研究的人，不求實在武術精神之真理處，像多年他教育的學生卡羅.葛西亞(Carlos García)也是一脈傳染壞的品德，來欺騙師長人眾，技藝尚末完成，自稱師父級，誘騙大眾認爲，他同我師父學習武術的，我師父都過世十幾年了,卡羅.葛西亞(Carlos García)從沒有見到他們，怎樣同我師父學武呢?武術要有誠心忠義孝悌精神，他們沒有這原則，不算是武術家，我這裏提醒西班牙想學武術的人，像這種人要小心注意不要受騙。因爲他兩人有段時間同我學習，怕外面人不明白他們早反叛面離開了，在此聲明。另外尚有一位用欺詐心來學武的人，叫凡路易.葛妹 (Juan Luis Gómez)，更心狼性毒魔鬼，作出欺師滅義傷天害理事，他不是學生不是為人有人性人類，我這裏提起這事情，因為武藝精神的內心世界，要到超人一等，而神質更需要進人聖人仙籍的百善奉行，諸惡不作，不要污姤別人感情，破壞人家家庭和睦，利用武術來達成自己貪慾害人欺世之目的，對於我一輩子練武教武的人，這種發生在自己學生中，這實在比教一隻豬還不值得，所以諠告學武術者，技術功力的進步是同樣人性向善良邁前的，心不正技無得也。騙詐和偽誘的功夫師太多。

我在本書修訂時，儘量將武術內的秘訣分開出來，用一顆愛心供獻給喜歡讀者，用武術技術和精神意志純正，引導讀者武技高強而人性也走到更善良愛心的神聖之地。

感謝由法蘭西斯哥.歐雷佛羅 (Francisco Orejudo) 帶領西班牙國分館各位學生在荷蘭，日本，挪威，西班牙，委內瑞拉完成這次的修訂本。現在，十年前的西班牙文再版，希望這次的英文版能夠使這種知識得到更為廣泛的傳播。本次翻譯由兩位委內瑞拉的學生編寫而成，並獲得兰伯各.瑪麗特 (Marit Ramberg) 以及英國學生們的幫助。

致謝學生及愛好武術的朋友，經過這麼多年來，還願意看這再版書，是對我們最大鼓勵和幫助，謝謝。

蘇昱彰
2014年 4月 21日
台北市

Author's Preface

IN 1991, EDITORIAL ALAS published in Barcelona the book *Pachi Tang Lang Chuan*. This book sold out soon and Mr. José Alas, head of the publishing house, asked me to prepare a new edition, given the great demand the book had amongst Martial Arts practitioners.

Over the following decade I set up a New York branch of the school and traveled to many countries sharing my knowledge. About ten years ago, in 2003, whilst spending time in Palma de Mallorca, I dedicated some of my time to the writing of an extended and improved edition of the book, together with the Director of the Center and other students.

In this second Spanish edition, I changed some historical details, and others regarding technique, which were not quite accurate. I also included complementary information in order to give readers, both old and new, a better knowledge about the truth of *Pachi Chuan*. The first edition of the book was written by Mr. David Conches under my direction, but the product was not entirely faithful to what I had envisioned. I had provided Mr. Conches with all the information, the documents and materials needed for the making of the book. His job would consist of transcribing and organising in the form of a book the information that I dictated, but the result was different. Besides his subjective version of my teachings prevailing, he also introduced material that I had not provided as well as ideas and thoughts of his own which I do not share and that have nothing to do with what I wished to transmit. I discovered that Mr. Conches had betrayed my trust, but when I realised the situation, it was already too late, and I found myself with the already printed copy in my hands, full of erroneous information and wrong historical and technical facts.

Mr. Conches likes the world of Martial Arts very much, but he does not like the hard work of regular training nor serious research, and this is why he does not really know the subjects about which he talks and writes; he simply gathers information about all sorts of Martial Arts and talks about them without having practiced them.

Carlos García, from Barcelona, was for many years Mr. Conches' student, and learned from him the casualness with which he talks about his "knowledge", without concern for his students and other readers trusting what he writes. Lacking the necessary qualifications, he has self-proclaimed himself a master, thus setting up a great lie within which he lives and to which he drags the people around him. Anyone who has had contact with Martial Arts knows, or should know, that the hierarchy of the lineage is transmitted from master to student. I have never given Carlos García the title of "master", but he misleads people by saying that he is one, and teaching without the authorisation of a real master. A proof of Mr. García's level of falseness is that he affirms having studied with my masters. He never met any of my masters. This is clearly a very grave matter, and I need say no more. I raise this warning so that people who are interested in Martial Arts know who they are dealing with.

The martial artist must subject himself to a code of ethics in which the principles of loyalty, justice, faithfulness, courage, kindness, respect and filial love towards the master prevail.

In this edition, many secrets concerning the techniques of Martial Arts are made public, so that all the readers who wish to do so may get to know about them and benefit from them.

I wish to thank warmly Mr. Francisco Orejudo and all the students from Holland, Japan, Norway, Spain and Venezuela, who have contributed to the production of this book. Now, so many years after the Spanish edition first appeared, I hope that this new English edition will make this knowledge available to a wider public around the world. This translation has been prepared under my direct supervision by two students who have been formed in Pachimen/Pachi Tanglang since their early youth, with help from the English students and Marit Ramberg.

Finally, I wish to thank all my students and all the lovers of Martial Arts who after so many years continue to be interested in my books, since with this interest you have also helped this book become a reality.

Su Yu-Chang
蘇昱彰
Taipei, April 2014

Translators' Preface

Every book has a story (*habent sua fata libelli*), and the story of this volume is certain to be instructive for the reader in more than one way. What you hold in your hand is the product of a labour of love now more than thirty years long.

It started in Venezuela in the late seventies, when Master Su had already consolidated the nucleus of advanced students of the Pachimen Institute. At least once a week, Master Su and a few interested and devoted students would gather to put in writing the proceedings of simple and traditional questions and answers sessions. The fruits of these gatherings, often lasting until very late Friday evenings, have eventually developed into three major publications: a manual of Taichi Chuan, *The Invisible Web* (1998), a commented translation of the *I Ching* (*I Ching, el oráculo*, 2002) and this book. It was also during these years that many of the photos included in this volume were taken. We still remember how Master Su once pointed out that while people were out partying on those weekend evenings in Caracas, we were taking advantage of all the energy they were releasing, and using it to pursue our studies.

Late in the eighties, when Master Su had consolidated the school in Venezuela and was already preparing to move to Spain, one of his Spanish students put together many of those accumulated materials and brought out the first edition of this work (Editorial Alas, Barcelona, 1991). Unfortunately, as detailed in the previous pages, that first edition ended up including a bizarre selection of foreign material, and many mistakes which eventually made urgent a new edition under closer supervision by the author. This huge task, assumed by Francisco Orejudo, head of the Majorcan branch, culminated with the enlarged and corrected second Spanish edition, which is the direct basis of the present translation.

The pains taken by Orejudo to bring this work to completion can not be overemphasized, and Master Su himself has repeatedly expressed his grateful satisfaction with the result. Throughout the nineties, when the school, now Pachi Tanglang, was becoming a truly global endeavor, Orejudo spared no means to follow Master Su around the world, submitting to him set after set of proofs, getting corrections and additions, finding all sorts of help from the branches in Holland, Japan, Spain, USA and Venezuela. Worthy of special mention is the diligent coordinating role played by Marit Ramberg, now head of the Norway branch of the school, in all stages of the production. More recently, the translators would warmly want to acknowledge her invaluable and ongoing support for this English edition.

Following in Orejudo's steps, we have sought at every stage of the work the editorial supervision of Master Su, who has taken the opportunity to correct some errors and to add the Chinese characters which we hope will be of benefit to a more international readership. Several valuable appendices at the end of the book will help to convey a more rounded vision of the current teachings of Pachi Tanglang International, whose headquarters are now back in Taiwan, under the name Taiwan Tatungshan Pachimen International Martial Arts Institute (台灣大東山八極門國際武藝協會).

The practice of 默念師容, "silent inward contemplation of the master", accompanied and guided us during our translation work, as well as many of the people who contributed to the birth and development of this book. It is in the spirit of this traditional practice, which alone can guarantee the transformative powers of Kung Fu, that we dedicate this translation to the blessed memory of Masters Chang Te-Kuei, Wei Hsiao-Tang, Li Kuen-Shan, Sang Tan-Chi and Liu Yun-Chiao, and their ancestors in the lineage. May this volume contribute to the sustained propagation of traditional Chinese Martial Arts in the way that Master Su has faithfully, rigorously and lovingly handed them down to us, indeed, for which we are ever in his filial debt.

Cristóbal Rodríguez   Juan Acevedo
Mérida, Venezuela   Cambridge, UK

Chapter 1

Chinese Martial Arts

> "Martial Arts?
> What does Art mean?"
> "24 hours a day."

IN RECENT YEARS there has been an increasing worldwide interest in Martial Arts. This has led the general public to begin to understand and value the benefits that derive from the regular practice of these remarkable movements, which in addition to being efficient fighting techniques have powerful health effects.

Due to this rising popularity, a true avalanche of Oriental, and non-Oriental, "masters" has spread through many countries around the world.

Participants in the 7th Pachi Tanglang International Seminar. Holland, 2002.

However, authentic knowledgeable transmitters of the ancient traditional knowledge become fewer every day.

Until relatively recently, only some Martial Arts like Judo, Karate or Taekwondo, were known to the Western world, and this knowledge rarely went beyond recognizing the name. Hence, even today, many people will mistakenly refer to a Kung Fu film or a Chinese martial artist in a picture as a Karate film or a Karate fighter, respectively. This is a mistake, since Karate is different from Kung Fu.

Master Li Kuan-Shan with Master Su Yu-Chang, 1960.

"Martial Arts" is a name given to a whole variety of combat methods and forms, the majority of which have it's origin in China. Currently, the newly reconstituted styles of continental China are known as styles of *Wushu*, while the term "Kung Fu" has come to refer to the traditional styles that are nowadays almost only found in Taiwan and in some western countries, due to the emigration of Chinese masters. Something characteristic of almost all traditional Kung Fu styles is that they include a great variety of techniques in which practically every part of the body is used to strike, push or knock down the opponent. On the other hand, the majority of Martial Arts known in the West are limited to using some techniques focused on using only certain parts of the body.

If we look at the countries around China, we will see that they all have their own Martial Arts: Karate and Judo in Japan, Taekwondo in Korea, etc. It is commonly believed that these systems are original to each of these countries, but that is not accurate. In fact, history tells us that Chinese Kung Fu is to be found at the origin and alongside the evolution of the most important oriental Martial Arts. Some of the more widespread systems in the West, like Karate, Kendo, Judo, Taekwondo, were effectively born in Japan and Korea, but they were based on Kung Fu styles. This sort of influence was common in former times, since China used to be the greatest power of the far East, and as such, the great exporter of cultural elements.

In the context of these cultural exchanges, when Chinese Martial Arts arrived in other countries, they were integrated into the local martial systems, and some techniques (kicks, throws, dislocations, punches) were emphasized while others were eliminated, to conform the new styles. This is the way Judo came to have only throwing techniques, Taekwondo concentrated on kicks, Kendo simplified the *Miao Tao* techniques, and Aikido, almost in the 20th century, essentially chose those of *Chinna* and *Pakua Chang*. Finally, Karate has its origin in Southern China, whose inhabitants traveled to Okinawa and Japan in general. For this reason, the names of techniques and postures in Karate correspond to those of the styles of Southern China.

This is historical fact and can be verified by looking into the genealogy of each system or in some documents that still survive in the archives of the most important Martial Arts federations and universities. This does not mean to say that these are not good, efficient and effective styles or methods. On the contrary, some of these possess the best techniques of the Chinese Martial Arts that gave them birth.

Sword from the Warring States period, 5th century BC.

Martial Arts developed as ways of preserving your own life, but they gradually incorporated medical and philosophical concepts that transformed them into marvelous tools for cultivating health. Currently, given that the Art of Combat has ceased to be a necessity, many "martial arts" styles are only practiced as sports, in national or international competitions. Others are learned to improve health and some, the least of all, still continue with the tradition of merging the martial, therapeutic and philosophic components. In any case, the regular practice of this type of exercise brings to the practitioner a general wellbeing that leads to his self-development.

Westerners wishing to learn an Eastern Martial Art may find themselves bewildered by the many existing "martial arts". Kung Fu in particular has a great number of styles and sub-styles. Willing to shed some light on this landscape, we will try to establish a classification that may serve as a guide for the interested reader.

1.1 Northern and southern styles

Given the great expanse of China, the first distinction we make is geographical. The most important natural boundary in China is the Yellow River, which lies at the origin of Chinese culture. It divides the country in two, the North and the South, and it has also served as a reference for a classification of Kung Fu styles. Generally speaking, we say that there are Northern styles and Southern styles.

Master Su in the Shaolin Temple hall of fame, standing next to the column where his name is recorded, 1982.

Northern China is dominated by great plains, and for this reason the horse has always been an inseparable part of the life of its people, as it continues to be even today. Horseback warfare induced the development of particularly long weapons. Combat took place in the open, and because people were of medium to tall height and with long legs, the Northern styles evolved using a lot of space for their performance as well as placing their emphasis on kicks and extended leg techniques. Arm techniques on their part, consist of long range punches or attacks.

Northern China has also distinguished itself as being the birthplace of some of the most illustrious minds of the country, like Confucius and Lao Tzu, and it is perhaps for this reason that the styles of the North have a greater number of techniques and that these are more complex.

The styles developed under these conditions are rounded, relaxed, of long stances and numerous techniques. The principal Northern styles are:

Chang Chuan, Cha Chuan, Lo Han Chuan, Liohoe Chuan, Ying Chua Chuan, Pachi Chuan, Tanglang Chuan, Hsing-I Chuan, Pakua Chang, Tai Chi Chuan, etc.

The South is dominated by large rivers, so for this reason fights would often take place on board a boat where more stability is required. Hence, in the styles of the South, stances are low and wide and leg techniques used are short with few kicks. The lack of space for combat and the shorter build of the people of the South of China contributed to the development of short to medium range arm techniques, and similarly, the weapons used are also short and often double. As a result of these conditions, the styles of the South are rather hexagonal, stance-centered, apparently tense, with short steps and wide stances, without too many techniques and using shouts to emphasize the explosive action.

Cover of a Japanese book on Tang Lang Chuan, published 2002.

The styles of the South include: *Pai Hou, Mou Cha Kuan, Choy Lee Fat, Hung Gar Kuan, Pek Mei* and *Wing Chun.*

In general terms, it could be said that Northern schools have an inclination towards technique and agility, while those of the South towards strength and roughness.

1.2 Internal and external styles

Another classification of Kung Fu which has become very popular in recent years, speaks of internal or external styles. These concepts have never been present in Chinese culture and have only appeared recently due to the lack of real knowledge of Kung Fu. In general, people think that if a style is practiced slowly or softly, then it is internal, and if it is fast it is external. This is a serious mistake. We will now shed some light on this matter by raising a few relevant points.

Let us start by saying that a great many fighting systems, with very different origins and characteristics, are gathered under the single title of Chinese Martial Arts. There have always been class differences amongst human beings and these differences have naturally found their reflection in Martial Arts. It is easy to understand that the technique of the Emperor's bodyguard cannot be equated to that of a peasant, since in each of these cases, defeat has a remarkably different importance from a social point of view. Thus, a distinction must be drawn within Martial Arts between those considered superior and those we could call of the common people. The difference lies both in the intrinsic quality of the teachings and in the time and dedication required to master them, and fundamentally on the possibility of finding an authentic master of the lineage who is willing to teach.

Although the common motivation for the development of Martial Arts was self defense, the achievements of each martial artist in his endeavor for greater effectiveness were different, thus giving rise to different schools over time.

In some styles — the most popular, which could be called "external" — the emphasis was put on the early learning of different techniques, such as

Opening of the government promoted gym at Lai Yan, Shandong, where master Li Kuen-shan was appointed director, 1934.

kicks, blocks, punches and evasions, with the aim of obtaining a minimum combat ability in a short span of time, and probably due to the lack of greater knowledge as well. Later, the practitioner who wished to improve his effectiveness and showed to be prepared to do so, was given access to the internal aspects of the art and the use of energy.

In other styles, which can be called "internal", the aim is not a mediocre effectiveness in the short term but rather an infallible destructive capacity. This may be achieved by means of the use of refined techniques for the management of energy, and it is for this reason that the nurturing of *Chi* is inherent to the practice from the very beginning. In other words, in these styles internal power takes precedence over external technique; although it is not exactly so, for once internal power has been adequately developed, one is automatically proficient in the "external" techniques.

Master Tu I-sai performing Chen Taichi Chuan Cannon Fist, 1966.

Learning an "external" system is relatively fast and attainable when the aim is to be able to use it in combat, since external techniques are easier to practice and develop. This is not the case with "internal" styles, where achieving some effectiveness requires great dedication for a period of time that is never under ten years. The difficulty of learning so called "internal" styles is increased due to the scarcity of competent masters in these styles. This, added to the time, dedication and patience needed to attain an adequate level in these systems, makes few able to master them.

The "internal" character of Martial Arts is inherent to the arts themselves from the start. Being combat systems, they produce wounds that must be cured, leading to the necessity of the knowledge of how to restore the health of the wounded; they are thus at the origin of medical arts and are indeed the cradle for their development. On the other hand, martial artists were repeatedly confronted with death, and as meeting death is one of the most efficient methods for achieving introspection, it was not unusual for martial artists to go into retreat in monasteries and to cultivate there the mystical and philosophical aspects of *Chi*.

In this context, all those Chinese martial artists who made it to an old age had usually accumulated significant medical and philosophical knowledge. This knowledge was secretly transmitted within the Martial Arts lineages, which were also lineages of doctors, philosophers and mystics. It is important to bear in mind that in extreme conditions, the effectiveness of a Martial Art may determine the line between life and death. Secrecy was hence essential to being able to have an advantage on the occasion of a confrontation.

Masters from various lineages confirmed, generation after generation, the relationship between the practice of certain movements and applying pressure on specific points with the improvement of health. They were able to develop the knowledge of the energetic body, becoming martial artists of energy or "internal" martial artists. This type of knowledge also allowed older martial artists to have an effective defense system with which to defeat younger opponents.

Master Su holding the Taiwan championship trophy, 1957.

The internal character of all styles manifests itself in *Nei Kung*. This is the name originally given to the internal energy work now known as *Chi Kung*. Every style of Kung Fu includes *Chi Kung* in its teachings, although its practice will vary. In the North, it is soft and flexible, while in the South hard and strong; they are *Chi Kung* but of different natures. *Chi* is used in the North to improve health and to foster longevity, while in the South it is focused on breakings and various demonstrations.

It can be said that the Northern school is the great internal one, itself having both internal and external aspects although emphasis is put in learning the internal before the external. The South is the great external one, and even though the internal aspect is also studied, it is of a different nature to that of the North. Due to the constant wars, in the South the practical or external aspect was taught before the internal, so as to be able to defend oneself in the shortest possible time.

In an authentic Martial Art, in Kung Fu, all aspects are present without any real possibility of distinguishing internal from external. First, movements set the energy in motion, this makes available an amount of energy which then generates the movement. When there is Kung Fu, the boundaries between internal and external cease to be.

1.3 Names and forms

Wushu or *Wu-I*, meaning literally "Martial Art", is the generic name of all Chinese Martial Arts. There are also those who call them *Wukung*, which means "Martial Work". Currently, the term *Wushu* is more common in mainland China, while in Taiwan *Kuoshu*, meaning "National Art", is the preferred term.

In China, all the above terms are used according to their meanings. In the West, however, the name Kung Fu has come to designate the traditional styles, while the term Wushu is applied to a new breed of martial arts developed in mainland China. The term Kung Fu does not necessarily refer to martial arts at all. Kung Fu could be translated as "Art of Movement", but it originally refers to a highly developed skill in any activity, acquired through dedication, time and effort; this utmost skill is what is meant by

Master Su performing an exhibition with three section staff, Taiwan 1968.

Master Su fighting against various weapons
at Master Liu Yun-chiao's Wu Tan gym, Taipei 1962.

Kung Fu. For example, it could be said that a doctor specialized in a given medical field has Kung Fu in that field; an eminent musician will have Kung Fu in music, and so on. We can see that the person who has practiced diligently the art of *Wushu-Kuoshu* for a long time following an adequate method, will have acquired Kung Fu in such an art.

The practice of Kung Fu usually follows three modes: empty handed forms, exercises with weapons and combat. Each of these may in turn be practiced individually, in pairs or in groups.

Kung Fu practice requires the joint use of body and spirit or mind in order to generate energy. To make the techniques of a Kung Fu system easier to learn, they are ordered in continuous sequences of movements called *Tao Lu*, "form". These forms are composed of characteristic movements of the style, and are ordered in a specific manner so as to build combat sequences which are easier to understand and grasp.

Originally, different styles were not classified into different categories nor were there established competition or combat rules; in order to prove the martial applicability of their knowledge, different Martial Arts schools would challenge each other to combat. Nowadays martial artists do form and combat exhibitions called *Chuan Tao* and *San Ta*, respectively.

The terms *Men* and *Pai* refer to a Martial Arts school, while *Chuan* is used for a form or style.

Nei Kung or *Chi Kung* would deserve a whole chapter to itself. All

Kung Fu styles contain a *Chi Kung* of their own, made up of characteristic movements of the system, performed in an isolated manner or in short sequences and composed for the development and projection of internal energy. In recent years, *Wushu* has dispensed with its own *Chi Kung*, viewing it as a discipline separate from the styles; this is a serious mistake. The lack of their characteristic internal work, of their *Chi Kung*, has brought about the degeneration of Martial Arts styles. Every Kung Fu school needs its own *Chi Kung*, otherwise it is not Kung Fu.

In the context of Kung Fu training, combat is known as *San Ta*, but *San Ta* is only one of the constituent parts of the teachings of a Kung Fu system, and it cannot be separated from the practice of the forms of the style, since it is in these that its combat techniques are condensed. The study must be complete, otherwise Kung Fu will not be achieved.

An exceptional photograph portraying, from left to right, sitting, Liu Yun-chiao (*Pachi, Pikua, Pakua*), Tsao Lien-huan (*Hsing-I*), Kung Pao-chai (*Pakua*), Li Ching-hoe (*Hsing-I, Pakua*), Sang Tan-chi (*Hsing-I*) and Chang Hsian-shang (*Lio Hoe Tanglang*); standing, Su Yu-chang, Chou Kao-shan, Fu Shong-nan, Uh Song-hua, Uh Un-chang, Shu Chia-chun, Adam Hsu, Huan I-nan, Yu Wen-tong and Chian Tsao-shu. Wu Tan, 1970.

Huang Ti, the Yellow Emperor.

Chou Wen-wang

Much of the *Wushu* that we see these days is closer to a Chinese opera performance than to an authentic Martial Art. Bodily movements of the opera performances had their origin in Kung Fu; they were adapted for the stage, and authentic movements were modified to make them more eye-catching and suited to theatrical aesthetics. Something similar is happening with current *Wushu*.

Although most of what passes as *Wushu* today is only an artistic sport, traditional Kung Fu can still be learned. Its practice under the guidance of an authentic master leads to the cultivation of health and builds up character, as well as being useful for self-defense.

If you want to study an authentic Martial Art, it is necessary to know the lineage of masters that guarantees its teachings. Many people talk about Kung Fu nowadays, but they are ignorant about who transmitted the teachings. They must look back towards the origin, to know if their masters are known in history. Making up names is very easy.

1.4 Historical review

The first evidence of the use of Martial Arts in China comes from prehistoric times, and they tell us about certain activities called *Shen Long Tien Ti*. The people of that time were nomadic hunter-gatherers, and the chief of the tribe taught the properties and usage of plants. They were always exposed to animal attacks and had to fight them to be able to survive. This circumstance fostered the creation of combat systems that consisted of isolated movements derived from the movements of the animals they were fighting. This is how Kung Fu was born. Another term referring to a prehistoric forerunner of Martial Arts is *Chao Ti*. It refers to hunting techniques that made it possible to knock down an animal, and that were later used in combat. But the first clear references to a martial art can be traced back to the times of Emperor Huang Ti (2697–2599 BC), the father of Chinese culture, also known as the Yellow Emperor. In his time, a group-combat system called *Chi Ho* was developed, gathering and giving structure to isolated combat movements, moving towards a superior Martial Art.

Chou Kung (Chou Wu Wang)

In those times, warriors wore leather cuirasses as protection and covered their heads with deer's heads. Since the existing weapons were not strong enough to penetrate these cuirasses, Huang Ti, thinking of a way to overcome this impediment, devised a weapon using bear's claws called *Hsiong Chang*. As the effective use of bear claws required a refined technique, he developed a sequence of movements called *Pa Men Hsiong Chang* (our *Pachi Chuan* lineage starts here). Given the name, it is likely that this technique was carried out by groups of eight men who would encircle the opponent and prevent his escape. Herein is found the origin of *Pachi Chuan*'s empty fist.

Huang Ti was also the inventor of the compass. It is said that, when in battle, he would always ride a chariot furnished with a revolving dummy which would always point to a specific cardinal point, letting him know in which direction he was heading.

The discovery of archery, during the Xia dynasty (2207–1766 BC),

Confucius

Kuan Kong plays Chinese chess while an arrow tip is extracted from his arm

was the great achievement of the military arts of this period in which the king Tou Han, the discoverer of jade, lived. Before archery was developed, people used spear-throwers. The legend has it that Tou Han, in his greed for ever more jade, abused his subjects in the search of the precious stone. Angry at his behavior, God made nine Suns shine over the Earth to get rid of the despot. The heat became unbearable and Tou Han, unable to remedy the situation, issued an edict offering great riches to whoever could eliminate eight of the Suns. A warrior named Houyi presented himself for the feat, being well known for his skill throwing javelins. However, no matter how much he tried, he was not able to reach any of the Suns. His tenacity did not have limits, and going back home he spent several days pondering together with his wife how to throw javelins more effectively. They were deep in such thoughts, walking through the forest that surrounded their house, when the wife moved a branch of a bush out of their way in such a way that when she let go it slapped Houyi's face, leaving him stunned. But this not only struck him physically, since he understood the potential force within a flexible branch. Losing no time, he took a straight branch, he tensed it using a string and tried until he finally managed to shoot an arrow into a great distance. Equipped with his new weapon, he went back to the palace and before the bewildered eyes of the emperor, he threw arrow after arrow until he brought down eight Suns. The emperor was so impressed by the power of the new weapon that he adopted it for his armies.

During the Shang dynasty (1765–1122 BC) horses and war chariots started to be introduced into warfare. Additionally, and coinciding with the first version of the *I Ching*, composed by Chou Wen Wang, philosophy is introduced into Martial Arts. It is in this period that Chang Tai Kong, a minister of the king, started to organize martial groups that studied formally different combat systems.

Kuan Kong

Chou Wu Wang, son of Chou Wen Wang, defeated the Shang in 1121 BC, thus founding the Zhou dynasty, the longest lasting dynasty in Chinese history. Chou Wu Wang was a great lover of Martial Arts. A military book called *Lio Tao* 六韜 or *Six Secret Teachings*, was written by Chang Tai Kong under his reign, and this was to be the first Martial Arts book. In this book there is a reference to the "Praying Mantis Soldiers", who were the personal guard of the emperor. This is the origin of the *Tanglang Chuan* style (Master Su's Praying Mantis lineage starts here).

Ta Mo

In the Spring and Autumn period (771–476 BC) an army General of the Kingdom of Wu, called Sun Wu (685–643 BC), wrote the *Sun Tzu Ping Fa*: "The Art of War". In this treatise, 36 war tactics are exposed, and a philosophical foundation is provided for the management of troops during wartime.

During the Warring States period (403–

222 BC), Lao Tzu authors the short philosophical treatise called *Tao Te Ching*, that would eventually lay the philosophical foundations of *Pakua Chang* and *Tai Chi Chuan*. Also from this period dates Confucius, who with his ideas enriched the *I Ching*, a book that is also part of the philosophical foundations of these Martial Arts styles.

Lao Tzu

After long years of war, China was united under the rule of the emperor Chin Shu-Huang, founder of the Qin dynasty (221–206 BC). In his time, philosophical systems and combat systems were united, the construction of the Great Wall began, ironwork techniques flourished and weapons of great quality were made.

It is under the Western Han period (206 BC–8 AD) that the great development of cavalry takes place, together with that of long weapons. The generalized use of the *Miao Tao* and the spear dates back to this period. Similarly, there is a great increase in the amount of private Martial Arts schools, which until then had been only state-run.

In the year 226 AD, a physician called Hua To wrote a book, entitled *Wu Chin Hsi* (*Movements of Five Playing Animals*), on health-oriented *Chi Kung*. An official military instruction book was also written in this time, in which appear thirty-six sword wielding movements as well as six hand movements and eight archery techniques.

The years between 220 AD and 265 AD are called the Three Kingdoms period, referring to the kingdoms of Wei in the North, Wu in the South-East and Shu to the South-West. The latter was founded by Liu Pei in the year 221 AD.

During this period lived an important figure, who is still venerated in our days as the father of Chinese Martial Arts. His name was Kuan Yu, and after his death he received the titles of Kuan Kong (Duke of Kuan) and Kuan Ti (Emperor Kuan). He is frequently depicted accompanied by his two sworn brothers, Liu Pei and Chang Fei, with whom he fought to establish the kingdom of Shu. It is said that Kuan Yu was already more than 50 years old and used a broadsword weighing 260 pounds when he started to spread the knowledge that made him the legend he is nowadays.

These three figures are represented according to their characters: Chang Fei in black, Liu Pei in white and Kuan Yu in red. Kuan Kong distinguished himself for his rectitude and honesty as a warrior and leader. This is why he became the patron of Martial Arts. The legend of his encounter with the surgeon Hua To has become very famous. It tells of the occasion when Hua To extracted a poisoned tip of an arrow from Kuan Yu's arm without him taking the *Mafeisan* drug (mixture of hemp and strong wine) to ease the pain. While Hua To scraped off the flesh contaminated with poison, Kuan Yu played Chinese chess. The speedy recovery of General Kuan very much impressed Tsao Tsao, his staunch enemy, who later captured the doctor to have him at his service, only to eventually execute him.

In the year 238 AD, Japan sent a mission of good will to the state of Wei. As part of the expedition traveled a doctor who brought plants, medicines and rice as gifts. The king was very satisfied with the presents and gave away two *Miao Tao*, each almost three meters long, hoping that they could use them in the harvest of rice. These were probably the predecessors of the current katanas or samurai swords, and the ones that gave origin to *Kendo*. Also in this period, there was a great increase in the popularity of Taoism, and *Tao In Chi Kung* (exercises to channel energy through the meridians) began to be practiced.

China found itself in the midst of continuous wars between the years

Master Liu (center left) with Master Su and his first students. Sitting before Master Su is Yu Kuan-hsing, his first student. On Master Su's right is Eduardo Ng. 1982

280 and 552 AD. For this reason, people were always armed; peasants and the poor, not being able to afford real swords, would carry wooden ones. A religious awakening also occurs during this period and in the year 495 AD, the king Hsiao Un Ti founded the Shaolin monastery. Shortly afterwards, the famous Taoist alchemist and philosopher Ke Hung, author of the treatise *Paoputzu*, founds the *Wu Tang Shan* temple, where *Pakua Chang* was probably born. These exercises are probably the first to have taken the form of a Martial Art, since they precede the ones taught by Bodhidharma (called Ta Mo by the Chinese) to the Shaolin monks in the year 500 AD.

Bodhidharma was an Indian Buddhist monk who traveled to China to teach *Chan* Buddhism. *Chan* Buddhism was stricter than the one known in China at that time. Ta Mo's attempts to convert the king ended with a conflict between the two, and with Ta Mo's confinement to the Shaolin Temple. There, Ta Mo dedicated himself to the practice of the techniques of *Chan* Buddhism. It is told that his discipline was formidable and that he spent nine years meditating in front of a wall. The temple monks tried to imitate him, but since they were not accustomed to that type of discipline,

Master Su at Lao Shan temple together with a 101 year old Taoist monk who is a master of *Tanglang Chuan*, 1990

Master Liu with his wife and Master Su, 1960.

their health would deteriorate after some time and they would fall ill. With the aim of improving the monks' health and resistance, Ta Mo taught eighteen breathing exercises based on primitive forms of Yoga that he had studied in India during his youth. So Ta Mo actually did not teach any Martial Art to the monks. The Martial Arts of Shaolin Temple developed later.

In those times, it was common for some warriors to retire to a monastery after leaving military life. It was also a custom that fugitives who had taken shelter in monasteries would be pardoned by the authorities for as long as they remained there as monks. So it was that, eventually, there were monks in every monastery that for one reason or another mastered some type of Martial Art. These monks taught the others and it was in this way that monasteries started to develop Martial Arts schools.

The famous Shaolin staff has its origin in the pole used to carry water buckets. The monks had to fetch water from the rivers, and they would use the staff to defend themselves when attacked by animals. This is how they developed the now famous Shaolin staff technique.

General Li Shu Min, who was sympathetic to Buddhism, tried to defeat the emperor and establish a new dynasty. He failed in his first attempt and was pursued by the army. He found shelter in the Shaolin Temple and with the help of the monks, well trained in the staff techniques, he managed to withstand the attack and eventually went on to defeat the emperor. This is how the Tang dynasty (618–907 AD) was established, under whose reign Buddhism and Taoism were largely promoted. Emperor Li offered great financial help to monasteries and their popularity increased accordingly; it was during this time that the Shaolin Temple gained its fame.

During the Southern Song dynasty (1127–1279 AD), China went to war against other nations. Consequently, military arts acquired great importance and Kung Fu showed great progress, thanks to the technological improvements taking place and because the soldiers were required to pass strict fighting tests in order to be promoted in the imperial examinations: the greater the skill, the higher the degree obtained. This favored the publication of several official Martial Arts treatises. Health oriented *Chi Kung* was popularized and a many new Taoist texts were published.

The most prominent martial artist of this period was General Yueh Fei, who studied the original *Pachi Chuan* and the spear under *Chou Tong*. He modified *Pachi Chuan* to adapt its movements for the combat of heavily equipped military units, thus creating *Hsing-I Chuan*. The newly constituted army was very effective and he achieved great victories.

In the 13th century, Genghis Khan invaded China with his Mongolian military might and founded the Yuan dynasty (1277– 1367 AD). Mongols tried to impose their own combat system and banned Kung Fu, the practice of which only survived in the mountains and isolated villages where tradition was maintained. The first use of gunpowder in Martial Arts dates to this period.

About the year 1368, the Chinese overthrew the Mongols and founded the Ming dynasty, which lasted until the year 1642, thus entering the modern age. A famous General called Chi Chi-Kuan (1528–1587 AD), victorious in battles repelling Japanese attempts to invade the continent, wrote in 1562 a military treatise on the main existing Kung Fu styles of his time called *Chi Hsiao Hsin Shu* (*New Book Recording Effective Techniques*). He mentions, among others, *Chang Chuan, Chen Tai Chi Chuan, Pachi Chuan* and *Pikua Chuan*.

Recording of a video in Japan. Standing next to Master Su is Noda Hisakata, director of the Japanese branch of Pachi Tanglang Martial Arts Institute

Towards the year 1644, the Manchu invade China founding the Qing dynasty (1644–1911). The Manchu were savage compared to the Chinese Han, and for this reason they tried to eradicate the Han culture they did not understand, including Kung Fu. Anyone knowledgeable in Kung Fu or who cultivated Kung Fu would be persecuted and executed. These circumstances brought important changes into Chinese Martial Arts. First, genealogies changed, because masters would not want to make explicit that their art had a Han origin and would instead say that they had invented it. Second, names of styles were changed: as it was impossible to keep the traditional names, people chose to assign names of animals or surnames of the masters who had preserved the styles. Third, and most importantly, the need to keep secret the origins of the styles prompted the adoption of the *Paisu* distinction as a warranty of loyalty. The *Paisu* oath involved both disciple and master, constituting a warranty of discretion that assured the master that he would not be denounced and would hence be able to speak freely and transmit his knowledge without fear of treason. The Manchu yearning for a culture of their own led to the proliferation of newly constituted Martial Arts, which consequently brought, on the one hand, a lot of competition between different schools and, on the other hand, the popularization of the practice together with an abundance of Martial Arts books.

Nevertheless, the Qing kept certain styles for their exclusive personal use. So it was that *Pachi Chuan* became the official system of the emperor's private guard, while *Pakua Chang* the style used by the palace guards. The last emperor of China, Pu Yi, was an assiduous practitioner of *Pachi Chuan*, learning from Master Huo Tien-Kuo (a disciple of Master Li Shu-Wen).

In the year 1912, Sun Yatsen (1866–1925) declares the establishment of the Republic of China (regime that continues in Taiwan today). Thus started the rapid and free spreading of all previously banned Martial Arts systems, the majority of which were taught at the newly established Nanking Central Kuoshu Institute. With the arrival of Mao Tse-Tung's People's Republic of China (1949), Kung Fu went underground

Group of students in Alaska. Standing behind Master Su is Kurt Wong

once again, and a great many Kung Fu masters exiled themselves to Taiwan, Hong Kong and the United States of America, where they transmitted their knowledge, salvaging tradition. Later, during the Cultural Revolution (1966–1968), Kung Fu was transformed into Wushu and in this new guise it gained unprecedented development. Emphasis, however, was put on standardization rather than on rescuing tradition, and the whole process was oriented towards making it a sport, leaving aside the authentic values of traditional Kung Fu.

1.5 Martial Arts today

Nowadays, many people talk about this or that style of Kung Fu as if they were experts, but very few know what Kung Fu really is. The first mistake is to describe a style as being external or internal. Every style needs internal and external work; you cannot study only one of these aspects. Authentic Kung Fu enables us to achieve the highest, to be able to use energy in such a way that one may finish the opponent with only one strike. Others encourage the breaking of boards or bricks with physical force, but they do not teach how to manage energy. One may still speak about Northern or Southern styles, both being internal and external although with different techniques and ideas.

Whoever is serious about studying Kung Fu needs a master with a lineage that goes back at least to the year 1744, which is when current names and genealogy begin.

Tournament in Caracas in 2001. Venezuelan students perform Yang Tai Chi Chuan behind Master Su

Chapter 2

History and Masters of *Pachi Chuan*

> A master must have a lineage, he must be a link in a chain of masters.

2.1 The origins

WE DO NOT KNOW who invented *Pachi Chuan*, but he is agreed to have been an historical figure. The first direct reference to this style goes back to 222 BC, when it is mentioned in an official military book, although without naming its creator. In a secret book of *Pachi Chuan*, its origin is ascribed to Huang Ti (2697–2258 BC), father of Chinese culture. Even though no direct reference to *Pachi Chuan* as a fighting system is made, it affirms that this emperor taught tiger and bear movements to his soldiers, and the energies of these two animals are present in *Pachi Chuan*. Also, official strategy books of the time describe Huang Ti's ideas on strategy and these are similar to those of *Pachi Chuan*.

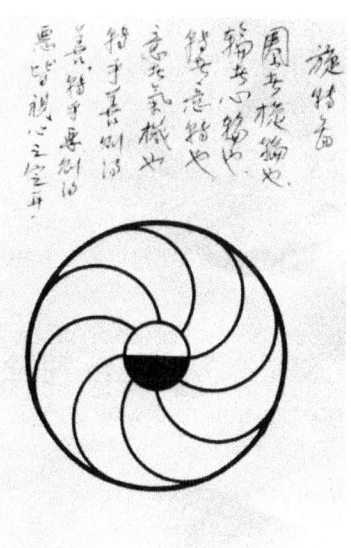

First ever drawing of the Wu Tan symbol and calligraphy, by Master Liu, 1962.

Yueh Fei's mausoleum at Sihu

The next reference to *Pachi Chuan* available to us dates approximately from 1120. In that time lived a general called Yueh Fei, who is said to have studied the style under Master Chou Tong. Yueh Fei taught *Pachi Chuan* to his soldiers, but had to modify it to adapt it to their limited movement, constrained by the weight of their armor and the little space between them while in combat formation. It seems likely that present day *Hsing-I Chuan* is this modified *Pachi Chuan* taught by general Yueh Fei.

There is a story about the first encounter between the still young Yueh Fei and the monk Chou Tong which highlights the qualities that must prevail in anyone who aspires to reach the highest levels of Kung Fu.

On a certain day, when Yueh Fei was going back home, he went past a bridge where there was an old monk trying to pick something up from the river. Yueh Fei approached the old monk and asked what had happened, to which the monk replied "my shoe has fallen into the river and I can't reach it. Could you get it for me?" Yueh Fei assented, jumped into the water without hesitation and caught the shoe, which he gave back to the monk. The monk thanked him for his kindness, but while holding the shoe in his trembling hands, it slipped and fell again into the river.

"Oh! I'm sorry. Please forgive my clumsiness due to my old age. Could you get me my shoe once more?," said the monk.

"Don't worry old man, I will get it," replied Yueh Fei smiling.

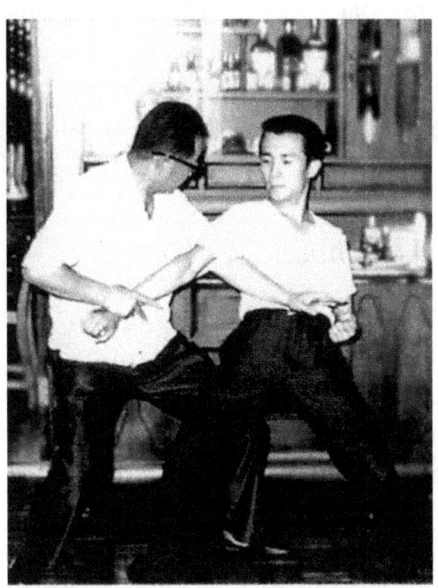

Master Liu shows a *Pachi Chuan* application with Master Su, 1962.

Master Su demonstrating *Ma Shu Shuang Chong Chang* position at the Parc Güell, Barcelona.

So jumping off the bridge once more he rushed to pick up the old shoe and gave it back to the monk. The monk thanked the youth again for his good will. Yueh Fei replied that it was nothing, and after saying farewell, started to walk away.

But the monk, watching him leave threw his shoe into the water and called him, "Young man! I beg you, help me again, I'm so clumsy and old that I have lost my shoe again." Yueh Fei turned smiling and asking the old man to sit down, reached for the old shoe for the third time and gave it to the monk. But the monk asked, "could you put it on my foot? I fear that with my clumsiness I may drop it once more."

Yueh Fei looked at him joyfully and knelt down, took the foot of the old monk and put on the shoe. Then he helped him stand up and offered to accompany him on his way to his village. Seeing the young man's lack of pretentiousness, and his patience and kindness, the monk admitted that the scene with the shoe had been a trick to observe his attitude and that he was actually the monk Chou Tong, famous for his skills in Martial Arts.

So it was that chatting along on their walk back to the village the monk felt so much sympathy for the young man that he took him as his personal disciple. He taught him *Pachi Chuan* and other systems, including group fighting tactics and the *Sun Tzu Ping Fa* (*The Art of War*), which would be of so much help to the future general.

2.2 Historical *Pachi Chuan*

It is said that *Pachi Chuan* came to be known as a superior Martial Arts system during the Ming dynasty (1364–1644). It was during this period that another general, Chi Chi-Kuan (1528–1587), wrote an official military treatise which is very important for Chinese history. *Pachi Chuan* is mentioned in this treatise, though nothing is said about its founder.

Cover of the Japanese magazine *Wushu*, 1991.

In 1644, the Ming dynasty (from the Han ethnic group) was overthrown by those who would establish the Qing dynasty (from the Man Ching ethnic group). This made the country fall into civil war. Everything related to the Han ethnic group was banned. Hence, for security reasons, many masters decided to change their names and those of their Martial Arts. This explains why the historical background of *Pachi Chuan* is not known prior to this period, as is the case with other Martial Arts, not because it does not exist, but because all traces were deliberately erased. For example, the name Shaolin Chuan was not used for a long time and only reappeared around the year 1912.

In 1912, after fading into the official oblivion of the Qing dynasty, *Pachi Chuan* reappears as well, thanks to the efforts of the government-founded Nanking Central Kuoshu Institute. With the advent of the Republic, this institute spared no means to trace historical data relating to traditional Kung Fu, eventually finding references to masters dating back to the beginning of the 17th century. In addition, we have relatively well known lineages going back to around 1644. In any case, *Pachi Chuan* as a technical

If you master the technique of the sword,
Then you are already in *Tao*.
The way of *Tao* does not need anything,
Just leave emotions and you will reach tranquility.

Grand Master Liu Yun-Chiao

term is historically attested since the Qing dynasty. We also know the names of two men who practiced *Pachi Chuan* during that period : Ting Fa-Hsiang (1615–1694) and Wu Chung (1712–1802).

Ting Fa-Hsiang's *Pachi Chuan* has survived to this day, although the line of his descendants is not known, either because it was kept secret or because it was lost. He gave his name to the style's first eight movements: the *Ting Tzu Pa Pu Suh*. His *Pachi Chuan* is slightly different from the one generally known, but even today it is possible to find people who practice it.

Wu Chung, from the Han minority, was a native of Shandong. He went to live in the province of Hou Pei in his youth, where he studied *Pachi Chuan* for several years with a Taoist monk who had changed his name to Lai. Regarding this change of name, there is a secret *Pachi Chuan* book that mentions someone called Lai Kuei Yuen as a teacher of the long spear. The Chinese character used for "Lai" in this case is the same as the one used when speaking of the Taoist monk Lai. "Kuei Yuen" is the title given to the champion of the national Martial Arts examinations. It is very likely that for security reasons the monk Lai did not want his real identity to be

Drawings from the secret book of *Pachi Chuan* written by Wu Chung around the year 1750.

known, especially given that he had reportedly served as an army general under the Ming dynasty. Later, Wu Chung furthered his knowledge through a disciple of Lai called Pi.

When he considered himself sufficiently prepared, Wu Chung went to *Chiang Nan* (name given in China to the Southern territories) to test his knowledge in *Pachi Chuan*. At that time, the Shaolin Temple had been burnt down and a new temple, founded in the South, had come to be known as Shaolin of the South. The temple was heavily guarded and numerous traps were installed to impede access and to prevent attacks. It was a custom for the best-known martial artists to go to this temple and test their abilities by trying to enter, but until that moment no one had succeeded. Wu Chung tried himself and not only did he succeed, but he repeated the feat three times. This came to be heard by the king, a great lover of Martial Arts, who called Wu Chung to his palace. Eager to know if all that was said about him was true, the king asked Wu Chung to fight against Mao Yun Mo, a high-ranking palace official who was a renowned spear artist. In those days, the tip of the spears was replaced by a ball of cloth covered with flour for friendly fights. Wu Chung, who was by this time an accomplished artist of the long *Pachi Chuan* spear, had no difficulty in touching Mao Yun three times, with the latter surrendering before Wu Chung's skill. From then on, Wu came to be known as "Wu Chung of the Saint's spear", becoming the most famous martial artist of the capital.

Wu Chung had only one daughter, Wu Rong, who was initiated by him. Wu Rong got married to a renowned Kung Fu master from the town of Luo Tong. A son was born from this union, but he inherited his father's surname thus bringing to an end the Wu lineage. Nowadays there are *Pachi Chuan* practitioners in Mang village, close to Tsang Zhou, who claim to be heirs of the Wu lineage. This, however, is not likely, as it was mentioned before that the Wu lineage came to an end after Wu Chung failed to produce male descendants. Nevertheless, Wu Rong did have an initiated student: Chang Kuo-Ming.

Chang Kuo-Ming, who came from the Mang district of the Hou Pei province, stood out because of his skill with the spear. Chang Kuo-Ming initiated his son, Chang Ching-Hsing, and the latter initiated his own son, Chang Yu-Heng. The three of them, from grandfather to grandson, are known for their use of the spear. Chang Ching-Hsing was hired by the Tientsin Wusu Kung Fu Association, while Chang Yu-Heng was an army instructor.

Chang Kuo-Ming initiated Huang Szu-Hai, who came from the the town of Luo Tong. Later Huang Szu-Hai initiated Li Shu-Wen, who came to be the most famous *Pachi Chuan* master of the late Qing dynasty and the Republic.

2.3 Li Shu-Wen

Li Shu-Wen (1864–1934) was a native of the town of Nan Liang. He practiced Martial Arts throughout his life and was never defeated in the numerous combats he held. He had a deadly fist and his foremost skill in the use of the long *Pachi Chuan* spear made him earn the name of *Shen Chiang Li*: "Li, the spear wizard".

In addition to being initiated by Huang Szu-Hai, Li Shu-Wen was also initiated in another *Pachi Chuan* lineage, that of *Chin Pachi Chuan*, from where the techniques of *Pachi Chuan*'s most famous weapon —the spear— come from. Since initiation in *Chin Pachi Chuan* was secret, it is very difficult to know its lineage. However, it is known that Chin Ming-Chi initiated Chin Tien-Shen and that Li Shu-Wen was initiated by the latter.

Portrait of the "spear wizard" Li Shu-Wen

Moreover, it is said that Li Shu-Wen studied advanced *Pikua Chuan* techniques with Huang Lin-Piao. This story is credible due to the fact that those who studied *Pachi Chuan* also studied *Pikua Chuan* and if Li Shu-Wen devoted himself to the in-depth study of Martial Arts, it is likely that he sought and learnt from other masters.

He worked as a Martial Arts instructor for an army general called Hsu Lan-Cho. Later, another government official called Li Ching-Lin employed him to go to Tientsin in order to teach army officers and instructors. Thus it was that he devoted his life to teaching, especially military men, training many students.

Li Shu-Wen had a reputation for being a dangerous man, and this was no exaggeration. Li challenged anyone who intended to show his Martial Arts skills, and his mastery was such that he would announce the technique that he would use and would warn the opponent to watch out for a particular attack, which he then employed successfully and often lethally. Indeed, his great skill led him to kill many of his adversaries.

He was not able to control his energy when he could not fight, and to calm himself down he would gnaw at rocks and hit trees that would later dry out. When eating chicken, he would eat even the bones, and when he practiced, the then common paper windows of Chinese homes would shake under the energy released, and sometimes even break.

On one occasion a student of his, the general Chang Hsiang-Wu, presented him with a pistol, but Li rejected it, saying that a pistol, because it killed from a distance, would not let him feel death, and so he preferred the spear.

Master Li Shu-Wen lived until his 70s. As he grew older, his behavior became more and more uncomfortable for the officers that employed him, and even Master Liu feared him. Then, hoping to get rid of him, general Chang Hsiang-Wu offered him money to go back to his home in Tsang Zhou, Hou Pei province. Master Li agreed to leave Huang Hsian, but he asked Master Liu to accompany him. By then General Chang had offered Master Liu a post as a secret agent, so Master Liu apologized and decided to stay.

Master Li Shu-Wen died shortly after leaving Huang Hsian. There are two versions regarding the circumstances under which he died. The first one tells of him going to Wei Shien and staying at a hotel which turned out to be owned by the son of an old adversary who had been killed by Li Shu-Wen. Thirst for revenge led the hotel owner to poison Li Shu-Wen, who died sitting in his hotel room. This is the version that Master Liu heard and later told Master Su.

The second version tells that Master Li Shu-Wen went to Tientsin, Hou Pei province, and settled in his nephew's house, which had been a gift of the emperor to the Li family. The nephew and his students would train regularly in the courtyard of the house and one evening in which Master Li sat down to see them train, he died of a stroke. Master Su heard this version from Master Li Zhi-Cheng, Master Li Shu-Wen's grandson.

Neither Master Liu nor Master Li Zhi-Cheng were present at Master Li Shu-Wen's death. These are only two versions of the story, and it is not possible to know which one is true, though it is certain that Master Li Shu-Wen's body is buried near the house where he was born in Nan Liang.

Picture taken in Nan Liang, 2003, by the tomb of Li Shu-Wen, with heirs of his lineage representing countries from all over the world.

2.4 Li Shu-Wen's successors

Master Li Shu-Wen's Kung Fu teachings may be divided into three types or levels, according to the period of his life in which he taught. A line of descendants survives for each of these periods.

One of his first disciples, and the one who succeeded him in the first level, was Huo Tien-Kuo. Originally from the town of Hsiao Chi, he had studied Martial Arts during his youth. Later he went on to study *Pachi Chuan*, *Pikua Chuan* and *Lio Hoe Ta Chiang* (Six Unions long spear) with Master Li Shu-Wen for more than ten years. His nickname was *Tie Kuo Po* (Iron Arm) and he came to be personal guard and *Pachi Chuan* master of Pu Yi, China's last emperor. Huo went to Tientsin and Changchun with the emperor and taught *Pachi Chuan* in his travels. This is why there still are many people who practice *Pachi Chuan* in Tientsin and Changchun. This line of descendants shows techniques of Li Shu-Wen's first period.

There is another line of teachings still practiced in many places and corresponding to Li Shu-Wen's second period. However, the *Pachi Chuan* coming from this line, as we see it today, differs considerably from the original due to changes and combinations that have taken place over the years. The transmitters of this line were Ma Fong-Tu and Ma Ying-Tu.

Ma Fong-Tu (1886-1976), from the Sino-Islamic Hui minority, had already studied *Tong Pei Chuan* when he started to study *Pachi Chuan* with Master Li Shu-Wen. He was famous for his skill with the double broadsword and he was accordingly refered to as "Double-Broadsword Ma" (*Ma Shuang Tao*). He graduated from Pei Yang University, was a member of the Republican Society and held several public offices. He was also the founder of *Ma Shu Pachi Chuan* (*Pachi Chuan* of Ma) and it is because of these changes that this *Pachi Chuan* began to diverge from the original, having broader stances, wider movements and longer steps. His four sons are still active and are referees in national Martial Arts competitions.

Ma Ying-Tu, Ma Fong-Tu's brother, had been a Martial Arts instructor in the army, where he had several positions and even became a general. Thanks to the Ma brothers, the army of *Hsi Pei* — name given to Northwestern China — became famous because of its skill in the use of the broadsword. They instructed their soldiers in the use of Martial Arts techniques, thus showing its effectiveness in war and helping them acquire great prominence within the army.

In 1928, general Chang Chi-Chiang of the *Hsi Pei* army founded the Nanking Central Kuoshu Institute, where the Ma brothers had a leading role. In the 18th year of the Republic (1929), Ma Ying-Tu got an excellent place in the first national Martial Arts examinations. From then on he worked as an instructor in the Central Martial Arts Gym and later served as Director of the Training Department, from where he made *Pachi Chuan* a compulsory course.

The third line of Li Shu-Wen's teachings corresponds to the *Pachi Chuan* that he taught Liu Yun-Chiao. This is the *Pachi Chuan* of Li Shu-Wen's mature age, when he was already 55 years old. Together with Liu Yun-Chiao also studied one of his father's employees called Li Chen-Wu. He was actually recruited when Master Liu started to study, so that the young Liu could have someone to practice with. Later, Li Chen-Wu would become the personal bodyguard of Mao Tse-Tung and his secretary, Chu En-Lai.

This third line remained unknown in China until recently, to the point that even Ma Ying-Tu denied its existence. In the 1960s, when one of Master Liu's Japanese students inquired him, Master Liu told him that if he wanted to know the truth, he should look for Ma Ying-Tu and ask him to talk to Li Chen-Wu, who was already Mao Tse-Tung's bodyguard. Thus the student went to China, contacted Ma Ying-Tu and told him the story.

Master Liu Yun-Chiao performs *Tcha Tu, Pachi Chuan*.

Ma contacted Mao's personal guard and managed to find Li Chen-Wu, who confirmed the story.

2.5 Liu Yun-Chiao

Liu Yun-Chiao was Master Li Shu-Wen's last student and hence the bearer of the teachings of his mature age. As mentioned above, Li Chen-Wu studied together with Master Liu, but he was not in fact a real disciple.

Grand Master Liu was born in 1909 in Chi Pei To, Tsang Zhou, Hou Pei province, into one of the wealthiest families of Tsang Zhou county. It was a family of high-ranking public and military officials, several of which had served in the governments of the Ming and Qing dynasties. Liu's father had only had daughters and it was only towards the end of his life that he received an heir, Liu Yun-Chiao.

As a child, Liu was of poor health, and this caused his father many worries, since losing his only son would mean the loss of the family's heir. It was in order to strengthen his son's weak constitution that he made him practice Kung Fu from an early age. Master Liu started studying with Chang Yao-Ting, who happened to be *Pao Piao* (bodyguard) of his grandfather and then governor of Tsang Zhou. Chang Yao-Ting taught *Mitzong Chuan* and *Taitzu Chang Chuan* to the young Liu, who worked hard and noticeably improved his health.

At that time, Tsang Zhou county was on the main route for those heading towards Beijing, and every martial artist or caravan guard going to Beijing had to pay his respects to the governor. This influx of people related to Martial Arts in one way or another made Tsang Zhou county be known as the "Home of Martial Arts".

Master Liu and Master Su, 1982.

Chang Yao-Ting became very old and when he could no longer teach young Liu, his father had to look for another master and called upon Li Shu-Wen, who was known as the best and strongest martial artist of the time. Li Shu-Wen accepted taking care of Liu's education under the condition that no one was to interfere with his work. Liu's father accepted the conditions and put his son in the hands of the new master.

From that moment on and for more than ten years, Grand Master Liu had to endure the severity of the training imposed by an already ageing Li Shu-Wen. This is how Grand Master Liu acquired all his secrets and techniques.

When he was only 17 years old, Li Shu-Wen took Liu Yun-Chiao out of Tsang Zhou for him to test his skills against other martial artists. Liu defeated all his opponents and thus earned the name *Hsiao Pa Wang*: "Little Tyrant King". Later they went to Huang Hsian, Shandong, to meet one of Master Li's old students, general Chang Hsiang-Wu.

Liu stayed in Shandong province as Chang Hsiang-Wu's guest. During the time he spent with the general, he had the chance to meet and study with the masters that visited the military base. It was there that he met masters Ting Tzu-Cheng and Kung Pao-Tien, from whom he learnt Liohoe Tanglang Chuan and Pakua Chang, respectively. With general Chang Hsiang-Wu he studied Tai Chi Chuan, the sword and the broadsword.

It was about this time that Li Shu-Wen died. Liu's father then summoned him back and sent him off to study at Beijing military academy. The end of his studies coincided with the start of the war against Japan, and having joined the Chinese forces, he was eventually taken prisoner. His fame as a martial artist had reached the Japanese, and he was forced to fight against them. Making a great display of his skills, he earned his captors' admiration, leading them to relax their surveillance over him. Master Liu eventually took advantage of the situation and put into practice his knowledge of *Chin Kong* —a technique for very high jumping— to flee the prison. The Japanese guards went after him and one of the soldiers found him hiding in a stream. He was attacked with the bayonet, but managed to grab it, knock the soldier down and kill him. Nonetheless, he received a wound in his arm that made him wary to teach any Japanese in the future.

Master Liu and Master Su, when the latter was 25 years old.

Master Liu eventually met his troops and continued his work as a secret agent. His secret name was *Tien Tzu* 001 and his actions had great influence over the events that took place in China in that time. He had to kill Sun Tuan-Huan, a general who intended to divide China by seceding from the South. He also had to kill Tan Sao-I, a former governor who wanted to surrender part of China to Japan.

Mao Tse-Tung's revolution seized power in 1949 and Chang Kai-Chek's republican government had to flee. The leaders of the republic entrusted Master Liu with the heavy golden seals that sanction the president and the secretary of the republic, for him to take to Taiwan. Without these seals, Taiwan would not be a country today.

Grand Master Liu worked for the party as a high-ranking officer, but despite his merits, he was not promoted to the rank of general. This upset him to the point that he took an early retirement, before he was 50 years old. Later, a chance meeting with Chang Hsiang-Shan, a *Liohoe Tanglang Chuan* master, brought about his return to the world of Martial Arts. Because of his extensive Martial Arts knowledge, Grand Master Liu

Last picture of Master Liu in Beijing in 1991, where he hands Master Su the documents that accredit him as guardian of *Pachi Chuan*.

was called upon to take care of the training of Taiwan's presidential secret service agents.

In 1968 he was invited to the Great Chinese Martial Arts Demonstration in Malaysia, where he demonstrated *Pachi Chuan*, astonishing the competitors from Taiwan, Thailand, Singapore, Vietnam, Hong Kong and Malaysia with his skill. This was the first time that China was represented abroad by a national team. Master Su and Master Adam Hsu also participated in this demonstration.

In 1971, Master Liu founded a Martial Arts magazine called *Wu Tang*, together with some of his students. They also founded the *Wu Tang Center for the Development of Martial Arts*, where Master Liu started to teach openly. His teaching activity in his school as well as in Taiwan's presidential secret service continued until his last days.

Although many excellent students were trained in his school, Liang Chi-Tsu, Adam Hsu, Su Yu-Chang and Chen Kuo-Chin were the most outstanding. Their teachings have spread throughout the world and today we find practitioners of their *Pachi Chuan* in South America, Canada, United States, Spain, Japan and other countries.

In 1991, already in poor health, Grand Master Liu visited continental China after forty years of absence. By the time he returned from the journey his physical condition had deteriorated and he died in Taipei on January 24th, 1992.

Master Liu, sitting next to his wife. Standing are Master Su, his children and a group of students from Majorca. 1991.

In the world of Martial Arts, Master Liu's feats have become legendary and were even the inspiration for a film's script.

Below, Master Su relates some anecdotes that serve as an illustration of the technique quality of one of the last Martial Arts masters to use them for what they were meant for.

> "When I studied with him, he used to tell us a lot about his life, about his fights and adventures. Many Martial Arts books talk about him, but I will only refer what I have witnessed."
>
> "I met him in 1963, when he was 51 years old. One day in that same year, I was studying in his house while it rained heavily and water ran nonstop through a leak on the roof. I saw him go out to the garden and leap to the roof using a *Chin Kong* movement to repair the broken tiles. I estimated the roof was more than two meters high."
>
> "Once, I went to the cinema with him and his wife. While we were queuing outside to get the tickets, a cyclist bumped into my master's wife and went on his way without apologizing. The man had barely advanced three or four meters when my upset master caught up with him in two strides and grabbed

him softly from both sides of the torso. The cyclist crumbled and fell to the ground unconscious. Master Liu then came back to the queue as if nothing had happened. Ten minutes later the cyclist was still lying on the ground, so my master gave me a signal to go with him to tend to the man. We approached him and my master brought him back to his senses with a simple kick."

"On another occasion, my master had a relative with a five or six year old child for a visit. My master started playing with the child asking him fondly to bite him. The child tried to bite his arm, then his back and finally his stomach, but it was impossible, he could not sink his teeth in. Instead he started to cry with a sore jaw. I always found remarkable that my master's body, without being fat, had a distinct roundedness and was full of energy."

"The following year, my master and I went to the countryside, to the house of one of his friends. The people of the area had the custom of having many dogs and one of my master's friend's dogs attacked him with a jump. My master gave it a fast but seemingly soft pat. The dog was sent two or three meters away and got up howling. A short while later it collapsed bleeding through the mouth and died."

"Several years later, in another visit to the countryside, my master taught me how to hit a dog to kill it. I was happy when I managed to put into practice the technique, thinking that I had gained command of my energy. However, my master told me that there was still a lot to learn, and to prove it he stroked a dog from head to tail and the dog only managed to walk a few meters before dying. Then I asked my master: 'what Kung Fu technique did you use to kill in this way'. My master replied that he had only used his energy to break the dog's gall bladder."

"Another time, during a meeting of the Chinese Olympic Committee, a famous Judo instructor (7th Dan) asked my master who was the Martial Arts director at the time. 'I am,' said Master Liu. 'Do you know Judo or do you only know how to punch?', rebuked the judoka. My master replied: 'I only

Master Liu Yun-Chiao performs the movement
Ma Shu Shuang Chong Chang of *Pachi Chuan*.

know that you are not capable of taking me down.' They both went down to the combat area, where my master stood on *Ma Suh* stance and demanded the judoka to try to move him. For three minutes, however hard the Judo instructor tried, he was unable to move Master Liu by a single inch. But not only that, the judoka fell to the ground exhausted and needed a week of rest to recover. When I asked my master what 'magic' he had used, he told me that it was the projection of infiltrating *Pachi Chuan* energy. Using this technique one may redirect the adversary's energy toward himself. 'That is why he didn't have any strength over me. His strength was diverted outwards,' said Master Liu."

2.6 Su Yu-Chang

Master Su started to study Martial Arts at a young age. He studied *Mitzong Chuan* and *Tanglang Chuan* with Master Chang Te-Kuei for more than 10 years during his childhood and adolescence. In 1957 he left his hometown Tong Shan, Tainan district, Taiwan, and went to the capital Taipei, where he worked and studied *Tanglang Chuan* with the great masters Wei Hsiao-Tang and Li Kuen-Shan. Back then, Master Su was also interested in the style Mitzong Chuan, so in 1960 he made contact with the great master of that style, Li Yuen-Tzu (1904–1972), and started to study with him. Li Yuen-Tzu was also who introduced Master Su to *Pachi Chuan*.

Grand Master Li Yuen-Tzu had studied *Mitzong Chuan* with Master Chen Yu-Shan, who had been a bodyguard of Sun

Master Su and Master Adam Hsu standing by Master Chang Te-Kuei.

Yatsen, the father of the Chinese Republic and leader of the uprising that overthrew the emperor. Master Li Yuen-Tzu had also studied *Shuai Chiao* (grabs and dislocations) with his father-in-law and great master Tong Chong-I. Furthermore, he had learned *Pachi Chuan* from Ma Ying-Tu, Li Shu-Wen's disciple, at the Nanking Central Kuoshu Institute. In 1929, he participated in the Martial Arts Tournament held at Shanghai, where he obtained the highest marks. When he graduated he became instructor at the Central Institute, as well as in the Army. Despite having taught many people during his whole life, he did not have a disciple that became his 'heir'. He nevertheless left some written works such as *The Meihua Broadsword*, *The Ching Ping Sword* and others. His father-in-law was very well-known for his skill in *Liohoe Chuan* (Six Harmonies Fist) and his *Shuai Chiao* techniques.

Between 1960 and 1962, Master Su did his military service and during that time he taught *Pachi Chuan* in a military school. However, he had not learned all the forms of the style, so when he left the army he looked for Li Yuen-Tzu to continue studying *Pachi Chuan*. Li Yuen-Tzu was ill and could not teach him, but instead told him about a disciple of the great Li Shu-Wen who was known as a high-class martial artist in Northern China and had apparently come to Taiwan to serve in the army. Upon Li Yuen-Tzu's suggestion to look for him, Master Su set about finding whether that master was actually in Taiwan.

Master Li Yuen-Tzu and Master Su in 1958.

In 1963, Master Liu Yun-Chiao was out for a walk in the new Taipei Park when he saw a man teaching *Liohoe Tanglang Chuan*. The image brought him fond memories, since he had learned the style in his youth. He approached the man and it turned out that he was Chang Hsiang-Shan, an old classmate whom he had not met for the past 30 years. This is how it was discovered that Master Liu was in Taiwan and many martial artists went to meet him. It was then that Adam Hsu, Liang Chi-Tsu and Su Yu-Chang started studying *Pachi Chuan* with master Liu.

From that moment on, Master Su became Liu Yun-Chiao's most assiduous disciple and managed to learn the whole *Pachi Chuan* system. In 1978 he left Taiwan and since then he has traveled all around the world disseminating the truth of Martial Arts.

In August 1991, Master Su Yu-Chang was staying in Beijing together with his children and some of his Spanish students on his way to a traditional Kung Fu competition in Jinan, Shandong province. Knowing that Grand Master Liu was in town, Master Su went to visit him. In the hotel where Master Liu was lodging, aware that he did not have much time left, he designated Master Su as guardian of the secrets of the lineage. Shortly after their return from the journey, master and disciple met again in Taiwan, where Master Liu handed over the secret *Pachi Chuan* writings.

Ten years have passed since the first Spanish edition of this book came out. Things have changed and today *Pachi Tanglang Chuan* schools exist in many countries; books and instructive videos have been published. *Pachi*

Tanglang Chuan's combat efficacy has been proved again and again in many competitions.

Beijing, 1993

Venezuela, 1996

Taiwan, 2000

Master Su is very well-known in Japan because of a series of comics that tell his adventures in Taiwan, while he taught a Japanese student called Matsuda.

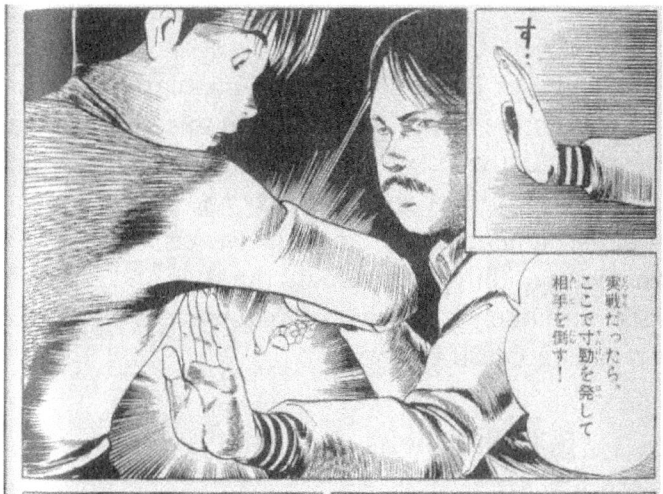

Pages of Japanese comics featuring Master Su.

Chapter 3

Pachi Chuan

> In *Pachi Chuan*, every technique is applied with maximum power, all the force is externalized. There is no such a thing as 'almost' in *Pachi Chuan*: its techniques represent the commitment to 'everything or nothing.'

What is the meaning of *Pachi Chuan*? The popular version says that the original name was *Pa Tze Chuan*. According to this, the style had this name because of the shape of the characteristic *Pachi Chuan* fist, which resembles a rake. The Chinese word for rake is *pa tze* and its pronunciation is very close to that of *pachi*, hence the change. However, *Pa Tze Chuan* would be a prosaic name with nothing to say about the style and rather inappropriate. *Pachi Chuan* is more likely to be the original name if we take into account the esoteric meaning that it conveys.

3.1 Simplicity and effectiveness

'Pa' means eight: eight places, eight points, eight directions or eight poles. 'Chi' means limit, extreme boundary, very (it is a superlative). In *Pachi Chuan* there are four body parts with two directions each, totalling eight poles or extreme points. The four parts are the head, the upper limbs, the torso and the lower limbs. The two poles of the head correspond to the

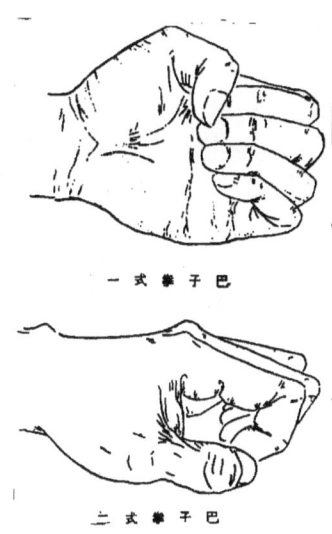

Master Liu Yun-Chiao's drawings of the *Pachi Chuan* fist.

right and left parietal bones; in the upper limbs, the poles correspond to the empty circles formed by the semi-closed fists (called *Pachi* fist); in the torso they are the outer regions of the hip (the iliac crests); in the lower limbs they are two secret places of the feet.

Although the origins of *Pachi Chuan* are not known for certain, a deeper analysis reveals it as a very mature style. It seems to be case that the creator, or creators, of *Pachi Chuan* extracted the most economical and powerful techniques and the most efficient training methods from various other styles, always choosing the best and aiming at efficacy. *Pachi Chuan* was constituted as an art for war, and then as now, everything related to war was studied to the minutest detail. The greater risks are thus exposed and the essential is retained while the superficial is discarded. This is how *Pachi Chuan* was formed, with such a selective refining of techniques that only one in a hundred was kept.

As a result of this strict selection, and contrary to what occurs in most other Kung Fu styles which have numerous and complicated techniques, *Pachi Chuan* uses only a few techniques that are characteristic because of their pureness, power and frankness. Instead of diversity and complexity, *Pachi Chuan* favors conciseness and apparent simplicity, giving always primacy to and following always the most pure and essential ways.

The use of *Pachi Chuan* in combat requires the application of all the energy.

Pachi Chuan is a style without ornamentation or excesses, its techniques are refined. If one were to choose a Chinese character to describe its philosophy, perhaps it should be 近 (*chin*), which translated literally means "near", alluding to *Pachi Chuan*'s ultimate objective: proximity, the shortest and fastest way to its goal, feet and hands using the most efficient shortcut to "open the doors" (terminology used to describe the penetration of the enemy's defenses). When a battle is waged in a war, troops and armed vehicles will not necessarily move through the routes people use in normal circumstances, nor will they limit themselves to the existing roads, they will take whichever path is the shortest and most direct. Likewise, *Pachi Chuan* takes the most direct routes, the "shortcuts".

Every technique is applied with maximum power, all the force is externalized. In *Pachi Chuan* 'almost' does not exist; its techniques represent the commitment to 'everything or nothing'. There is a Chinese proverb used to illustrate this attitude: "When the lion attacks the elephant, it uses all his might. When it attacks the rabbit, it does so just the same." *Pachi Chuan* is black and white, everything and nothing, it means staying always alert and sharp with a firm intent on destroying the enemy.

It is a style that may change in an instant from very soft to very strong, from very slow to very fast. Energy and spirit must be together during the whole execution of a form. This is something very special and fascinating about this style. It is possible to feel an intense contrast between the strong and the soft, the instantaneous change from absolute calm to the most powerful explosion of force.

The secret of the style consists in learning how to concentrate all the body's energy on any one point, which is not necessarily the fist or the foot. It is this concentrated energy that may kill, physical strength being of secondary importance. Another fundamental characteristic of the style is

Group of participants of the first international seminar of the Pachi Tanglang Martial Arts Institute. Pocono, USA, 1995-1996.

the great speed and force developed in very short distances. In *Pachi Chuan* one single strike is deadly.

Penetration in combat has three steps. The first before physical contact, the second with the first contact and the third when the force of the strike is transmitted. In most Martial Arts these three aspects are independent and are studied separately. In *Pachi Chuan*, on the contrary, each movement has all three elements: the energy of one strike does not stop until it reaches its target. These compact training techniques are representative of the economy and philosophy of "proximity" of *Pachi Chuan*.

3.2 Studying *Pachi Chuan*

The attitude of someone who undertakes the study of *Pachi Chuan* should be like the style itself: serious and practical. *Pachi Chuan* benefits health and, when practiced at a high level, it can also be very appealing. It is a superior Martial Art for the serious martial artist. Whoever is not prepared for great dedication, effort and devotion will not be able to practice this style. Furthermore, the study of *Pachi Chuan* has a special characteristic: if practiced seriously and with dedication, one may attain the highest: in Taoism, Tao, in Buddhism, Nirvana.

Without the proper attitude, studying *Pachi Chuan* may prove to be very difficult. This is a very little-known style partly because the first steps in its study are different to those of other styles due to its sobriety and its apparently simple movements. We could compare it to an aged whiskey

First group of students of the Pachi Tanglang Chuan Martial Arts Institute in Japan, 1991.

International seminar of the Pachi Tanglang Martial Arts Institute. Holland, 2001.

whose subtleties cannot be appreciated by everyone. To be able to feel the benefits of *Pachi Chuan* one must be willing to persevere, since they do not become apparent in a short time. Other styles with rapid and varied movements give the impression of having received good results in a short time. On the contrary, with its short and simple movements the aim of which is to project energy, *Pachi Chuan* does not show results in a short period of time. In *Pachi Chuan*, internal energy is felt more than the external movements. Consequently many more years of practice are required to be able to appreciate it.

The rush and 'magic recipes' for 'fast and easy' learning have come to dominate the Martial Arts of our times. This approach to Kung Fu has, unfortunately, lowered the quality of Chinese Martial Arts. Without an adequate basis and a step-by-step training there is no substance to the forms. Knowing the movements without knowing the applications transforms them into a Chinese dance. A whole style may be learned in a single day ignoring the traditional steps needed to acquire a true command of Kung Fu. However, mastery of a single style requires years of dedication. Many "masters" appear nowadays, people who believe they know the art of a style just because they know a few forms. Today someone studied with me, tomorrow he goes about proclaiming to be one of my best students and to have studied under my masters. Such people do not carry the essence of the Art.

Initial training is crucial, since solid foundations are as essential to high levels of *Pachi Chuan* as good excavations and solid foundations are to tall buildings.

Since *Pachi Chuan* is a style without many forms, it may become monotonous or boring if training is not sustained onto the point where the energy arises. This is why many *Pachi Chuan* students simultaneously study other styles, to overcome this stage with relative ease. Someone studying *Pachi Chuan* from an early age does not need to study another style. However, according to the ancient tradition, it is important for *Pachi Chuan* to be studied together with *Pikua Chuan*. This is because *Pachi Chuan*, being a style with short-distance attacks,

Master Su together with his son, Su Wei-Jen, holding the championship trophy awarded at the first Jinan International Traditional Martial Arts tournament. China, 1991.

short displacements, very strong, tough, aggressive, *yang*, needs the complement of a style characterized by longer range combat, softer, calmer, *yin*. That style is *Pikua Chuan*. It was Li Shu-Wen who fostered the joint use of the two styles and established the simultaneous teaching of both. This is what made him the best, a fact proved and definitely established through his actions.

While *Pachi Chuan* should be complemented with *Pikua Chuan*, it is not important to practice it together with other styles. If so done, nonetheless, results may be obtained faster.

The study of *Pachi Chuan* is focused from the start on energy management. At the beginning, practice is oriented towards concentrating all the energy in one point, which is the vertex of a triangle. Once this stage is mastered, one must learn how to apply the energy according to the vertices of a square, in every direction, like a bomb explosion. Then one moves into the circle, learning how to manage energy within a circular shape. The opponent will thus be unable to understand your intentions or to foresee where the strike will come from. At this stage one is able to produce both soft and strong energy with any part of the body. Many people think that to be devastating one must use strong energy, but one may also be devastating using soft energy. Control of soft energy together with strong energy is a masterly achievement of the highest levels of *Pachi Chuan*.

Chapter 4

Learning *Pachi Chuan*

> The study of *Pachi Chuan* is more difficult than that of other styles because the management of energy is essential in order to perform the movements correctly. If a *Pachi Chuan* strike does not carry internal energy it is not authentic *Pachi Chuan*, even if it carries mechanical energy. A true Master is necessary to become able to manage internal energy, because internal energy is invisible.

From an esoteric point of view, the two characters in the name *Pachi* describe the various concepts that constitute the universe in which the learning of the style takes place.

4.1 *Pachi*: Eight extremes

Pa, in Chinese, means eight. In *Pachi Chuan*, the number eight refers to several concepts that must be known by whoever hopes to attain the highest levels of its study.

Pachi, eight extremes

The first concept refers to the parts of the body that establish the energetic configuration in the practice of *Pachi Chuan* and which constitute the essential points of the flow of energy. These points have a role in any combat action of *Pachi Chuan*. More details about these eight points will be given later.

The number eight also appears, very importantly, in the eight learning stages of *Pachi Chuan*, which will be described in the next section. Its philosophical description is given in terms of the eight trigrams. Its energetic description involves four energies of essence and four energies of spirit. The plane is defined in terms of the eight directions, while space-time is likewise described using eight parameters: above and below, left and right, forward and backward, weight and thought.

The techniques of bodily movement also revolve around the number eight, hence that the ultimate form of *Pachi Chuan* is *Pa Ta Chao Su*, "Eight Secret Movements."

On the other hand, the term *Chi* in the name *Pachi Chuan* implies that one must go to the limit. This defines the objectives of *Pachi Chuan*. One must be able to expand oneself towards the outside and reach infinity, while at the same time being able to concentrate oneself inwardly into an infinitely small and elusive point.

4.2 Learning stages of *Pachi Chuan*

In other styles, the student will first study the movement alone, and only later will he go into the management of energy. In *Pachi Chuan*'s approach, the student will start directly dealing with energy. Its method starts with the preparation of the body by means of the practice of stances. Then the focus is on the development of energy and force. Finally, the flow of energy is studied. Once this is done, the energy must be strengthened to the limit, and this will determine the practitioner's level.

The study of *Pachi Chuan* may be divided into nine stages which develop as the student progresses. These nine stages indicate the practitioner's level in terms of the quality of his energy and his capacity to manage it. The nine stages are the following:

Master Su performs the Tiao Ta Ting Chou position. Picture taken in Cang Zhou, birthplace of Pachi Chuan, 1982.

1. *Fang Song Tzu Jan* 放鬆自然: Natural relaxation of the body, seeking the original energy.

2. *Shen Chin Pa Ku* 伸筋拔骨: Stretching of the tendons and joints so that the energy may reach every part of the body.

3. *Wu Shing Chi Ching* 五行氣勁: The body energy may be transformed into the energy of the Five Elements.

4. *To Chin Ku Mo* 透筋骨膜: The energy goes into the tendons, muscles and organs.

5. *Shan Shi Ku Suei* 滲洗骨髓: The energy cleanses the bone marrow and may be projected outside the body.

6. *Wu Chi Kuei Yuen* 五氣歸原: Secret transmitted only to *Paisu* students.

7. *San Tsai Chi Ting* 三才聚頂: Secret transmitted only to *Paisu* students.

8. *Tien Ren Ho I* 天人合一: Secret transmitted only to *Paisu* students.

9. *Tao Shen Wu Chi* 道神無極: Secret transmitted only to *Paisu* students.

It is customary for only the two first levels to be taught to non *Paisu* students. The term *Paisu* here means "initiated student", but the significance of being a *Paisu* student will be explained later.

The nine stages are mentioned here so that their existence may be known. However, of these nine stages, only the first five may be comprehended in some way, the others lying within the realm of the spirit, beyond rational grasp. For this reason, their realization is conditioned by having the necessary level and being amongst the *Paisu* students.

The practitioner who has reached the first two stages will have reached the essence of Kung Fu. The body of the one who reaches the stages three and four will have been transformed into that of a saint, and he will have the level of a master. If the practitioner reaches stages five and six, he will be a saint and will have *Chinkan Ti* (body and mind as strong as a diamond). At stage seven, the practitioner will have a body of *Lohan*. At stage eight the spirit reaches *Pusa* and finally, at stage nine, *Tao* or nirvana is attained.

On the first two stages, the land and the materials for building the house are obtained. With *Wu Shing Chi Ching*, building works begin. Traditionally, more than ten years were required to reach *Wu Shing Chi Ching*. Then at least another ten years were needed to go through the next four stages. Nowadays, however, the Master speaks more clearly and we have resources such as videos, which make a more detailed study possible, so one might not need so much time to reach a high level.

Due to the incapacity of the beginner to move the energy, the path of study starts with what is available to him or her, namely, the movement of the body. Hence, all the stages, and specially the first two, correspond to various types of increasingly sophisticated physical activity that foster the transition from mere bodily movement to the movement of the energy.

4.2.1 *Fang Song Tzu Jan*. Natural relaxation

During the initial stages of the study of the management of the body and of physical strength, the student falls into unnatural patterns of body usage.

Master Su performs *Shen Ching Pa Ku* in *Chi Ma Su* stance

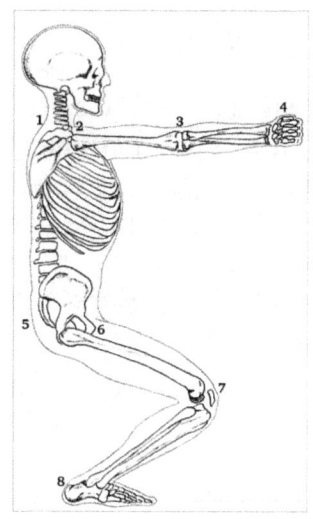

Location of the "Eight Places"

It is therefore necessary to transform such patterns into movements with technique, and to cultivate a natural capacity for relaxation, in order to dispel the tension accumulated due to performing incorrect movements and working with unnatural energy.

Fang Song means relaxing in order to let the energy flow. Without being completely relaxed it is not possible to have a powerful *Fa Ching*. Using *Fang Song* one may achieve strong and natural movements.

The higher the tension in the practitioner, the greater the tendency to lift the energy and the body upwards. To be able to attain relaxation eliminating the unnatural tensions, it is necessary to lower the body and the energy. This is done by means of *Fang Song*.

To attain *Fang Song*, the physical and mental efforts are focused on letting oneself go without obstacles, specially downwards. The "precipitation" or "sinking" energy (*Chen Sui Ching*) is the most characteristic sign that relaxation is being gained and the emergence of a feeling of having a center is its most immediate achievement.

Tzu Jan means "natural". There are two things which must become natural when starting to study Kung Fu: the movement of the body and the thoughts of the spirit. Someone who approaches the study with the wish of finishing fast or wanting to know a lot, is already mistaken because he has a preconceived idea and is also anxious; his thoughts are not natural. When the student has his own ideas, a conflict with the teaching is bound to arise; this is why the natural spirit requires patience. Similarly, since the body already has its own movement, there are fixed ideas of what the movement is, and these ideas may conflict with the movements being taught; this is why movements must be natural. In order to transform movements into real movements, they must be natural. In other words, they must be soft. Soft does not mean slack or slow: it means relaxed.

4.2.2 *Shen Chin Pa Ku*. Stretching the tendons and separating the joints

The second stage of learning and a fundamental part of the practice of *Pachi Chuan* is a technique called *Shen Chin Pa Ku*. Its aim is to increase the separation of the ligaments of the joints, in order to bring about the elongation of the tendons. The practice of this technique also helps to dispel tensions and to stay relaxed, preventing the stagnation of energy anywhere in the body. This is one of the most important secrets of Chinese Martial Arts, because someone who is not able to acquire *Shen Chin Pa Ku* will never be able to manage his energy in the right way. In general, it is recommended to study this technique before the age of 35–40, as at this age the body starts to naturally lose its strength, and the meridians start to stabilize, making the expansion of energy and the study of *Shen Chin Pa Ku* more difficult.

The intervention of the Master is necessary to be able to gain proficiency in *Shen Chin Pa Ku*, otherwise it is very difficult. *Shen Chin Pa Ku* aims to stretch all the fibers in the body, and to amplify the consciousness of all of them, hence that it should be done in a spiral motion. To develop such consciousness, eight points of reference are established throughout the body. Focusing the attention on these points it is possible to be aware also of the spaces separating them, thus establishing the global perception of the body of the meridians. This focusing of the attention and this attempt at stretching the body starting from these points is the basis of *Shen Chin Pa Ku* in *Pachi Chuan*. Their importance is such that they give the style its name: *Pa* — eight, *Chi* — extreme energies.

The *Shen Chin Pa Ku* technique is simple in principle, since it just consists of adopting one of the several stances of the style and making a mental scan of the eight points, focusing the attention on each one of them. At the same time, one tries to stretch the point itself and the intermediate parts, until acquiring an awareness of the whole body in that stance. The conjunction of the spirit (thought) and the body (stretching) in all the points simultaneously fosters the circulation of energy and thus the awareness of the energetic body.

There are eight points of reference distributed throughout the body, from head to feet. Two of these are single, that is, they are formed by a single point, while the remaining are double. Their location coincides with the joints. Since the capacity for movement of the joints is varied — they can be stretched upwards, downwards, sideways, they can be opened or closed — the characteristics of the stretching of the points is different for each stance. In the section dedicated to the postures of *Pachi Chuan* are specified the characteristics of *Shen Chin Pa Ku* corresponding to the stances *Ma Suh* and *Tan Shan Suh*. *Shen Chin Pa Ku* must be applied in any movement where *Fa Ching* is applied.

EIGHT EXTREME PLACES OF THE BODY: Pachi Ta Chang 八極大槍

The teaching of the *Shen Chin Pa Ku* techniques and the eight places from where action is taken on the body is what proves the Master's intent to teach the real fundamentals of *Pachi Chuan*.

- 頭 **Toh – Head** The first reference point is a single one and is located at the back of the neck, between the shoulder blades, below the prominence of the 7th cervical vertebra (*Ta Tsuei* point). Its area of influence spans from the *Pai Huei* point near the crown of the head down to the *Huei Yin* point at the perineum. It is tensed by the stretching of the neck when the chin and the collarbones are drawn back, arching the shoulder blades and moving the perineum downwards. On the one hand, this point blades and pulling the perineum downwards. On the one hand, this point controls the head, and on the other, it is part of the control mechanism of the shoulder blades, the collarbones and all the muscles around them.

- 肩 **Chien – Shoulders** The second point of reference is double and is located on the shoulders. These points are upwardly related to the first and downwards related to the arms. The movement of the shoulders comes from the shoulder blades, this is why taking care of the movement of the shoulder blades is important. If the movement of the shoulders is not natural, the body becomes restless and tense.

肘 **Chou – Elbows** The third point of reference is located on the elbows and is related upwardly with the shoulders and downwardly with the forearms. The elbows are where the energy coming from the body is transmitted to the hands. They are also responsible for placing the hands in the appropriate position, in accordance with the energy transmitted. This is why the *Shen Chin Pa Ku* of the elbows is important, so that the energy is not blocked and may reach the hands.

手 **Shou – Hands** The next point of reference is located on the wrists and the hands closed into the *Pachi Chuan* fist. It acts upon the hands and it is related to the elbows through the forearms. When talking about the hands, it is important to keep in mind the two basic positions they may take: the fist and the open hand. When the hand is clenched, the energy changes according to the orientation of the fist; when the hand is open, the energy follows the position of the fingers. This makes it possible for the body's energy to reach the tips of the hand while practicing *Shen Chin Pa Ku*.

These four points of reference constitute and act directly upon the upper body, that is above the diaphragm. They also act indirectly upon the lower body, acting as a counterpoint with the lower body's movements.

The points of reference of the lower body are similarly disposed:

尾 **Wei – Coccyx** The fifth point of reference is single and is located at the coccyx. This point changes the movement of the spine so that it can generate the body-energies desired. The spine is the axis of the body energy.

胯 **Kua – Hip** This point is double. Its importance lies in the fact that it carries the body weight. The energy between the trunk and the legs is transferred through this point. The movement of the hip plays an important role in the up-down, front-back and left-right flow of energy. If the *Shen Chin Pa Ku* of the hips is not done correctly, the general agility of the body is hindered.

膝 **Ti – Knees** The seventh point is located at the knees, controlling the thigh and the lower leg. The health and the strength of the body are reflected in the knees. The correct practice of the *Shen Chin Pa Ku* of the knees fosters an increase in the endurance of the body and the energy.

足 **Tzu – Feet** Finally, the eighth point is located at the ankles, heels and soles of the feet. It controls the feet and the legs. This point together with the first and the fifth constitute the axis of the body, as well as the global *San Tsai* that will permit the transformation of the whole body into a fighting weapon in the more advanced stages of study. The body-energy (that is, energy of essence, not that of spirit nor of energy) starts in this last point, this is why at least five forms of *Shen Chin Pa Ku* of the feet should be practiced.

Participants of a *Pa Kun* course in Alaska

The practice of *Shen Chin Pa Ku* leads to an awareness of the constitution of the body as the system of points and intermediate parts, and hence to the capacity of acting at will upon any part of the body. This configuration of the body is actually the one established by the meridians and is manifested physically by means of the tendons.

A student at this stage of learning will be able to manage his body as one whole system and will have an energetic potential, since perhaps even unknowingly, a body of energy will have been constituted. Nevertheless, he will still be ignorant of the techniques for managing that body of energy.

In the *Pachi Chuan* system there are five ways of projecting energy. These are, *Chen Sui Ching* (sinking), *Suh Tzu Ching* (cross), *Chan Suh Ching* (spiraling), *Pao Fa Ching* (explosive) and *Toh Hua Ching* (penetrating). Even if the movements for projecting energy are practiced, without mastery over *Shen Chin Pa Ku* the manifestation of energy is not possible.

4.2.3 *Wu Shing Chi Ching*. Energy of the Five Elements

As we have seen, the first two stages deal, so to speak, with the preparation of the physical condition. In those two stages the body is prepared for the management of energy: firstly, energy is made available by relaxing the body; then, by means of stretching, it is made to circulate through all possible paths. With this, the student has the land and the materials ready for building the house. Now the construction work can begin.

In the third stage, *Wu Shing Chi Ching* is studied: the management of the energy of the Five Elements. The aim at this stage is to develop the capacity to use the energy in a functional and specific manner. By mastering the movements of different parts of the body, particularly the torso, the energy that was made available by means of *Fang Song* relaxation and that was brought into circulation through *Shen Shing Pa Ku* stretching, is now set in motion.

The human body is equipped with a *Natural Energy*, but due to everyday life movements and thoughts it manifests itself as non-natural energy. Natural Energy as such lies outside the human domain; hence, for it to be perceived and used in our human domain it undergoes a process similar to the refraction of light to become Five Natural Energies. The original light is blinding and cannot be perceived; it needs to separate into colors for human perception to take place.

In the human domain, the manifestation of the Natural Energy as natural or non-natural takes place by means of the Five Energies. Our non-natural activities are characterized by one or more of these Five Energies, which have been displaced from their original location in our bodies through the seven Inherited Spirits. This displacement of the Five Energies is necessary for life to continue, since it is by means of that displacement that we relate to our surroundings and we carry out activities. However, this shift of the Five Natural Energies from their original places, which is temporary during early childhood, becomes permanent: our bodies are reconfigured by adopting wrong postures and our minds by memory and the never-ending internal dialogue. Thus, the original centers are deprived of energy, bringing about restlessness, illness and finally death. The aim must therefore be to bring the Five Energies back to their original places with their ensuing reunification and manifestation as Natural Energy. The way of bringing the Five Natural Energies back to their original places is through very specific movements that are to be practiced with equally specific thoughts.

The use of energy in Kung Fu is conditioned by the proper arrangement of the Five Energies in their original places. Only then do they flow and become usable. Otherwise, energy is scattered in the form of bodily tensions and dissipated thoughts, and it cannot flow, let alone be projected out of the body.

This is the real starting point of learning the management of energy proper. In *Pachi Chuan*, the study of the energy of the Five Elements consists of the practice of postures and movements that together with the corresponding thoughts lead the natural energy to surface.

As the student advances in the practice of the movements of the Five Energies, it becomes apparent which of these is more favorable to him or her and may thus be developed more easily, fostering the others to follow suite.

There are actually very few Kung Fu styles that include movements of all Five Energies. This is why it is common to hear that a certain master has one very good punch, but nothing is said about the others.

It is necessary to know the movement and the thought corresponding to each energy to be able to make it surface and learn how to use it.

In *Pachi Chuan* there are two terms related to *Wu Shing*: *Wu Shing Chi Ching* and *Wu Shing Fa Ching*. *Wu Shing Chi Ching* refers to the matter of the energy, which is the Five Elements. *Wu Shing Fa Ching* refers to the five ways of projecting energy. They are studied in two different ways.

4.2.4 *To Chin Ku Mo*. Energy in any point of the body

In the fourth stage, *To Chin Ku Mo*, the practice is oriented towards the management of the energy of the Five Elements within the body. The practice of *To Chin Ku Mo* gives the practitioner the capacity to make the energy circulate through the fourteen meridians and to send it to any part of the body. This makes it possible to act upon the nerves, hormones, glands, etc. By means of the energy, one comes into contact with the interior of one's own body and it is possible to know the state of our organism.

Although in the previous stage the student is already capable of projecting explosive energy, when this stage is mastered the complete management of explosive projection is achieved. Furthermore, the mastery of *To Chin Ku Mo* makes the body capable of receiving strikes without any damage.

4.2.5 *Shan Shi Ku Suei*. Cleansing the marrow

In the fifth stage the practice is oriented towards the cleansing of the marrow. The bone marrow is where the global spirit of the body resides. If one is able to act upon the marrow, then one is able to manage the spirit. This enables management of the energy flow and enables a global circulation of the body energy, not subject to pre-established paths but as an energetic field that may interact with external energy fields. By means of this technique, energy may be projected outside of the body as well as put into contact with external energies and absorb them. Energy may also be used as a protection to block any type of aggression.

In China it is said that whoever achieves this level is a *Kung Fu Sage*. From here on, one goes into matters of the Spirit.

The ultimate learning stages of *Pachi Chuan* are not explained here because their understanding escapes those who lack the energy needed to imagine them.

Group of Pai Su in Holland, 2001.

4.3 *Pachi Chuan* and *Pikua Chuan* forms[1]

It is not necessary to learn all the forms of *Pachi Chuan*; the master will teach the more important forms according to the characteristics and skill of the student.

The forms *Ting Tzu Pa Pu Suh*, *Chinkan Pa Suh*, *Lio Ta Kai*, *Lio Chou Tou Chuan* and *Ta Pachi Chuan* are well-known. However, *Pachi Lienhuan Chuan* was not known by Li Shu-Wen's first disciples because this form was created by him in his last years, when his energy had reached higher levels. Li Shu-Wen realized that what is important is *Kung Li* 功力, the skill developed by means of intense training, and he reorganized the *Pachi Chuan* forms accordingly. *Pachi Lienhuan Chuan* was formed by combining *Chinkan Pa Suh* with *Lio Ta Kai*. Li Shu-Wen created a basic form for all students and five other versions, one for each energy, with the aim of helping students practice the energy that they most need to develop. He applied the same pattern to the spear form *Pachi Ta Chiang*. Li Shu-Wen also created the form *Ing Shou Chuan* with the help of Huo Tien-Kuo, combining the forms *Lio Chou Tou Chuan* and *Lio Ta Ying Chia Chuan*. This is the essence of the *Pachi Chuan* of Li Shu-Wen's last years, and he taught it as such to Master Liu Yun-Chiao.

Similarly, Master Su Yu-Chang has created the forms *Kaimen Chuan*, *Chinkan Chuan*, *Fong Mo Chang Chuan* and *Hsiong Hu Hoe I Chuan* with the aim of making practice easier. In the new forms there are no variations of the basic movements. Instead, new sequences are established to expand the training with alternatives better suited to the teaching needs of today.

All forms are trained in three versions with the aim of achieving increasingly higher levels of energy. The movements are basically the same, but the order and the way they are performed varies slightly. The training of *Pachi Chuan* starts with "calm steps" (*Suh Pachi*), where the movements are done slowly, providing a solid basis. Later, the "lively steps" (*Huo Pachi*) are studied, where the movements are performed faster, making their use in transmitting energy in combat possible. Finally, "bodily conversion" (*Fua Shen*) is practiced, where one strikes with the body; this is a secret technique from which it is very difficult for the opponent to escape and which may cause death. These three types of practice are called "calm *Pachi Chuan*", "dynamic *Pachi Chuan*" and "converted *Pachi Chuan*". In fact,

---
[1] For a complete list of forms see p. 301

these are different ways of performing steps and movements and of using the energy, in order to attain lower or higher levels of skill.

With the first way of practicing, the aim is to achieve *Fa Ching* (projection of force and energy). With the second, the aim is *Hua Ching* (continuity of force and energy) and *Kan Rou Shiang Chi* (union of hardness and softness). Finally, with the third, the aim is *Toh Hua Ching* (piercing force and energy) and *San Tsai Chi Ching* (union of spirit, energy and essence to move to a superior level).

4.4 The traditional transmission in Kung Fu. *Paisu* students

According to the tradition that has survived to this day, it is required that the student become a *Paisu* to be able to study the higher levels of energy control. In the world of Chinese Martial Arts this is the name given to those who in our cultural context would be called "initiated students". They represent the links of the lineage chain and are guarantors of its survival.

The *Paisu* is not only present in Martial Arts but in all arts. Traditional schools of music, medicine, religion, etc., all have this figure. The existence of initiated students has been characteristic for the traditional transmission of knowledge, not only in the East but also in our culture.

Anyone can become a *Paisu*, however not all those who claim to be one are in fact *Paisu*. For example, in the first Spanish version of this book, the person responsible for its transcription claimed to be a *Paisu* without actually being one. Many things written in that book were of his own creation. Being a *Paisu* demands having a certain disposition and spirit that were lacking in that case. Being a *Paisu* carries a reciprocal life-long commitment to integrity and honesty between the master and the student.

Commitment is necessary, because if one aspires to Power, one must be able to claim it and must know how to use it. With the aim of crystallizing this mutual commitment, a ceremony is carried out where the master opens the energetic connection of his age-old lineage, enabling the flow of knowledge. Without this flow it is very difficult to reveal all that lies hidden in the movements of a Martial Art. Furthermore, every Kung Fu has non-evident details that are very difficult to discover if not through a master. *Pachi Chuan* is a method of self-defense, but this is only a consequence, since in essence it constitutes a very technical and sophisticated system whose movements are an example of management of cosmic energy and thus of human energy. The application of these techniques leads to the enjoyment of a clearer spirit, a stronger energy, a healthier body, and ultimately, obtaining the *San Tsai Chi Ching* (union of spirit, energy and essence to reach a superior level).

4.5 The essential forms

Traditionally, masters condensed the knowledge related to the details of a form's management of energy in verses or songs that were transmitted to the *Paisu*. These verses are encoded and they require direct contact with a master to be interpreted, as well as having an appropriate level of Kung Fu.

Being aware that we live in different times and being faithful to the open spirit that characterizes him, Master Su has decided to reveal some *Pachi Chuan* poems that until now were only bestowed on the heirs of the lineage. In ancient times, the verses were transmitted using the *Pa Ku Wun* language, which had very abstract concepts and was of difficult comprehension, while at the same time it portrayed the literary knowledge of the author. Taking into account the fact that Martial Arts songs should focus on explaining the content of the execution of the form, Master Su has made great changes to render them easier to read and understand. Thus, the content of Martial Arts movements is expressed more broadly and clearly so that those interested may understand everything. The result is a set of simple, concrete and relatively easy to understand verses.

Below are brief descriptions of the forms that make the basis of *Pachi Chuan*, together with the poems written by Master Su. These forms are also featured in the different videos published by Master Su.

4.5.1 *Ting Tzu Pa Pu Suh*. Eight steps in T form

In this context, the Chinese character Ting 丁 does not refer as usual to an individual human life, but refers instead to the shape assumed by the *Fa Ching*, that of the letter T. More explicitly, 丁 here means triangle.

The *Ting Tzu Pa Pu Suh* is the first step in the path of *Pachi Chuan* learning; it was conceived to build a foundation. It is constituted by eight parts that include the eight basic steps. It develops the management of energy in T shape, the triangle energy: three points together and applied

Master Su in the Forbidden City

in a correct way. This type of expression of energy could be likened to what is known in physics as vector sum of forces or sum of linear forces.

The first two learning stages of *Pachi Chuan* are developed in this form: *Fang Song Tzu Jan* and *Shen Chin Pa Ku*. This allows for the first three types of *Fa Ching* to be put into practice: *Chen Sui Ching* (sinking), *Suh Tzu Ching* (cross), *Chan Suh Ching* (spiraling). In the *Ting Tzu Pa Pu Suh* we find the foundations for the future development of *Pao Fa Ching* (explosion) and *Toh Hua Ching* (penetrating).

In some cases, when the student has previously practiced other styles correctly and is able to use the first three types of *Fa Ching*, this stage of learning may be skipped. Accordingly, Master Su learned this form for the first time from Master Li Yuen-Tzu, but years later, when he started learning *Pachi Chuan* from Master *Liu Yun-Chiao*, he was taught *Chinkan Pa Suh* from the start. Master Su then asked Master Liu why he had not started by teaching him the Eight Steps in T Form as he did with new students. Master Liu replied that since he had studied Praying Mantis for a long time, he already had the basis provided by the "T Shape". Then Master Su told his master that he had actually already practiced the method of the "T Shape" and showed him how he had learned it. After watching him,

Master Liu told him that it was authentic, but he still corrected some of the movements to make them perfect.

Similarly, Master Liu had studied *Chang Chuan* and *Mitzong Chuan* from a very early age, so when he started studying *Pachi Chuan* under Master *Li Shu-Wen*, they went through the "T Shape" quickly and went on to study *Chinkan Pa Suh*.

Verses of Ting Tzu Pa Pu Suh

Ting Tzu Pa Pu Suh confronts with three points
Liver energy is used in the fist of *Tzen*, pushing forward as a blast of air.
The energy of the *Ta* hand comes from the confluence of liver and kidney
The dragon descends stirring the cloud with its ribs and its spine
The majestic tiger keeps vigil over the abyss, sinking energy of the kidneys
Split the mountain with the palm of *Pi*, rotating waist and spine in a spiral
The circular hand surrounds the body, the heart and the stomach.
The Hero with sensitive hand tries to catch the wild horse, energy of the lungs
The tiger assaults, *Chi* of *Tan Tien*
Projection is accumulated in the triangle followed by the diamond
The secret of *Pachi-Pikua* is thus transmitted
Real learning is obtained by respecting the Master and following the rules.

4.5.2 *Chinkan Pa Suh*. Eight movements with energy like a glittering diamond

Chinkan Pa Suh literally means "Eight diamond movements". This name makes reference to the pattern of energy management. If in the *Ting Tzu Pa Pu Suh* it is a triangular (vectorial) handling of energy, as indicated by *Ting Tzu* (the character *Ting*: 丁), here it is a matter of dealing with it in a manner likened to the glitter of a diamond, *Chinkan*. The energy is no longer limited by the vertices of a triangle, but is inscribed within a square, that is, it is a matter of *Pao Fa Ching*, explosive projection of energy that expands like the glitter of a diamond.

Verses of Chinkan Pa Suh

Relaxation gives rise to softness. Softness in not relaxation.
The energy of softness gives rise to strength; strength contains sofness
Strength and softness are complementary: the perfect energy
Strength and softness are attained by means of relaxation and calmness.
The study starts with relaxation in the *Ting Tzu Pa Pu Suh*
The basis is established with the three points of *Ting Tzu Pa Pu Suh*
Chinkan Pa Suh provides force to the whole body
The secret is revealed by stretching the tendons and the bones
The Five Elements of *Chinkan* are projected explosively:
The two sides of the liver energy provide the energy of wood
For the energy of the heart, the chest must be extended upwards
The horizontal rotations of the diaphragm please the spleen and the stomach
The shoulder blades are brought forward so that the energy of metal may shine
The *Chi* of the kidneys is brought down as water over earth
Shape of a bear, stance of a tiger, shoulders and arms of an eagle-monkey
Pachi-Pikua, scarce treasure in the world!
This is the starting point for the betterment of the tendons and the cleansing of the marrow
The Five Elements and the Three Sages help the spirit and the ideas
Obtaining wisdom and attaining Tao means finding the truth of Martial Arts
The Yu-Chang lightning thus teaches his secret.

4.5.3 *Hsiao Pachi Chuan*. Small *Pachi Chuan*

Hsiao Pachi Chuan, also called *Pachi Chia* (static *Pachi*), is practiced on three levels.

The first level is for training the basis: from relaxation to natural softness, from softness to stability (solidness, resistance), and finally tendons and bones are stretched by means of a secret *Chi Kung*. The second level is for practicing the transmission of energy, starting with the movements of *Tsun Ching* (short range strike, from a one inch distance), *Tsun Na* (thrust starting with the hand already touching the opponent) and *Tsun Toh* (similar to the former but the energy goes through the opponent), to be able to reach the secret of the energy of the Five Elements and unite internal and external energies.

Later on, the three forms of transformative energy (*Hua Ching*) will be practiced, soft in the outside and strong in the inside, to strenghten internally. This is achieved using the secrets of *Shen Chin Pa Ku* and the *Chi Kung* of the Five Original Energies.

Verses of the Hsiao Pachi: "Striking the oil" poem

The first *Hsiao Pachi* provides a basis, stretches bones and tendons with relaxation as starting point

In the second *Hsiao Pachi*, the Tao of energy unites the Five Elements

Receive, gather and strike from very close; short energy coming out; you must explode

Everyone has something to keep and something to give; *Pachi Chuan* keeps the hidden energy of *Lienhuan*

The third *Pachi* helps the tendons, cleanses the marrow: it is the spirit and the essence, the Five Original Energies

The sage master of the right school teaches his secret. The journey of this lifetime is now justified.

4.6 Detailed description of two forms

4.6.1 *Ting Tzu Pa Pu Suh*[2]

• 1 • 撐捶式 *Cheng Chuei Suh*. Support-push fist. Liver

Secret poem

The sage pushes the vessel leaving the force behind
Shape of a bear, a heavy step falls down
Empty step (*Shi Suh*) rotate the waist forward
Fist that thrusts, elbow that grazes the liver, the armpits are opened.

♦

Kidney energy for Liver. Use Bear Step (*Hsiong Pu*) and Deployment Step (*Nien Pu*). Think of the Liver finger.

1. Lift the right foot by lifting the knee. Take care that the foot does not go higher than the other knee. Go down with the weight of the body, making Bear Step sound. Lift the left heel with the toes touching the ground. The right hand moves upwards. A triangle is formed by the fingers, the elbow and the shoulder. Inhale.

Hsiong Pu: Right foot must be well grounded, from the heel. When lifting the left heel, the knee must be bent slightly forward, using the hip and the thigh. Keep your head back, pulling the chin inwards

---

[2] For descriptions of the different stances and steps mentioned in the following, see 5.2 and 5.3.4.

and stretching up. The ribs on the right side are opened while on the left they remain closed. The right wrist is bent and the fingers point upwards. Sinking energy.

2. The left foot is brought forward by stretching the knee (*Chuan Chiao*, see 126). The toes touch the ground. At the same time, the right hand is brought forward by rotating the waist. Keep the breath in. The weight falls; lower and bring forward the coccyx. The foot goes forth towards the center, with the extended toes touching the ground slightly. The right arm, pushed forth by the twisting of the waist, is stretched from the elbow towards the center and the fingers are kept vertical at the height of the eyes. The left elbow is stretched back and downwards, lowering the shoulder and helping the twisting of the waist. The chin is pulled inward, stretching the neck upwards. The head is kept facing forward while the shoulders rotate. The right hip is turned backwards while the left is turned forward as if wanting to come out. The spiraling energy is prepared.

3. The left foot is brought slightly forward. The waist is turned back to its natural position while the left foot goes into *Tan Shan Pu* stance with the weight lowered. The right foot is dragged slightly forward falling into the *Chi Ma Pu* stance. Simultaneously, the left fist comes out from below the right hand in the form of *Li Chuan* (see p. 115). When the hands are crossed, the right hand is brought backwards at the level of the waist. The left arm in "mouth of the tiger elbow", the shoulders aligned, the armpits open. Liver energy. Exhale.

Special explanation to (2): The Deployment Step (*Nien Pu*) begins. Spiraling energy. The foot goes forward with the toes stretched forward and downward. The coccyx comes out, the right foot rests well on the ground, the knee starts to extend and the arm starts going forth. The hip is relaxed and turns pushing the leg forward.

Special explanation to (3): The toes touch the ground. The waist and the hips turn forward, the heel turned rapidly to rest on the ground is in command. The support to the foot is given by the external edge of the foot from the toes to the heel. The rear foot moves into *Ma Pu* stance pushing downward. At the same time, the right arm is stretched backward while the left has arrived completely extended. The kidneys are brought out and the coccyx inward. The ribs are open in the front and closed in the back, the fist stretches, the shoulder blades are lowered, the elbow is stretched and lowered placed slightly forward so that it is in line with the rest of the body. The head faces forward, aligned with the shoulders. There is a brief pause. Energy circulates through the *Ying Chi* circuit: lungs, stomach, liver (see p. 149).

The movement is repeated switching sides.

• 2 • 塌掌 *Ta Chang*. Crushing hand. Kidney

Secret poem

The rooster stands on one foot, the palm holds up the sky
Both hands push down, grinding step
The hand comes out with liver and crushes with kidney
Receive and come out in a distance as short as one palm.

♦

1. Prepare by inhaling then exhaling. The right foot steps strongly, going slightly forward with Bear Step; the weight is lowered. At the same time, the left foot is lifted with the tip up, in the stance of the Cold Rooster. Also simultaneously, lift the right hand with the Support Palm (*Tuo Chang*, see p. 130) facing upwards. A triangle is formed by the palm, the elbow and the shoulder; the weight is on the right foot.

Bear Step: the foot must rest well on the ground from the heel. The tip of the other foot is pulled upwards while the heel is pulled down. The knee is bent slightly forward. The ribs are opened stretching upwards with elbow. The hand is horizontal and the wrist is bent sharply as if against the rising hand. The rear elbow is closing the left ribs. The head is upright and slightly back, pulling the chin inwards.

2. The left foot goes forward in *Chuan Chiao*, without touching the ground. At the same time, the right hand changes to a crushing position and goes forward. The left hand also goes forward with the fingers over the right wrist. The waist rotates to the left and the right part of the ribcage goes forward. Inhale.

The left foot comes out, pushed forward and towards the middle by the knee, as if pulled from the heel. The right hand is turned over its axis pushing down as if to overcome a resistance while the left one placed over the right wrist. The elbows and the left foot stretch towards the middle.

3. The right foot, as if screwing in, pushes forward while the left one also goes forward. With the Wind Mill Step, the stance becomes *Chi Ma Pu* of water. Both palms push down with the left one going forward while the right one goes by the *Tan Tien* touching it and rests beside the waist. Both hands as tiger claws. The left hand, elbow and shoulder as well as the right shoulder should be aligned. Exhale. The left side of the ribcage should go forward and down. The elbows come down stretching the shoulder blades downwards.

It is important to focus the attention on the claw hand that goes down touching the *Tan Tien*. *Ta Chang* uses energy of liver, lungs and, finally, of the kidneys going down. Think of the kidney finger. At first, Spiraling Energy is used, and then Sinking Energy. Energy circulates through the *Wei Chi* circuit (see p. 149).

The movement is now repeated on the other side.

- 3 • 降龍式 *Chiang Long Suh*. Stance of the descending dragon. Shoulder blades and waist. Kidney to Heart

  Secret poem
  The dragon descends stirring the cloud as it moves its tail.
  Open the chest by moving the waist and the spine.
  Change shape and change your step to reach Heaven
  The fist aims to the sky
  Lift the wind, move the tree.
  The dragon moves its tail.

♦

1. The right foot does the Bear Step and all the weight of the body is lowered. The left heel is lifted while the toes touch the ground on the Cold Rooster stance, *Han Chi Suh*. The right hand is simultaneously brought to a claw shape and rotated clockwise moving upwards to block. Exhale. Sinking energy.

2. The left foot goes forward in piercing form (*Chuan Chiao*) forty-five degrees to the left to fall into *Chi Ma Pu*. The upper body does not move. The waist is turned so that it is aligned with the right hand and the left elbow and this line is perpendicular to the one formed by the feet in *Chi Ma Pu*. Inhale.

   The inverse Spiraling Energy is prepared by focusing on the *Tan Tien* and extending the Sinking Energy. The hips are opened by moving them forward as if drawing them together. The shoulder blades are also opened.

3. The left foot, being well grounded, is unwounded forward and the waist turns with the right side towards the back. The right foot is brought back by drawing a quarter of a circle to fall into *Pai Pu*, forming a 90° angle with the left foot. The heels are aligned in a *Tan Shan Pu* stance. At the same time, the left fist comes up towards the right hand, which in turn is brought to the waist. Both hands and both feet must be aligned and the inclination of the body must be of approximately 45° with respect to the floor. Exhale.

The inverse Spiraling Energy is developed. It goes up through the left leg, from the kidney to the heart; the energy of the heart is moved with the liver. The waist must be rotated, the ribs and the armpits are opened, the empty sternum points outwardly, the shoulder blades and the hips are drawn backwards, the neck is stretched to help the energy go up, the *Tan Tien* pushes outwardly. The shoulder blades are stretched by pulling the right elbow downwards and the left fist upwards.

Now repeat on the other side.

- 4 • 伏虎式 *Fu Hu Suh*. Stance of the tiger that subdues. Ribcage, shoulder blades, spine, Kidney.

  Secret poem
  Yin and Yang moving the arms followed by grazing steps.
  The hungry tiger leaps to eat, it catches three times.
  The wild tiger awaits by the abyss. Sinking Kidney energy. Descend.
  The *Lohan* saint subdues the tiger and defeats it majestically.

  ♦

1. Feet together, inhale. Put the right foot forward in *Tan Shan Pu*, exhale half of the breath. The left hand rises with the palm facing up and the arm extended and rotating. The right hand is placed at the height of the left elbow, touching it, with the palm facing down.

2. The right hand rises with the palm facing up, the left hand with the palm facing down touches slightly the right elbow. Exhale.

1 and 2 are *Yin Yang Fong Kai Chang* (陰陽封開掌 — Yin-Yang palms to open and close). Yin energy of Liver and Lung together.

3. The left hand is lifted with the palm facing up. Inhale. When the hand comes up, the fingers are in front of the left shoulder.

4. Both feet go forward with the "Friction Step". The left arm is rotated and slightly drawn back with the the hand as "Hook Palm", the fingers pointing forward. The right hand is below the left elbow with the palm facing down.

One inhales for step 3. Then in step 4 all the energy of the air is distributed throughout the body, pores of the skin and hair, all relaxed.

5. The left arm grabs forward with a circle. The arm must be completely extended while the circle is drawn downwards with force.

6. The right arm grabs forward with a circle, similar to the previous one but wider. Bring the left foot forward with the "Piercing Step", *Chuan Chiao*, without touching the ground.

7. Move forward without stopping, drawing an even wider arch with the left arm and grabbing downward in this manner. At the same time, the left foot falls and the *Panma Suh* stance is adopted. The left hand is next to the knee as a tiger claw. The right hand is also as a tiger claw, but is placed forward. The wrists are bent upwards, the coccyx is stretched with the anus upward and forward. The head is turned forward and slightly upward with tiger eyes. Optionally, the sound "Hn" may be used. Exhale.

This is part of *Meng Hu Pa Shan* (猛虎爬山 — the wild tiger climbs the mountain). Lungs and Kidney energy. At first, the energy circulates laterally through the *Ying Chi* circuit (see p. 149), the ribcage is moved and left and right become united. The hands rotate. Then the energy moves downwards, vertically. The three claw movements must draw arches, each larger than the previous one, and following each other in a continuous motion. In the final step, suck in with the anus. The ribcage is lowered and the gaze is upward. Up-down energy, Yin and Yang are distributed. Spiraling and diving/sinking energy are used. The spine is used. First, the forward jump with the shoulder blades towards the back. Then, in a tiger position, the shoulder blades and the elbows push down the energy that is trying to come up from the feet. The coccyx is lifted inwards. The hands as claws should be lower than the knees.

Repeat on the other side.

• 5 • 劈山掌 *Pi Shan Chang*. The palm splits the mountain. Shoulder blades

Secret poem

The ribcage opens and closes both pushing hands.
The mischievous dragon plays with water arousing myriads of waves.
The comet reaches the moon, and it advances cutting through the mountain.
Eagle and bear argue, making the mountain resound.

◆

1. Feet are together and knees bent. Initially, the palms are facing up with the arms extended forward at a height between the chest and the abdomen. Inhale.

2. The right foot falls in Bear Step while the left foot is lifted with the tip upwards and both hands are brought towards the waist with force. The palms face forward and graze the waist while having a hook shape. Inhale. The rear part of the ribcage is stretched and drawn back.

   The weight rests on one foot, the shoulder blades are drawn back, palms face forward, fingers pointing down, elbows back.

3. Bring forth the left foot as *Tan Shan Suh*. Advance with spiraling energy. Both hands push vigorously from the elbows which are closed. The palms face forward and are at the height of the chest and the shoulders. The fingers are separated from one another and point up; energy is focused on the ring finger. The back part of the ribcage and the shoulder blades push forward. Exhale. Lung energy.

4. Both feet are rotated backwards to form *Pai Suh* (*Tan Shan Suh* with the body rotated backwards) with the help of the hips, which also rotate. The left arm is lowered and placed vertically stretching down so that the hand is at the level of the hips. The right arm is bent up so that the right hand is at the level of the left shoulder. Inhale.

The extended arm, which is parallel to the torso, is stretched down so that the shoulder blade is brought down and forward. The bent arm is pushed up from the elbow. It is important to keep the energy within the plane formed by the body. This is a forward movement with backward moving shoulder blades.

5. Steps 5 and 6 are executed non-stop. The left arm traces a circle from below, rising and going forward, and eventually falling while splitting with the edge of the forearm. The right arm traces a circle from above, descending and going back. The shoulder blades and the hips are closed at the back, while at the same time the weight shifts forward into *Tan Shan Suh*. The *Tan Tien* is stretched.

6. The waist and the feet rotate. The right foot *Pai Pu* moves forward and to the right to land in *Tan Shan Suh*, perpendicular to the former direction. The right arm continues to move from behind, forward and up, *Lun Pei* (strike in circular motion). The left arm is down and balanced. Make sure you do an inverted exhaling in this step. Step of closed pelvis (closed energy).

7. The arms move uninterruptedly. The right arm splits downward with the palm, and continues until it reaches the left armpit. Inversely, the left arm moves up from below until it touches the right shoulder. Both arms and palms split embracing. Energy in inverted cross. Exhale when the arms strike the body. The final movement is of the shoulder blades. The arms shoot out, then open and then cross each other.

Repeat on the other side.

Splitting mountain arm, *Pi Shan Chang*, is of Lung energy. Lung energy comes from the heart, goes through the lungs and descends to the kidneys.

7

The movements of the shoulder blades, opening and closing, going up and down, are important for the Lung energy. When coming out, the energy must be elastic (as a rebound) and it must be exact. The projection of energy is as spiral and as cross. It is important to move the hips and the waist.

- 6 • 圈抱式 *Chuan Pao Suh*. Embrace. Shoulder blades and waist. Spleen. *San Tsai Chi Ching*

    Secret poem
    The eagle flips majestically turning its breast-waist.
    The green dragon with endless motion embraces the pillar.
    Rotate the waist, tighten the abdomen, energy of Spleen-Stomach.
    The Roc spreads its wings and flies free.

1. Start with *Tan Shan Suh* with the right arm splitting to the right, with the waist and the torso rotating 45°. Then the left arm descends extended until it reaches the left leg so that later a circle is drawn upwards and back, defending with a hook. *Han Chi Suh.*

2. Without interrupting the motion, the left arm is lifted until the fingers are at the height of the face. The left knee is lifted, *Tu Li Suh*, the right arm is lifted at the back, stretched.

3. Bring forth the left foot placing it opened at a 45° angle. At the same time, the left arm moves forward drawing a circle in a diagonal and catching with a hook, moving until it is parallel to the right arm. *Tan Shan Suh*. Inhale. Waist and shoulder blades.

4. The right arm comes forward at the height of the face, splitting in a circular motion. The left arm simultaneously comes forward, splitting in an arch.

5. The right foot comes next to the left one in the "Cold Rooster" stance. At the same time, the arms cut horizontally and embrace (*Pi Pao*) slamming the torso. Energy of "suction" (retain the air while compressing). The arms rebound to separate. Shoulder blades go forward.

   Energy of Spleen-Stomach combined with Lung energy. Open like a pocket by inflating the diaphragm.

6. Bring forth the right foot with *Nien Pu* to land in *Chi Ma Pu*. At the same time, both arms open in a circular motion at the height of the shoulders with the palms facing up. Open and stretch. Exhale.

   Close like a pocket, squeezing the diaphragm. Energy of Spleen-Stomach with Lung energy.

Repeat on the other side.

In these movements (*Chuan Pao*) the most important thing is the rotating motion of the stomach and the spleen for the diaphragm; the opening and closing, inflating and deflating as principles of the movement of the diaphragm. One must think that the hands reach beyond and that the energy goes right there.

- **7** • 探馬掌 *Tang Ma Chang*. Seeking palms, left-right. Liver and shoulder blades, Lung

    Secret poem
    Searching palms, left-right, jump forward.
    One foot after the other, supporting palms, the horse jumps over the river of the abyss.
    The black bear shows its claw with the force for moving a mountain.
    The hero subdues the wild horse with its superior energy.

♦

1. Inhale. The left foot stamps loud in Bear Step. The right foot touches the ground with the toes, *Han Chi Suh*. At the same time, the right hand is lifted with the elbow bent so that the palm strikes against the right shoulder and produces a sound. The left hand is open below the right elbow. Exhale.

    The elbow must be high so that the ribcage is opened and the shoulder blades are closed backwards; the hand touches the back. The other shoulder blade is open towards the front, with the hand next to the armpit. The weight is concentrated in one foot, the other one with the heel up. Kidneys protrude. The lower the stance the better.

    1

2. The right arm is extended towards the front, drawing a circle as it descends. The right elbow descends with force while the right hand blocks pushing down, going by the middle of the chest and down to the waist. Inhale.

3. Bring forth the right foot as *Tan Shan Suh*. At the same time, the right hand goes forth with the fingers pointing forward, in a piercing motion. The left hand is placed next to the right forearm. While one hand goes forward, the corresponding shoulder blade is pushed forward and the other one is pushed back, and then vice versa. Exhale half the air.

4. Bring forth the left foot as *Tan Shan Suh*. The left hand brushes the back of the right hand making a sound and pierces forward. Exhale the rest of the breath.

Movements 3 and 4 are Lung movements. They correspond to the rear part of the ribcage and to the shoulder blades. Take and give; left and right.

5. Without changing the leg stance, change the palms so they are now facing the sky. The right hand below.

6. The right palm strikes the left one and both are lifted together. The right foot simultaneously advances half a step with *Ting Pu* step. Left foot in *Shi Suh* (empty or light foot). Inhale. The rear part of the ribcage is sunk in, the rear is closed; shoulder blades go backwards.

7. The left foot advances into *Tan Shan Suh*. At the same time both hands are turned with the left one in front and the right one pushing behind. The palms face forward and the thumbs cross each other. Exhale. The rear part of the ribcage should come out, the shoulder blades should move forward. The chin should be tucked in, the neck stretched.

Now the right side.

- 8 - 虎抱式 *Hu Pao Suh*. The tiger's embrace. Shoulder blades and diaphragm. *Wu Shing Chi Ching*

  Secret poem
  Ascend together, descend together, fire and water are united
  The sovereign king stretches the arch, elbows to the front and to the back
  Steal the step, steal the fist, unite at the *Tan Tien*
  The wild tiger turns its body and a pair of *Peng Chuan* are released.

  ♦

  1. Inhale. The right foot, in Bear Step, stamps loudly. Left foot touches the ground with the toes, *Han Chi Suh*. At the same time, both hands, closed as *Pa Tze Chuan*, are lifted so that the fists are next to the ears. Compress. Sucking energy. The weight should be at the back, resting on one foot. The elbows bring the shoulder blades back.

  2. The left foot is brought forth in Bear Step, stepping with the weight lowered. The body rotates to the right. At the same time, both hands strike downwards, at the sides of the pelvis. Cold Rooster stance (*Han Chi Suh*). Exhale. Descending Kidney energy. It is half a deployment step, landing with the toes as the fists are lowered and the shoulder blades are brought forth and down.

  3. Both hands are brought forward, extending the arms. The hands are open with the palms facing up, one over the other with the right one on top. Inhale.

  The shoulder blades are opened towards the front.

4. The right foot moves back to land in *Chi Ma Pu*. Both hands strike the *Tan Tien* and move apart to the sides. Exhale.

   The elbows draw circles as they go down and back and then up and forward. The shoulder blades rotate with the the elbows. The hands scratch and strike the belly.

5. The right foot goes behind the left one, grazing the ground with the sole and producing a sound. The two closed fists cross each other and strike the *Tan Tien* as the arms twist. The right hand should be below the left one and should strike forward. Inhale.

The legs are crossed as well as the arms. The diaphragm is twisted and shrunk, reducing its diameter. The fists go one upwards and the other one downwards, twisting the arms. The shoulder blades are opened and rotate. The ribcage is completely closed.

6. The whole body rotates towards the right in *Mo Pan Pu* (grinding step), placing the right foot in front to land in *Chi Ma Pu*. The hands move apart from each other as *Peng Chuan*, upwards with the little finger on top. Exhale.

The diaphragm unwinds and expands. The ribcage is opened and the shoulder blades rotate towards the front. This position is called "Union of the Five Energies".

Now start with the left side.

4.6.2 *Kaimen Chuan* two-man form

Once the eight series of the *Ting Tzu Pa Pu Suh* have been learnt, the student goes on to learn *Kaimen Chuan* (linking form of the *Ting Tzu Pa Pu Suh*) and its two-man form. In this section we will treat the two-man *Kaimen Chuan* directly.

The *Kaimen Chuan* form was created by Master Su with the aim of making easier the study of the first stages of *Pachi Chuan*. In the following pages we show only the first of the four sequences.

J. A. Bonilla (in the white jacket) performs the *Kaimen Chuan* part of the two-man form, while G. Arroyo (in the black jacket) performs the attacking side. To study the movements of *Kaimen Chuan* it is advised to follow the student in the white jacket.

• 1 • Greeting and opening

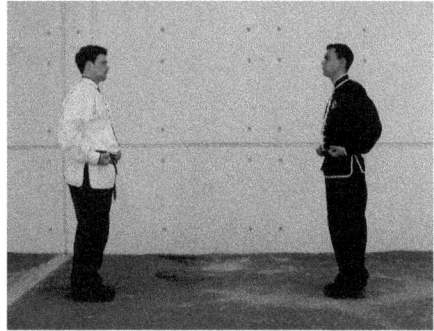

PACHI TANGLANG CHUAN 95

5

6

7

8

9

• 2 • 撐捶式 *Cheng Chuei Suh.* Support-push fists.

10

11

12

13

14

• 3 • 塌掌 *Ta Chang*. Crushing hand.

15

16

17

18

Front view

• 4 • 探馬掌 *Tang Ma Chang*. Seeking palms, left-right.

19

20

21

22

23

24

25

26

27

28

29

• 5 • 虎抱式 *Hu Pao Suh*. The tiger's embrace.

30

31

32

33

34

35

36

PACHI TANGLANG CHUAN

37

Front view

38

39

40

41

42

43

44

• 6 • 伏虎式 *Fu Hu Suh*. Stance of the tiger that subdues

45

46

• 7 • 劈山掌 *Pi Shan Chang*. The palm splits the mountain.

61

62

• 8 • 圈抱式 *Chuan Pao Suh*. Embrace.

63

64

65

66

Front view

• 9 • 挑打頂肘 *Tiao Ta Ting Chou*. Elbow towards the back.

72

• 10 • 伏虎式 *Fu Hu Suh.* Stance of the tiger that subdues

73

74

75

76

• 11 • 降龍式 *Chiang Long Suh*. Stance of the descending dragon

Start of the Left Side

- 12 • 撐捶式 *Cheng Chuei Suh.* Support-push fists.

- 13 • Presenting the elbow and concluding.

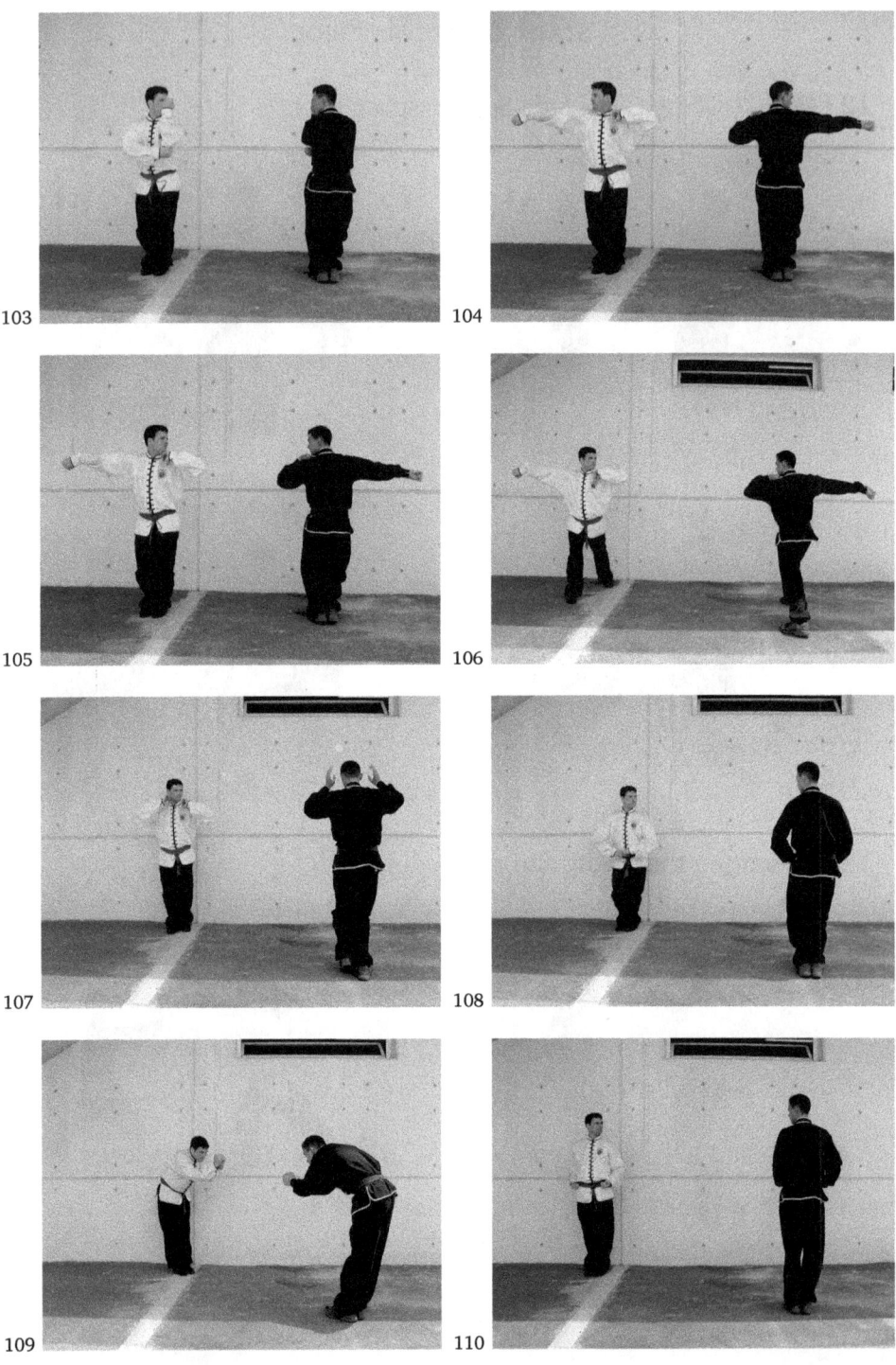

Chapter 5

Pachi Chuan Techniques

> It is very difficult to find a master, but finding one is worthless if no effort is made to assimilate his teachings.

Each technique in *Pachi Chuan* can be applied in five different ways. These are: striking with the hands, kicking, throwing, grabbing and piercing. Striking with the hands includes many types of hand techniques. Kicking includes the study of stepping. Throwing includes projections and impacts using specific parts of the body. Grabbing in *Pachi Chuan* means harming a muscle or a tendon, and also the breaking of bones. Piercing means pressing specific points of the body that affect the opponent in a specific way. Although it might not seem obvious, each *Pachi Chuan* technique includes the possibility of these five different ways of application. Now we are going to introduce the terms used to explain the secrets of these techniques.

◆

The techniques of *Pachi Chuan* are mainly related to two animals: the bear and the tiger. *Pikua Chuan*, on the other hand, is related to the eagle and the long-arm monkey. Both styles share two supporting animals: the snake and the horse.

The fists and steps come from the bear. The "bear fist" is a combination of fist and claw, that is, the hand is halfway closed, with an empty space in

Cover of the *Wushu* magazine, 2002.
Master Su is demonstrating Teh Shan Kao

the middle. The claws and the back come from the tiger. The tiger is also evoked by the postures. The waist should be like the snake. In Martial Arts, the waist should have good mobility, to the left and to the right; it should be agile like the snake. The "snake waist" is for making the energy move in a circle and for kicking with great force. The horse provides stability and speed in long-range steps/displacements. *Pikua Chuan* is for striking from afar while *Pachi Chuan* is for striking from a close distance. The energy of *Pikua Chuan* moves in wide circles, while in *Pachi Chuan* it moves in small circles, like a drill.

5.1 Fists

The *Pa Tze Chuan* is a fist known for thousands of years; we find it in ancient military documents. It is a special fist, being halfway between an open hand and the closed fist. Its shape resembles the shape of a garden rake. Since the fingers are only partially closed, it has a very adaptable form. Thanks to these features, tension is eliminated from the execution of techniques and the flow of energy at the moment of impact is favored. The fist resembles the claw of a bear because bears have very large and fleshy paws. What is characteristic of this fist is that it does not become tense and it integrates Yin and Yang, softness and hardness, thus allowing for its use in a number of small techniques that harm the opponent in specific ways. In *Pachi Chuan*, the fist and the palm do not have the strike as their sole purpose. In general, they are accompanied by some sort of push or exertion of pressure that is associated with one or more energies.

Accordingly, it may be said that the Lung is for pushing, Liver is to displace pushing, Kidney is for pushing down and Heart is like producing a spark. This fist is the result of a very long process of refinement to make the human hand a formidable, adaptable and devastating weapon.

Ying Chuan

Pachi Chuan has several types of fists:

仰拳 **Ying Chuan** Fist with the palm facing up. Energy is projected directly and at a short distance. This fist is applied forward and is ineffective otherwise. The energy used is that of the Lungs. The shoulder blades must be used to be able to project the energy at a short distance. It is not important if the arm is extended or bent.

俯拳 **Fu Chuan** Fist with the palm facing down. It strikes directly. *Fu Chuan* is performed with the *Pachi Chuan* fist (semi-closed). It uses energy of Stomach-Spleen; the diaphragm must be moved so that the energy rises to the shoulders and shoulder blades. The energy is then divided: Yang energy goes to the side that is going to strike while Yin energy goes to the other side as an auxiliary. When the hand meets the target, it closes completely and energy comes out. It is a special *Pachi Chuan* fist.

立拳 **Li Chuan** Fist with the palm facing inward. The energy originates at the ribs; Liver energy. To manage the energy, the ribs must be opened and

Fu Chuan

closed. This fist is used only laterally. The wrist should be stretched so that the energy may go through and reach the index and middle fingers.

Li Chuan

Rooshuen Chuan

螺旋拳 **Rooshuen Chuan** Spiraling fist, also called 鑽拳 (Tzuan Chuan). Energy comes from the *Tan Tien*, rises to the sternum and, finally, reaches the hand. The fist comes out rotating as the arm is stretched, finishing with the little finger facing the nose. At the same time, the weight of the body is lowered towards the feet.

摔拳 **Tsai Chuan** Downwards spiraling fist. Kidney energy is used. The position of the spine determines whether the movement is Yin or Yang. The coccyx manages the spine. It is sometimes combined with Heart energy, or with Stomach-Spleen energy. The movement of the coccyx is the defining factor.

Tsai Chuan

5.2 Stances

Stances help strengthen the legs and the lower part of the back. They provide a base and are to the Martial Artist what the roots are to a tree: the deeper its roots are, the stronger the tree will be. The inner power of the human body comes from the earth, hence the student who has a strong base will have developed deep roots and will have great strength. The legs and the lower part of the back determine the strength that the upper body can have. Someone who does not have strong enough legs will obviously have deficient techniques.

The importance of the stances in *Pachi Chuan* is due to the fact that only from strong stances can the student embody the different energies and execute the different techniques.

5.2.1 The twelve methods of stance training (Suh 式) in *Pachi Chuan*

Suh (式) means the posture and the way of standing. It is the most important of the fundamentals to be learned in any Martial Art.

The names of the stances are formed by adding the word "Suh" to one or more terms that somehow describe the characteristics of the stance. For example, "Chi Ma" means horse-rider and "Chi Ma Suh" is the horse-riding stance. This stance resembles in the position of the legs someone riding on horse-back.

Stances are virtually the same in all Kung Fu styles, only the frequency with which each one is used varies. In *Pachi Chuan*, the most important stances are *Chi Ma Suh* and *Tan Shan Suh*. Additionally, there are ten other stances that must be mastered. Together they form what is called the twelve methods of stance training in *Pachi Chuan*. The practice of these methods not only strengthens the legs and the lower part of the back, but is also of great importance for the learning of *Shen Chin Pa Ku* (stretching, see above, p. 58).

The twelve stances of *Pachi Chuan* are the following:

1.	騎馬式	Chi Ma Suh	Horse-riding Stance
2.	登山式	Tan Shan Suh	Mountain-climbing Stance
3.	拗步登山式	Au Pu Tan Shan Suh	*Tan Shan Suh* with the torso turned to one side
4.	吞塌式	Tun Ta Suh	Backwards *Tan Shan Suh*
5.	半馬式	Panma Suh	Half Horse-riding Stance
6.	獨立式	Tu Li Suh	One foot Stance

7. 虛式	Shi Suh	Empty Stance (one grounded foot and one empty foot stance)
8. 並立式	Pin Li Suh	Bent legs together and weight in the middle
9. 坐盤式	Tsuo Pan Suh	Sitting with entwined feet Stance
10. 跪膝式	Kuei Ti Suh	One leg kneeling Stance
11. 不丁不八式	Pu Ting Pu Pa Suh	Neither "T" nor "Eight" Stance, natural
12. 寒雞式	Han Chi Suh	Cold Rooster Stance

騎馬式 **Chi Ma Suh** *Chi Ma Suh,* the horse-riding stance, has a Yin and a Yang form of practice. In its Yin form, *Shen Chin Pa Ku* (stretching) is practiced. Firstly, the legs are separated keeping the feet parallel; the distance between the feet is determined by the length of the leg, from the foot to the knee. The cervical vertebrae should be stretched as if being pulled by a wire from the top of the head. The shoulders must be lowered and the elbows and fists should be extended towards the front. The hips should be brought slightly forward so that an equilateral triangle is formed between the coccyx and each knee and heel. The joints of the hips are opened and the knees are brought slightly inward. By bringing the knees closer to each other, the joints of the hips are opened, thus enabling the circulation of energy from the *Ren Mo* and *Tu Mo* meridians. Finally, the toes should press against the ground as if trying to clutch the ground.

Chi Ma Suh

The energy should be stored in the abdomen, at the level of the *Tan Tien*. It is also important to mention the kidneys; the lower ribs should cross them if the stance is done correctly. If the kidneys are not completely lowered, the abdomen will be very tense. The coccyx must be tilted forward so that the kidneys can descend. All this causes the circulation of energy from the *Ren Mo* and *Tu Mo* meridians. This stance also has a dragon movement, characterized by the arching of the spine to manage the *Tan Tien*. In this way the movements of the waist and of the spine, that is of Yin and Yang, are integrated, thus bringing the *Tan Tien* into play.

In the Yang form of *Chi Ma Suh*, *Chen Sui Ching* (sinking energy projection) is practiced.

登山式 **Tan Shan Suh** In *Tan Shan Suh*, the mountain-climbing stance, the projection of energy in form of a cross and in form of a spiral is practiced. In *Tan Shan Suh*, the distance between the feet is the same as in *Chi Ma Suh* but they are placed slanted. It is important that the front leg is bent so that the knee is in front, forming a triangle with heel and coccyx. If the front leg is not

Tan Shan Suh

properly bent, the force of the strike given in this stance will be restrained, whereas if done well, the strike will be projected much more towards the target. Furthermore, if the leg is not properly bent, it is very easy to be knocked over. With the front leg well bent there is much more stability when absorbing an external force. The *Tan Shan Suh* stance is always used to project energy while attacking.

The *Tan Shan Suh* stance has a few variants:

拗步登山式 **Au Pu Tan Shan Suh** This stance is *Tan Shan Suh* but with the torso turned to one side, forming a cross with respect to the legs. With this stance the energy projection in form of a cross is practiced. The difference between this stance and *Tan Shan Suh* is that in *Tan Shan Suh* the torso is facing forward, while in *Au Pu Tan Shan Suh* one seeks greater range with the strike by twisting the torso so that the hand, elbow and shoulder of the striking arm are aligned with the rear shoulder and elbow. These five points of the body are important

Au Pu Tan Shan Suh

to be able to project energy and force when using this stance in *Pachi Chuan*.

This is the stance used to practice energy projection in form of a cross. The *Shen Chin Pa Ku* of cross projection starts in *Chi Ma Suh* and moves into *Au Pu Tan Shan Suh*. The head is turned and the neck is stretched so that the chin is aligned with the shoulder. The shoulders, lowered and perpendicular to the line of the legs, are stretched in opposite directions. They interact with the torso by opening and closing the armpits: the front armpit should be opened while the back one should be closed. The elbows and the wrists also help to open and close the armpits. The front wrist should be completely stretched, the rear one bent. The coccyx pushes inward when the stance is Yin and outward when it is Yang. The hips are tightened as if trying to compress themselves if it is Yin, and the opposite if it is Yang. The knees are separated by stretching them, bending one ever more and pushing towards the front and towards the heel, the other stretched ever more pushing towards the back and towards the foot. One of the ankles should be increasing bent while the other should be increasingly stretched. The energy should arrive at the fist after passing through the shoulder and the elbow. The fist should be stretched forward and when it strikes it should go even further.

In the **Yin Au Pu Tan Shan Suh**, the rear leg is brought forth as the torso is twisted and *Chan Suh Ching* (spiraling projection) is applied. In this case, the energy rises from the leg. The step draws a triangle and the force for the attack comes from the foot.

Tun Ta Suh   Pan Ma Suh

吞塌式 **Tun Ta Suh** This stance is similar to *Tan Shan Suh* but with the torso turned towards the extended leg. A similar stance is *Pu Tue Suh* (仆腿式, Low leg stance), with the difference that in the latter the body is even lower, so much that the hands can reach the ground. It is important not to let the torso lean towards the back but rather to the front.

半馬式 **Panma Suh** The half horse-riding stance is done starting from *Chi Ma Suh* and rotating one foot 45° outward. The weight is no longer in the middle but distributed 60% on the rear leg and 40% in the front leg. This stance is also known as *Shih Liu Suh* (Four-Six Stance).

Tu Li Suh

獨立式 **Tu Li Suh** On the one foot stance, the sole of the foot must be in contact with the knee. The aim is to strike with the knee and at the same time guard the extended leg against an eventual strike.

虛式 **Shi Suh** In the empty stance the front foot is only lightly touching the ground, stepping "falsely", with 90% of the weight on the rear leg and 10% on the front leg.

並立式 **Pin Li Suh** The feet are together and the legs bent to form an equilateral triangle (the knees, heels and coccyx). The weight is in the middle. This stance is frequently used in *Pachi Chuan*.

Shi Suh　　　　　　　　Pin Li Suh　　　　　　　Tsuo Pan Suh

坐盤式 **Tsuo Pan Suh**   In the stance "sitting with entwined feet" the distance between the feet is the same as in *Chi Ma Suh*, the front foot is opened towards the outside, the rear knee is bent towards the ground without touching it, the heel of the rear foot is lifted. In the the Praying Mantis style, this same stance is called *Yuhuan Suh* 玉環式 and there is a stance which is also called *Tsuo Pan Suh* but is different in that one sits completely on the rear foot.

Kuei Ti Suh   Pu Ting Pu Pa Suh   Han Chi Suh

跪膝式 **Kuei Ti Suh**   The single kneeling leg stance is similar to *Tan Shan Suh* but with the rear leg bent.

不丁不八式 **Pu Ting Pu Pa Suh**   The neither "T" (丁) nor "Eight" (八) stance is like *Chi Ma Suh* but with both feet rotated 45° towards the front.

寒雞式 **Han Chi Suh**   The Bear Step can be practiced in the Cold Rooster Stance. This stance is very similar to *Shi Suh*.

5.3 Applying the different parts of the body

5.3.1 The head

The parts of the head that are used to strike are lateral parts and the middle of the crown of the head. The angular part may also be used in a shaking motion, which can be done forward or backward.

Chin Kan Ting Men head technique

1

2

3

4

5.3.2 Basic *Pachi Chuan* elbows

There are three basic ways of using the elbows in *Pachi Chuan*:

纏肘 **Chan Chou** The "wrapping elbow" is an attack oriented towards the back. That is, with the back part of the elbow, one pushes backwards. Kidney energy is used to strike towards the back.

献肘 **Shen Chou** "Show the elbow" strikes towards the front. The diaphragm is used to do the spiraling movement towards the front. Stomach and Lung energies are used.

頂肘 **Ting Chou** Here the strike is lateral and upwards. The technique starts with the *San Tsai* energies, which rise to become Heart energy and strike upwards.

5.3.3 Three basic *Kao* ("leaning") techniques

The *Kao* techniques may use any part of the torso to strike, mostly the shoulders and the hips, where the energies of *Wu Shing Chi Ching* and *San Tsai Chi Ching* are used. The basic *Kao* is done with the shoulders. There are three basic ways:

貼山靠 **Teh Shan Kao** "Use the shoulder to push the mountain" is a bear movement. It is done with the rear part of the shoulder. This movement is characteristic of *Pao Fa Ching* (explosive energy).

擠身靠 **Chi Shen Kao** In *Chi Shing Kao* one uses the central part of the shoulder. In this technique it is important to use *Chen Sui Ching* (sinking energy). It is used to strike the middle of the torso of the opponent. It can be used to block against an attempt at hugging.

Teh Shan Kao

1

2

3

4

Chi Shen Kao

穿身靠 **Chuan Shen Kao** In *Chuan Shen Kao* one strikes with the front part of the shoulder. The movement is similar to the one made to put on a heavy coat: one needs to swing the coat in order to fit one arm first, and then the other. The energy is projected in a spiral.

Chuan Shen Kao

5.3.4 Feet

The feet are used profusely in the *Pachi Chuan* style, to kick and to take penetrating steps. The steps in *Pachi Chuan* come from the horse. The details for a proper use of the steps are secret, but some of its characteristics can be observed by looking at the way steps are taken in *Suh Pachi* and *Huo Pachi*. There are not so many kicks in *Pachi Chuan* due to the fact that it is short range combat style.

• 1 • Kicks

Pachi Chuan has a variety of kicking techniques, but they always use the heel to strike. This style does not use the instep/top of the foot to strike because the aim in *Pachi Chuan* is to focus the energy in one point; this is a skill that is developed with practice.

Fu Ren Chiao   Pien Chuang Chiao   Chuan Hsin Chiao

斧刃腳 **Fu Ren Chiao** It is like an ax that cuts wood. The kick is ascending and rises at the most to the level of the knee.

扁撞腳 **Pien Chuang Chiao** It is a sideways kick always aimed at a height above the knee; it can reach as high as the head. The foot is always horizontal, with the toes pointing inward.

穿心腳 **Chuan Hsin Chiao** It is an ascending kick that rises frontally with three possible targets: the heart, the chin or the head. The foot is placed vertically, with the toes pointing up.

鈎腳 **Kou Chiao** It is a hook-like kick that uses the rear part of the heel to catch. It does not rise above the knee and it may be done inward or outward.

連環腳 **Lien Huan Chiao** Continuous kicks in a jump, alternating the left and right legs. One can do combinations of two of the kicks mentioned above.

Kou Chiao

• 2 • Steps

Pu Fa (步法), stepping techniques refer to the way of changing foot positions. With a proper use of steps, the energy can be made to reach any part of the body. The change of position may be toward the front, toward the back, up, down or sideways.

In *Pachi Chuan*, the ways of performing a step and how to change positions (*Pu Fa*) is of utmost importance. This is due to the fact that *Fa Ching*, that is, energy projection, requires that the upper and the lower parts of the body become one. In *Pachi Chuan* it is very important for the steps to be penetrating, *Chuan Chiao* (穿腳). The penetrating steps are characteristic of *Pachi Chuan* and are essential to mobilize the energy in the direction of the movement. The execution requires that the knee is active and that it takes the lead before the foot. In this manner, the spirit and the weight are brought forward in the direction of the movement. It is very important for the weight to guide the movement, and not to drag it. In general, all the modes of managing the energy, as well as all the basic energies, are present in each step, even if some steps are more characteristic to one of the modes.

The principal *Pachi Chuan* steps are the following:

擦步 **Tsa Pu** The Friction Step is done with the feet together; the step and the force must go together in the strike. One should stay low when moving forward, in a gliding manner. It is linked to Heart energy.

跟步 **Nien Pu** In the Deployment Step the front foot rotates so that the heel falls in its final position before the weight settles upon it. The energy comes from the hips. It is characteristic of the Liver energy but has variants for each energy. It is characteristic of the Spiraling Energy.

磨盤步 **Mo Pan Pu** In the Grinding Step both feet are simultaneously moved with a vigorous twisting of the waist. This movement is done with the energy of the whole body. Explosive projection of energy. Stomach.

細步 **Kun Pu** In the Tying Step, the opponent's leg is immobilized by the action of the knee and the foot. The movement is done using the internal part of the foot. The coccyx is used.

搓步 **Suo Pu** The Barring Step is similar to the previous one. the opponent's leg is immobilized using the knee and the foot, but here the external part of the foot is used. The coccyx is used.

提籠換步 **Tilong Huan Pu**   This is called "Carrying the lantern" step. The front foot is drawn back while the rear one moves forward. This step is used to change the body's position and to move the energy in a circle so that the opponent is unable to find us. The waist is very important.

熊步 **Hsiong Pu**   For the Bear Step, all the weight falls on one leg. Sinking Energy projection. Kidney. It is also known as *Ten Pu* 墊步.

擺步 **Pai Pu**   For the Pendulum step, the body pivots on the front leg while the rear leg is displaced in circular motion. The backwards Spiraling Energy projection is applied.

沈墜步 **Shen Tuei Pu**   For the Earthquake Step, one stands on the toes first, and then the weight of the body is swiftly transferred to the heels as they touch the ground. Sinking energy.

塌殿步 **Ta Ten Pu**   The Crushing Step may be done with only one foot or with both at the same time. What is important is to use the middle of the sole of the feet. Lung Energy.

The above mentioned steps are very important. In addition, there are other more complex steps that are part of the *Huo Pachi* and are considered to be very secret. Mastering these more complex steps indicates that *Huo Pachi* has been achieved. For information, here are the names of some of these steps: *Chi Hsing Pu Hua* (Seven Stars Step), *Tzuo You Pen Hua Pu* (left-right changing steps), *Chin Tuei Lienhuan Pu* (Forward and backward linked steps), *To Liang Huan Tzu Pu* (steps to secretly substitute the good spine with a bad one), *Yi Shing Huan Pu* (Magic steps), etc. Mastering these steps not only raises the quality of our *Pachi Chuan*, it also means that our body will be transformed, and will gain a superior quality, like the body of a saint. The opponent will fear such a martial artist, since he will not be able to locate him nor follow his displacements. After many years of traveling around the world, Master Su has never met or heard of anyone who knows about these techniques, let alone who has mastered them. They are now only guarded by him.

5.3.5 Palms

It is possible to use one palm alone or both at the same time. The basic palms are the following:

摔掌 **Suai Chang** The Shaking-off Palm strikes with the rear of the palm. *Tan* energy movement is used so that energy may be taken up to the tip of the fingers.

Suai Chang

劈掌 **Pi Chang** For the Splitting Palm, the arm moves downward drawing an arch. The strike is with the edge of the hand. A similar palm is *Chie Chang* 切掌, the difference being that the arch drawn is smaller. In both cases, the movement starts at the ribs. Liver energy.

推掌 **Tuei Chang** For the Pushing Palm, the entire surface of the palm is used. It may be done with one or both hands. Lung energy.

按掌 **An Chang** The Downward Pushing Palm also uses the entire palm. However, this technique is rarely carried out with both hands. It is a descending movement; Kidney energy.

Pi Chang Tuei Chang An Chang

掇掌 **Tuo Chang** The Raising Palm is performed using the hands in an ascending motion. It can be done using one or both hands at the same time. Heart energy.

伸掌 **Shen Chang** The Stretching Palm is performed pushing forward with the edge of the hand. This technique is used with steps going backward. Liver energy.

刁掌 **Tiao Chang** The Lever Palm is done with an ascending movement. The energy must reach the hand and to achieve this, the elbow is used. The hand should be in a vertical position with the thumb touching the index finger. Ascending *Wu Shing Chi Ching*: Kidney, Liver and Heart.

Tuo Chang

Tuan Chang

穿掌 **Tuan Chang** For the penetrating Palm, both hands are stretched and the fingers are used to strike. Two or more strikes follow each other continuously, with the hands sliding one above the other. This technique may be done with the palms facing up or down. Energy of *San Tsai Chi Ching*.

For a better understanding of these descriptions, see the photographs of section 8.10. *Pachi Chuan* and *Pikua Chuan* are studied together in Master Su's school. The two styles have the same palm techniques, with the same names.

5.3.6 Sacrum-Coccyx

The sacrum-coccyx (*Huei Yin*) is linked to the Kidney energy. When throwing an opponent, the sacrum is used at the end of the movement with a flexing and upward motion. It can also be used to lower the body weight in a sitting-like movement (*Tzuo* 坐). A closing or barring movement (*Pu* 蹼) may also be done.

5.3.7 The back

The *Pachi Chuan* techniques of the back are of the tiger, while in *Pikua Chuan* they are of the long arm-monkey. These techniques are the following:

通揹功 **Tong Pei Kung** The back is stretched laterally; left and right sides of the back are extended and opened. This is a monkey technique. If the back is not opened laterally, then the energy will not reach the fingers. This technique also lets the energy be projected further away.

拔揹功 **Pa Pei Kung** The back is stretched lengthwise. This is a tiger technique. The upper and lower part of the back are united by the spine, so when these are stretched, the spine is filled with energy that flows all along its length.

5.3.8 The hips

The hip (*Kua Ta* 胯打) can be used for thrusting movements (*Chi* 擠), for rebound movements (*Tan* 彈) and for lifting the knee (*Kai* 開). When wanting to throw an opponent, the hip is used to lift first and then to drop the adversary to the ground.

1

2

3

4

5

6

5.3.9 The knees

The knees (*Ti Ta* 膝打) can be used to strike with an ascending movement; this is called *Ting* 頂. *Kuei* 跨 is downward movement, as when kneeling. The sideways strike with the knee is called *Ti* 提.

Ting Ti, upward use of the knee

Chapter 6

Power and Energy in *Pachi Chuan*

> In *Pachi Chuan*, the force of the strike does not fade until it has reached its target.

Pachi Chuan has a variety of special features that possibly make it the most powerful Martial Arts style, as far as the management of internal energy is concerned.

Opening of the first branch of Pachi Tang Lang Martial Arts Institute in Tong Shan Hsiang, Taiwan, 1961.

6.1 Character of the energy in *Pachi Chuan*

It should be noted first that the projection of power in *Pachi Chuan* differs from other styles where after every attack one must take a new stance to be able to strike again. The time this change of position takes must be reduced as much as possible, because this transition is dangerous. In *Pachi Chuan*, the power of a strike does not decrease until it has reached its target. In order to achieve this, the body as well as the energy are used to strike with continuous force, and thus to pursue the target. *Pachi Chuan* does not allow any "empty" transitions of which the opponent might take advantage.

Secondly, movements in *Pachi Chuan* are not only strong physically: they require internal energy (*Nei Ching*). This is why someone who studies *Pachi Chuan* does not need to study other methods of developing internal energy; this style already contains very effective such methods.

Thirdly, all the attacks in *Pachi Chuan* are aimed at vital points of the body of the opponent. An unrelenting practice of *Pachi Chuan* makes the strikes very dangerous for the adversary as they may cause permanent damage or might cause even death. Someone who studies this style does not need to study which are the vital points, because it suffices to master the movements.

Something particular about *Pachi Chuan* is the discharge of internal energy towards the outside of the body. Generally, *Pachi Chuan* is considered to be a powerful style that consists only of powerful techniques. However, *Pachi Chuan* actually includes soft techniques within strong ones. In other words, in the real *Pachi Chuan* a powerful technique will suddenly change to a soft one and a soft technique will change to a powerful one. This is something very difficult to master. It is relatively easy to switch from one powerful technique to another powerful technique, or from a soft one to another soft one, but a great skill is required to be able to switch from a very soft technique to a powerful one in an instant.

One of the most sophisticated techniques of energy management in *Pachi Chuan* is *Ting Hsin Chou*. When executing this technique, a vibration should be felt throughout the body, as when a bomb hits the ground. This technique is of a very high level, since things do not vibrate without a reason. With this movement, *Pachi Chuan* not only projects energy, it can also suck it up again. It is like when a bomb explodes: the expansive force creates a vacuum which then has a sucking force. For this reason it is said that although physical force may be interrupted, the intent does not cease. Although it is inevitable that a pause occurs between two projections of energy, there should never be an interruption of intent. Due to this continuity of intent, energy changes from hardness to softness to come back with reverberations caused by the contraction of the body. In other words, the contraction and expansion of the body produce both types of energy: hard and soft. However, it is not good for the energy to change from hard to soft or vice versa repeatedly. Consequently, it is very important to understand the management of *Chi*. Once the energy has been set in motion, it is brought back by means of the *Ting Hsin Chou* and thanks to the contraction of the body.

6.2 The different ways of projecting energy in *Pachi Chuan*

As previously stated, the management of energy is essential for the correct execution of movements in *Pachi Chuan*. This is because the effectiveness of the style relies on the capacity of mastering *Fa Ching*, that is, the projection of energy. This is why *Pachi Chuan* must be executed with force.

The energy from different parts of the body may come out in different ways. The study of the management of energy is done by means of very precise techniques that are taught in stages and according to the level acquired. The aim of the first step is to fill the *Tan Tien* with energy and to then make it circulate throughout the body and even outside of it.

There are five forms of *Fa Ching* or projection of energy. These are:

BASIC LEVEL

沈墜勁 **Chen Sui Ching** Falling or sinking energy projection.

十字勁 **Suh Tzu Ching** Projection of energy in the form of a cross.

纏絲勁 **Chan Suh Ching** Spiraling energy projection.

INTERMEDIATE LEVEL

爆發勁 **Pao Fa Ching** Explosive energy projection.

Advanced level

透化勁 **Toh Hua Ching** Penetrating or infiltrating energy projection.

These five ways of projecting energy constitute the complete range of ways of managing energy in Martial Arts.

6.2.1 *Chen Sui Ching*.
Sinking and condensing energy and force

Chen sui means sinking. This is the first energy of *Pachi Chuan*, for which Kidney energy is used. Energy goes in a descending motion and is called sinking, falling or concentrating energy projection.

Chen Sui Ching

The movement of every part of the body is oriented towards the ground. It should reach the ground and even go beyond it, making the movement very stable and giving rise to a reflecting or rebounding force from the ground, which adds to the action-reaction principle. "Below" needs "above": there is the ground and there is your own substance. When something falls and hits the ground it produces a rebound that returns the energy through the substance of the object, like an echo. The reflected energy will be different according to the substance of the body that strikes the ground, and that energy will be useful depending on this substance. If the rebound does not find an echo in the bodily substance, then it will be damped down and will not reach anywhere.

The energy of the body is normally not focused in only one place. However, with this type of energy projection, it becomes concentrated. The weight descends to the ground and the energy is concentrated in the *Tan Tien*. This is why with this technique the energy not only descends, it is also concentrated.

The center plays a prominent role in the execution of this type of energy projection. The center of the movement is controlled by the coccyx. In other words, the coccyx is the center of the sinking energy projection and, consequently, it is the basis that controls the power. With a weak basis it is not possible to develop energy at all. It is the coccyx then, that manages the rebounding energy coming up from the heels. It will orient it upwards, downwards or sideways, always through the legs. Once the starting point is fixed, the energy can be developed.

This is the basic energy present in every movement of *Pachi Chuan*. It corresponds to the force of gravity and it helps the other energies. *Chen Sui Ching* is energy of water, but there are different types of water energies, each one corresponding to each of the Five Elements. Wood is like the roots of a tree; Metal is molten metal; the energy of Fire is related to petroleum and other liquid fuels; etc.

Every movement of *Pachi Chuan* carries a sinking energy that corresponds to one of the Five Energies. *Chi Ma Suh* is the characteristic stance for this energy; its basic energy is that of Water, but as mentioned above, it can also have energy of Metal, Wood, Fire or Earth.

Our body has a variety of liquids: blood, urine, tears, saliva, mucus. They are all water. The energy of Water comes from the movement of the liquids of the body.

This energy is the first and most important, since without mastering *Chen Sui Ching* the other techniques can not be mastered. Nowadays, there are styles which use very high stances. Possibly, in those styles the management of *Chen Sui Ching* was not originally known, and it is because of this that they cannot make energy descend.

6.2.2 *Suh Tzu Ching*
Projection of energy in the form of a cross

Usually, as a consequence of daily habits, people tend to concentrate a larger share of energy on one side of the body (left or right); this happens in the upper and lower body. This is due to the fact that people use one side more than the other. Something similar happens with the attention, since people pay more attention to what happens in one area of space than the rest. With *Suh Tzu Ching* we complete and make our movements and attention uniform in all directions. This characteristic of the cross energy projection makes fighting against multiple adversaries possible, while the condensing energy projection is only effective in one-to-one combat.

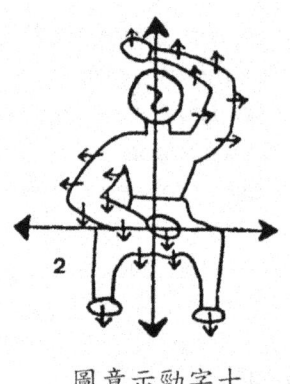

Suh Tzu Ching

With the cross energy projection, energy is projected upwards and downwards, left and right, simultaneously and with equal force, as if stretching in these four directions simultaneously. The sinking energy projection serves as a starting point for projecting energy in the form of a cross. With the *Suh Tzu Ching* it is possible to move the energy with equal force in the four directions, reaching the limits of the body and beyond.

By means of the cross energy projection, inward or outward movements are generated: from the center of the body towards its most external parts, and hence to the limits of the energetic body; or from the most external, represented by four points that form a cross, towards the center. This type of energy projection is governed by the Liver energy, Wood. However, as with the sinking energy, there are movements in which it occurs under the light of the other four energies. The most characteristic stances of this type of energy projection are *Au Pu Tan Shan Suh* and *Tun Ta Suh* (see p. 120).

6.2.3 *Chan Suh Ching*. Spiraling energy projection

With *Chan Suh Ching*, energy is projected in a spiraling manner. Every part of the body performs a spiraling movement with the aim of focusing all the energy in a single point. If force is projected linearly, it diminishes easily after covering a certain trajectory as it does not have the possibility to continue its path. In order to avoid this, the energy must be moved in a spiraling manner throughout the body. This keeps the energy constantly moving, and even though it reaches a point where it gets concentrated, it does not stop there, it can move further in another direction.

Suh Tzu Ching

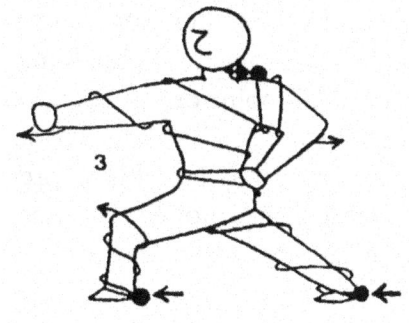

圖意示勁絲纏

    The spiral starts in the heels, it rises through the legs, and it is when it reaches the hips and the coccyx that it takes the intended direction, subsequently triggering the movement of the upper body which is controlled by the shoulders. The hips also turn, though this must be done uniformly, making sure that both sides turn equally and that the head, the coccyx and the heels are aligned vertically, forming the axis of the spin. The circle can be big or small, but the smaller it is, the better and faster the projection of energy will be.

    The energy of the body should spin in order to attain more force. This spin also gives the energy the capacity of producing forces in any other direction instantaneously, in a stable and enduring manner. This makes the management of energy more agile, sensitive and versatile.

Pao Hua Ching

The spiraling energy projection takes energy from one side of the body to the other. If it starts at the right side of the body, it will finish at the left side, and vice versa. It can also be performed going backwards. The typical stance for this type energy projection is *Tan Shan Suh* and it corresponds to Liver energy, although it can be of the other elements as well. The *Au Pu Tan Shan Suh* stance that moves the rear foot is also used (see p. 119).

What we have described is the best known aspect of the spiraling energy projection, which is present in almost every Kung Fu style and in many sports. In addition, there is another aspect of this type of energy projection. This is about making the energy come out through a very small point of the body, and then expanding it outwards in a spiral, thus shaping, as it were, a cocoon of energy. This technique is used for protection and may possibly be present only in *Pachi Chuan*. By mastering this technique, a sort of energy rebound is produced that acts as an earthquake over the opponent and knocks him down.

6.2.4 *Pao Fa Ching*. Explosive energy projection

Explosive energy projection is obtained by using simultaneously the previous three types of energy projection. The union of these projections makes the energy come out of the whole body vigorously, even through the pores of the skin. This is a secret technique of energy management, and it is specific to the *Pachi Chuan* style. Both this technique and *Toh Hua Ching* are very difficult to execute. They require years of practice and are in any case rarely taught. For this reason, only three types of energy are mentioned in other branches of *Pachi Chuan*. It is because I master these techniques that I can talk about them.

Contrary to the first three modes of managing energy, which involved the Five Elements, this mode is performed with only one element. A specific material is necessary for *Pao Fa Ching* to be executed.

In order to use *Pao Fa Ching* it is a prerequisite to have a strong body, especially the internal organs. Otherwise, it is not possible to cope with the energy. This state of necessary physical strength is acquired during the stages previous to *Pao Tsa Ching* (爆炸勁, another name for explosive energy projection). It is such that we can correct any health issue of our body. With the Explosive energy projection it is possible to reflect a received strike adding our own energy to it. Under these conditions, the state of our body is such that it is all but invulnerable.

Pao Fa Ching is executed expanding the body. Energy and force are projected outward as an explosion.

6.2.5 *Toh Hua Ching*
Penetrating or infiltrating energy projection

One of the last forms of energy projection in *Pachi Chuan* is the penetrating energy projection. Here, the projection is done in such a way that it pierces. This form of energy projection represents the union of soft and hard energies within the body, energies which can also come out of the body. To use this type of energy projection, many years of practice are required. It is, as a matter of fact, the natural consequence of a persevering practice of *Pachi Chuan*.

Toh Hua Ching

This type of energy projection can be soft or hard. For example, if someone hits us in the chest, we can absorb and disperse the force of the strike throughout the body, so that it is no longer concentrated at the place of impact. On the other hand, if we strike someone in the chest using this type of energy projection, all the force of the impact will reach every part of the body of the opponent. An explosive strike of Penetrating energy looks very soft and gentle, but Spiraling energy is doing its work within. When this energy penetrates the body, it goes through it and reaches the other side.

Mastering the Infiltrating energy projection enables us to disperse the opponent's energy before it reaches us and it gives us the ability to project our own energy so that it reaches the opponent. With this method it is also possible, on the one hand, to absorb the natural energy of our surroundings, and on the other, to make our own energy come out of our body so that it is united with the former.

Mastering this type of energy management, the highest of all, provides the Martial Artist with a tool of the highest level which enables him to reach any set goal within the range of human energetic possibilities: from the most simple goal of everyday life, to the most esoteric. The achievement of such possibilities is not however guaranteed by merely mastering these techniques of energy management, just as having a lot of money does not guarantee it will be spent in the most appropriate way.

The fourth and fifth of these types of energy projection are secret. They are very difficult to master, because they require the complete study of the style and the development of its energies, which is in itself very difficult. At present, only Master Su, and possibly one of his brothers in study, are capable of putting them into practice.

Photo montage illustrating what Toh Hua Ching may achieve.

Master Su was once in the countryside with some of his students and they asked him to demonstrate the use of the Infiltrating energy. Master Su then approached a goat, touched its head and gently slid his hand towards the back of the goat. The goat fell to the ground, lifeless. There was a doctor among the students who insisted in carrying out an autopsy of the goat to see what had happened to it. So they went back to the city with the goat and in the examination they found that the spine of the animal had been deformed and that it had torn its gallbladder.

For *Toh Hua Ching* to be applied, one must look at the person or animal straight into the face to determine where are the weaknesses in order to apply the appropriate energy.

The Infiltrating energy can produce shock waves in the blood and other body liquids of the opponent, which are propagated throughout the body and reach the heart and other vital organs, causing their collapse. It is also possible to act upon the energetic circuits of the body through the nerves. Surely, some people will think that all this is no more than storytelling, others that it is actually magic. However, mastering this technique is possible if one studies with a competent master.

6.3 Energy and its flow

In the previous section we have described the five ways of managing the energy, both inside and outside of the body. Since energy is the basis of *Fa Ching*, we will now describe the nature of energy itself.

Even though the body's energy is originally one, it acquires different qualities or characters as it circulates through the body, depending on the place where it originated. This process of acquiring different qualities occurs according to five general regions, each of which has sub-domains. Each can be activated by means of specific movements of the body.

In Martial Arts in general, and in *Pachi Chuan* in particular, the projection of energy always starts in the feet and legs, it is shaped in the torso, and it is managed with the hands—this is not to say that energy cannot be projected through any part of the body. For each of the five basic energies there is a position for the feet, a motion of the torso, and a position of the fingers that will trigger it. The knowledge of the techniques that distinguish the flow of energy, together with the knowledge of the five ways of projecting energy not only puts energy at the martial artist's disposal, but it also makes him capable of using it in specific ways.

The flow of energy follows two systems:

五行氣 – **Wu Shing Chi** Energy of the Five Elements

三才氣 – **San Tsai Chi** Energy of the Three Sages.

Each energy originates at the sole of the feet, according to the place determined by the *San Tsai* (Spirit, Energy, Essence); it then rises to the *Hsia Tan Tien* to be united with the *Shen Tien Chi* (natural energy of the body); it continues to the *Tsong Tan Tien* to be united with the *Hou Tien Ching* (non-natural energy of the body, the availability of which requires training the body). Energy is thus shaped while it moves through the body, and its echo is felt in one of the fingers at the moment of its projection.

For an in-depth treatment of these ideas, we refer the interested reader to the book *The Invisible Web*[1], where some of these concepts are explained in more detail.

6.3.1 *Wu Shing Chi*
The energy of the Five Elements

There are a few principles that, if followed while executing the movements of *Pachi Chuan*, lead to the circulation of the energy of the Five Elements.

---

[1] Su Yu-Chang, *The Invisible Web*, Asociación Europea Pachi Tanglang Chuan y Tao, Mallorca, 1998.

Without adhering to these principles it is not possible for the Five Energies to flourish and, consequently, without supply of energy, the projection of *Chi* is not possible either.

The concept of the Five Elements is part of Chinese Philosophy since ancient times. The five elements are earth, wood, fire, metal and water, and each element corresponds to a part of the body. In the following a brief description is given of what each of these elements represents and its relation to the practice of *Pachi Chuan*.

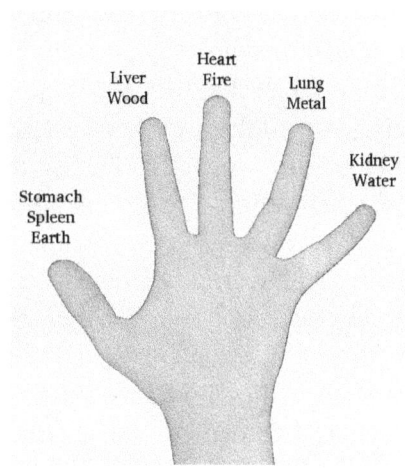

Correspondence between the Five Elements and the fingers

Earth corresponds to Stomach and Spleen. These two organs lie at the level of the diaphragm, which should be twisted and stretched. They correspond to the thumb. The movement of these organs is managed by the turning of the hands around the central axis of the arm. This turning motion is guided by the thumb. When executing a movement of Stomach or Spleen, we must twist these organs following the lead of the thumb. The feet give their support based on turning movements as they follow the circles of their outer edges. Attention must be paid to the knees, because as they stabilize the lower body, they contribute to the movement of the diaphragm. The shoulder blades should also turn.

Wood corresponds to Liver and to the index finger. Liver energy circulates along the sides of the torso. When executing a Liver fist, the ribcage should open in order to let Liver energy flow out. The stance is based on the edge of the foot and the use of the hips is fundamental. The shoulder blades are drawn apart and made to bulge, forming as it were, the trunk of a tree.

Fire corresponds to Heart and is represented by the middle finger. In order to make the *Chi* of Heart manifest, the center must be emptied. The center refers to the middle of the chest: the sternum, where the directions of forces oppose each other, one upwards and the other downwards. If the center of the torso is not emptied, the *Chi* of Heart will not be projected. This *Chi* is projected by stretching the middle of the torso, guided by the middle finger which points upwards. It is very important to pay attention to the feet. This energy is managed by resting on the tip of the toes. The neck should be stretched and the shoulder blades should be brought closer towards the back.

Metal corresponds to Lung and to the ring finger. In order to project Lung *Chi*, it is important to open the palm of the hand and to have the fingers separated. The shoulder blades play a central role since Lung energy cannot be projected if they are not well placed. The correct position is to have them drawn slightly forward. The elbows are also important since they should touch each other. The step is performed with the center of the foot empty.

Water Water, finally, corresponds to Kidney and the little finger. Kidney *Chi* is projected downwards and is guided by the little finger, which is also oriented downwards. It is important that the lower back should be protruding, and the fist is pointing downwards. The management of the coccyx and the stance based on the heels is fundamental. The shoulder blades should descend.

6.3.2 *San Tsai Chi*. The energy of the Three Sages

This is the name given to the trinity that makes the flow of energy through the body possible. This trinity comprises Spirit, Energy and Essence (*Shen* 神, *Chi* 氣, *Ching* 精). The body has several related trinities that in most cases involve the joints: in the arms there are wrists, elbows and shoulders; in the legs we have ankles, knees and the hips; in the body as a whole, there are the articulations of the neck, the coccyx and the ankles. The *San Tsai* that is mirrored on the feet is of special importance. The correspondence is as follows:

1. Spirit: front part of the foot, including the toes.

2. Energy: central part.

3. Essence: back part, including the heels.

San Tsai is very important for a good management of energy. For displacements, in particular, it is essential. In many steps, such as *Ten Pu* or *Tsuo Pu*, the energy of the Three Sages must be taken into consideration.

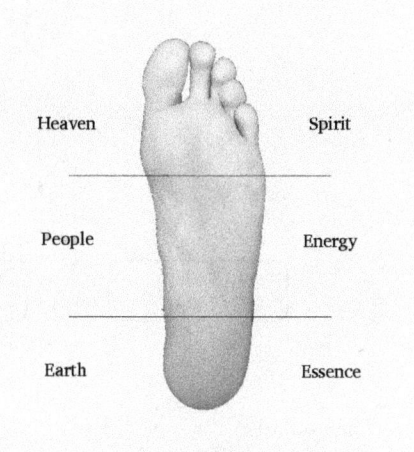

When standing on the front of our feet, we exercise and strengthen Spirit, and we move Fire *Chi*. When our feet rest on the heels, we strengthen Essence, that is the part of the body that corresponds to Kidney and Water *Chi*. Energy refers here to the interaction of the previous two, and it corresponds to Metal. The energy of Wood, Liver, arises when the foothold is based on the edge of the foot, from toes to heel. Earth, Stomach-Spleen, integrates the whole foot with a rotating foothold that engages the entire sole of the foot.

6.3.3 *Wei Chi* and *Ying Chi*

Wu Shing Chi and *San Tsai Chi* also designate the two circuits through which energy is channeled: through them both circulate the two kinds of energy that maintain the body: *Wei Chi* and *Ying Chi*. *Wu Shing Chi* is the vertical cycle, while *San Tsai Chi* is horizontal.

The *Wu Shing Chi* circuit is vertical, Yang, and *Wei Chi*, the "defensive energy" of breath, moves along its course. This energy comes from the breath, from what is absorbed by the lungs. The lungs draw in air together with subtle aid; this cycle is not possible without breath. When circulating upwards, it goes through the ascending order Kidney–Liver–Heart. When circulating down, it follows the descending order Heart–Lung–Kidney. The circulation of this energy is set in motion when we perform vertical movements, in order to direct the energy up or down.

In contrast, the *San Tsai* circuit is horizontal, Yin, and *Ying Chi*, the "food energy", circulates through it. This energy comes from food, from what is absorbed through the mouth and the stomach. The *San Tsai* of the *Tsong Tan Tien* is a movement of energy starting from the Liver at the left, then through Stomach-Spleen at the center, until the Lung on the right,

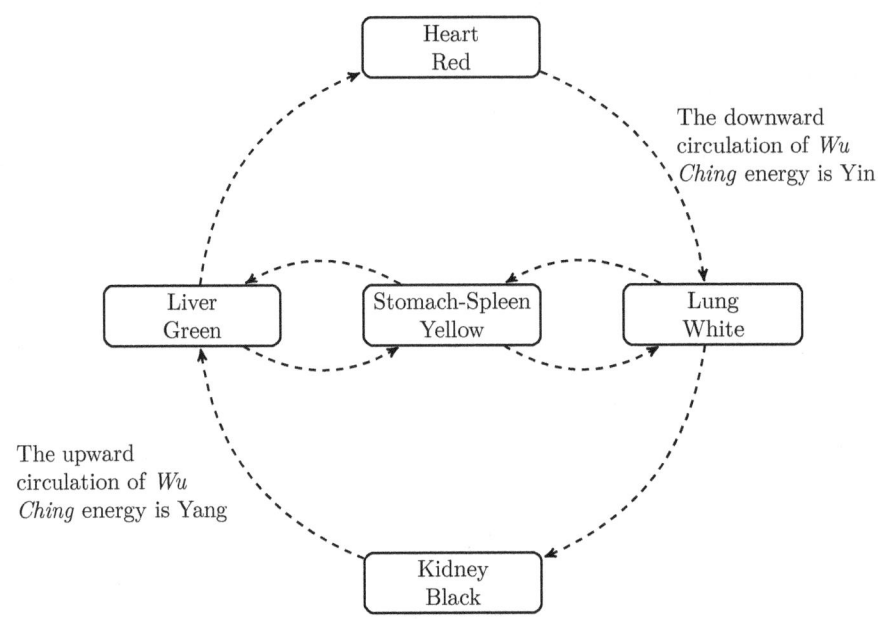

The circulation of *San Tsai* energy in the Lung–Spleen–Liver direction is Yang, while in the Liver–Spleen–Lung direction it is Yin

and then returning through Stomach-Spleen to Liver. The management of energy by means of horizontal and lateral movements uses this circuit. It is very important to unite this cycle with that of *Wu Shing Chi*. The transformation into different energies takes place in the *Tsong Tan Tien*.

The execution of any movement requires taking into account one of these circuits of energy, or both simultaneously. The Martial Artist who is able to manage well these two energy circuits will be able to control his breathing and nutrition: he is protected.

6.4 Combat application.
Techniques for applying energy in *Pachi Chuan*

The mastery of the movements that bring out and make available the energy of the Five Elements, together with the ability to put into practice the five methods of energy projection, bring the martial artist to a condition where undertaking personal defense is finally possible. However, it is still necessary to have a knowledge of the specific techniques for using energy to this purpose.

There are twelve *Pachi Chuan* techniques that project energy in the guise of a punch, a push, a thrust, etc. These techniques consist of movements of the extremities or of the torso that constitute the final stage of the application of energy. Every movement of *Pachi Chuan* should include one of these techniques, otherwise it can not be considered part of the style. Each of these techniques requires the use of one or more of the five projections of energy.

These techniques are:

1. 彈 Tan Elastic
2. 捅 Tong To penetrate
3. 砸 Tza To grind, to crush
4. 挷 Peng To rebound
5. 捼 Tsuai To knead
6. 吐 Tu To pierce
7. 喊 Han To yell (startling sounds)
8. 擊 Ji To attack
9. 挨 Ai To withstand, resist a strike
10. 挫 Tso To sand
11. 擠 Chi To push-reject, compress
12. 靠 Kao To lean

彈 **Tan — Elastic** This technique has the energy of a bow. An elastic energy is produced, similar to the one of a tense bow when it releases an arrow. It can be executed using the arm, the hand, the foot, the leg or the torso. The spine should bend and stretch so that its elastic rebound comes into play. It can be executed with the five types of energy projection. It is also known as *Wu Kong Ching* (五弓經): Five Bow Projections.

捅 **Tong — To penetrate** This technique has the energy of a battering ram. The battering ram is a device used since ancient times to break through doors, which consists of a log or beam. Hence, energy breaks through, penetrates. The arm is the characteristic body-part for the application of this technique. The extended arm, as if turned into a staff or a spear, is used as a battering ram. A strike with the arm completely extended conveys the energy of the body directly, and an appropriate movement of the rest of the body gives it greater range. The best type of energy projection for this technique is the Spiraling energy projection. It is used in short-range attacks, for the application of *Tsun Ching* (striking from a one-inch distance) and *An Ching* (technique used when already in contact with the body of the opponent). Added to the force of the strike is the weight of the body. It is said to be "the hand that comes out as a staff" (*Chu Shou Ru Kun* – 出手如棍).

砸 **Tza — To grind, to crush** This technique uses a descending demolishing energy. The arms are used in such a way that they fall one after the other. It can be executed doing a step forward or backward, which increases its efficiency. Sinking energy projection is characteristic for this technique. It is used for breaking the bones, joints or nerves of the adversary.

挷 **Peng — To rebound** This technique uses the energy of the spine in a lengthwise orientation. It is similar to the forces developed by a peasant when using a pitchfork to throw the ripe grain, or when using a shovel to move a load of soil. The strike comes from below as if it was rebounding. The rear leg plays an important role, as it supports the body-weight and makes the execution of the technique possible. In the Praying Mantis style there is a technique with the same name, but the movement itself is different.

搣 **Tsuai — To knead** This movement is similar to kneading dough to make bread. The wrists are used, usually in a descending motion. When applying this technique it is important to perform the characteristic twist of the wrist used when kneading dough, be it upwards or downwards. This technique can also be used in a defensive manner: if the opponent grabs hold of any part of our body, we can perform *Tsuai* of the body, somehow like a tremor, freeing us from the adversary's grasp.

吐 **Tu — To pierce** A protruding part of the body is used to strike. The energy is applied using the fingers, the elbow, the shoulder, or some other angular part of the body. The force is concentrated into a small area, usually aiming at breaking bones, or targeting vital points.

喊 **Han — To yell** Yells are used to reinforce the projection of energy. In the *Pachi Chuan* style there are three sounds: *Hn, Hah,* and a secret one, *I-Ya. Hn* is a sound that comes from the chest and goes out through the nose. It involves the energies of the Five Organs and the lungs should expand. It can be used defensively as it boosts the resistance against strikes.

Hah is used in other circumstances. It is a vocal sound generated by contracting and expanding the diaphragm. Its energy comes from the *Tan Tien*, and the abdomen must be contracted to produce this sound.

I-Ya is a secret sound. It requires the mastering of the circulation of energy through the meridians. This is a superior technique which is used together with, and controling, the Infiltrating energy projection.

It is important for the sounds *Hn* and *Hah* to be executed by the *Pachi Chuan* student in the first stages of learning. At an advanced level they are no longer vocalized, as it is enough to produce them in the mind (*Yi* – 意). The sounds *Hn* and *Hah* are very effective in helping our energy to develop faster. Furthermore, they help remember which energy corresponds to each movement they accompany. In the context of competitions, they function as *Hang* (哼 sounds that impress) and thus help to win.

擊 **Shi — To attack** Energy is applied by linking together several attacking movements, one after the other, very fast, and all of them forward. This technique is of paramount importance in *Pachi Chuan*. It is a principle of this style to push until the end in every attack; no punch that is thrown is retrieved before reaching its target. Every attack has its defined aim, a specific point which must be reached. The *Shi* technique develops a continuous flow of energy towards the objective.

挨 **Ai — To withstand a strike** The energy is concentrated following the flow proposed by the opponent, thus creating a void that is then used to make the definitive counterattack. This technique is present in a characteristic tactic of *Pachi Chuan* called *So Shen Fa*, which is usually kept secret because it seems to go against the spirit of the style. *So Shen* means to surrender. The opponent is made to believe that one has given up, and is enticed to attack with full power, reaching to a point of no return. It is then that we release all our force and strike back with a final attack to destroy the opponent.

Another application of *Ai* can be executed when the opponent reaches us with a strike. In this case, making use of *Pao Fa Ching* (Explosive energy projection), the energy of the adversary is assimilated and then returned amplified, like a ball that bounces back.

挫 **Tso — To sand** Energy is applied by rotating any part of the body like a sanding disc. The forearms, the arms, the hips, etc., can all be used. This technique has two functions, the first is to come out against an incoming strike with a twisting motion that diverts the energy of the opponent while hitting him or her at the same time. The second is used when a strike has reached our body: by making use of *Tso* we can diffuse the energy of the opponent, making it slide by.

Tso is typically used to attack especially sensitive parts of the adversary. It produces an effect similar to being electrocuted with a high voltage, or to the scalding produced by boiling water poured over the body, which can cause death.

擠 **Chi — To push-reject** This technique is used upon physical contact with the adversary, in particular when someone is grabbing us. *Chi* involves the contraction and expansion of the body, hence its use when there is no space between the bodies. *Chi* is also used while performing *Pachi Ta Chang*, the Eight Places (Toh 頭, Chien 肩, Chou 肘, Shou 手, Kuei 尾, Hua 胯, Ti 膝, Tzu 足). The energy of *Chi* can reach anywhere.

靠 **Kao — To lean** Different parts of the body are used to strike, such as the shoulders, the hips and the back. The weight of the body is thrown against the opponent, just as one throws a rock or a ball. *Kao* is one of the most important techniques of *Pachi Chuan*. Using this technique, once the *Pao Fa Ching* and the *Toh Hua Ching* have been mastered, one can cause the death of the adversary in the blink of an eye.

6.5 "Doors" in *Pachi Chuan*

The concept of "door" in Martial Arts refers to the degree of proximity of the opponent. There are five outer doors to reach the center. The first two doors are the hands and the forearms. At the second level lie the arms and the elbows; at the third are the shoulders; at the fourth are the sides of the torso. The meridians of the "Small Celestial Circle" (see p. 168) lie at the center.

One must try to penetrate as far inside as possible when attacking, as the further we reach, the better are we positioned to strike, and the least able is the opponent to fend off a strike. While defending, one must therefore try to keep the opponent at the outer doors, as strikes at the center are definitive.

6.6 Energy and technique in various Martial Arts

One might assume that *Fa Ching* (energy projection) would be the same in all Martial Arts, but this is not the case, because the use of the five forms of energy projection is different in each case. Sometimes, the first and the third types of energy projection are combined; sometimes 20% of the second is combined with 30% of the first and 50% of the third; some styles use only mechanical force, without any internal energy.

The energy of the body and the basic application and projection techniques are the same in every style of Martial Arts, but the training and the teaching vary from style to style. A style which is complete will develop all five forms of energy projection, while an incomplete one will only develop a few.

Although in every Martial Arts style all the techniques that are used in the combat application of energy have self-defense as their aim, the movements that constitute these techniques are usually different. For example, the Praying Mantis style also has the five types of energy projection, but the movements of the Praying Mantis style are very different from those of *Pachi Chuan*. This difference is due to the fact that the five types of energy projection are used to develop the twelve characteristic techniques of Praying Mantis. The same happens with *Pakua Chang*: the twelve characteristic techniques for applying energy of *Pakua Chang* are derived from the five forms of energy projection. Whoever masters several styles, such as *Pachi Chuan*, Praying Mantis and *Pakua Chang*, will be able to use the energy application techniques of any of those styles.

There are not many, however, who are knowledgeable in more than one style; and among these, only a few can execute the movements of each style in such a way that they can be unmistakably recognized as such. Often, when watching a Martial Arts film, we hear the "villain" boasting that he knows many styles, but the techniques displayed turn out to be the same because there is only one Martial Arts director behind the scenes. There are also people who say that they know several styles: Monkey, Cat, Shaolin, Tai Chi Chuan, etc., but they all look alike when performed. The Shaolin style looks like Monkey Shaolin, Tai Chi Chuan looks like Monkey Tai Chi Chuan, the Cat style looks like a Monkey Cat. What this shows is that that person is not able to manage each energy distinctly. Making a comparison with water, we see that there is water in wine, in paint, in soup, in ice, in the steam that makes machines work. However, when drinking wine, no one would say that he or she is drinking water, just as no one thinks of the steam when watching the movement of a machine that draws its energy from a steam engine.

An authentic master is capable of executing different styles using the same five original energies and show the well defined identity of each one. When a real master shows the Praying Mantis style, everyone should be able to recognize it as such. Furthermore, it should be possible to identify who were his or her masters, because a serious student should equal the original, or surpass it if possible.

Pachi Chuan and *Pikua Chuan* have been practiced together since antiquity. Their energy and combat techniques were used together in training, but the movements and energy of each style were never changed.

Master Su is a living example of this, having mastered the energy of several styles. He has also formed the *Pachi Tanglang Chuan* style, incorporating the energy and spirit of *Pachi Chuan* into *Tanglang Chuan* so that the latter, already strong, is even stronger and complete. But he has done this without changing any of the ancient movements nor the original energy of *Tanglang Chuan*.

The energy manifested in each style is the same, but produces, nevertheless, very different sensations. The energy of *Pachi Chuan* feels very stable, and when performing movements of the style it seems as if it wanted to expand throughout the body like an explosion. In the Praying Mantis style, the energy is felt as it travels through the body, and when performing movements of the style, it comes pelting out like rapid gunfire. In *Pakua Chang* the sensation is that the energy of the body is always united with the natural energy of the Universe; when coming out, the energy is like the current of a river, ceaseless and unwaivering.

6.7 Effects of energy in Martial Arts

The ultimate aim of a Martial Art is to reach the opponent and finish him. Often this implies striking. When striking something in any context, the most important thing is to know what our target is (a wall, a person, a tree, etc.). In Martial Arts, strikes are aimed at animals, be it human beings, tigers, dogs, etc. Some of the things animals have in common are blood, a body, energy, and breath. Due to this, there are three ways of striking; all three related to the energetic body, but each with a different effect. Accordingly, there are three possible targets in Martial Arts:

1. 氣 *Chi*. External and internal energy.

2. 穴 *Shue*. Blood and body.

3. 陰陽兩不接 *Yin Yang Liang Pu Chie*. Where Yin and Yang cannot be together. It can also refer to specific points of the body through which the person relates to Nature.

Striking the Chi Action is exerted upon those points that control the energy of the human being. For example, it is possible to interrupt the opponent's breath by striking or acting on specific points, thus causing death. In wrestling we see an external application of this type of action, in techniques aimed at strangling to prevent the intake of air (external *Chi*). There are higher level techniques that take away the opponent's energy with a strike, as if pricking a ball. This is achieved by applying *Pachi Chuan* techniques where the strike is aimed at the interior of the opponent's body, thus cutting the circulation of his vital energy (internal *Chi*).

Striking the Shue Action is exerted upon the material body. Our body contains blood, which has a liquid nature. By appropriately projecting energy it is possible to produce a million waves in the opponent's blood flow that cannot be withstood by the heart and therefore cause death. Similarly, if a nerve is struck and torn, the brain receives a deadly impact. Applying this type of technique is very dangerous, because its effects may not be immediately felt. One might feel well for hours or even days after receiving such a blow, and then suddenly fall dead. This is because a blocking element is introduced in the circulatory system and, moving along, it eventually reaches a point where it impedes the circulation of blood.

Striking the Yin Yang Liang Bu Chie Two incompatible vital points are simultaneously pressed, producing a shock. The body has "echoes" and if two of them are pressed at the same time, a deadly reaction is triggered.

There are also points that are indispensable for connecting the organism with the natural external energies. Hence, another possibility is to strike such a point in order to prevent the opponent's body from absorbing Nature's energy, producing death within a short term. This is just as a plant dies because of spending too much time without sunlight. It is also possible to strike a specific point to make the opponent's vital energy escape the body, like the air comes out of a punctured tire.

Every strike in *Pachi Chuan*, *Tanglang Chuan* or *Pakua Chang* aims at one of the aforementioned targets.

6.8 *Chi Kung* of *Pachi Chuan*

This *Chi Kung* has 8 series of movements and 95 technical movements. The names of the 8 series are:

1. 獻肘式 – *Shen Chou Suh*. Offering the elbow.
2. 提籃式 – *Ti Nan Suh*. Carrying the basket.
3. 聽風式 – *Ting Fong Suh*. Listening to the wind.
4. 敬酒式 – *Ching Cho Suh*. Offering a cup of liquor.
5. 叫門式 – *Chiao Men Suh*. Knocking at the door.
6. 看書式 – *Kan Shu Suh*. Reading the book.
7. 拉弓式 – *La Kong Suh*. Drawing the bow.
8. 抱肘式 – *Pao Chou Suh*. Hugging the elbows.

Pachi Chuan's *Chi Kung* is special for elongating the tendons by means of spiraling twists. It opens the joints and it can reach as deep inside as the bone marrow. It is a superior *Chi Kung* and it is called *I Ching Hsi Ku Kung* 易筋洗骨功.

This *Chi Kung* is based on spiraling twists of the body. All our limbs and the torso, all parts of the body are able to turn in a twisting motion. This motion can be done to the left or to the right. We can imagine that if a cross section were to be made of any of the limbs, of the torso or of the neck, a *Tai Chi* should be revealed, twisting ever more. The greater the twisting motion, the greater the force of the Yin or Yang energy. In *Pachi Chuan*'s *Chi Kung* it is very important to learn how to use these energies.

The energy obtained is very different depending on the sense of the rotation. The symmetry of the shoulder blades, the hips, the ribcage, the extremities, and of the body as a whole, make it possible for the two sides to be twisted in the same sense or in opposite sense. For example, both legs can be twisted inward, both outward, or one inward and the other outward. The clockwise rotation is Yin and the counter-clockwise rotation is Yang. The important thing is that the tendons, muscles and bones are all turned, twisting and stretching. If the twists are properly executed, energy will flow, otherwise it will stay blocked.

It is also important to keep in mind whether the energy of a given Element is Yin or Yang. For example, when doing a movement of Metal, if it is Yin, it will correspond to the lungs and energy will circulate through the inner part of the arms, where the Lung meridian lies; if it is Yang, the energy will circulate through the outer part of the arms, where the Intestine meridian lies. The rotating movement should draw a circle in the appropriate manner. It should be clockwise if it is Yin and counter-clockwise if it is Yang. Similarly, the sense of circulation of energy depends on which meridian it is going through: toward the hands if going through the Lung meridian and toward the torso if through the Intestine meridian.

If the palm pushes downward, it is a Yin movement, so Yin Lung energy should be made to circulate through the Lung meridian, which starts at the chest and runs through the inner part of the arms until the thumb. The energy moves spiraling as the arms are stretched and twisted clockwise. Here, *Tan Shan Suh* is used to shift all the energy forward. If the palms are upwards, it is a Yang movement and *Pu Ting Pu Pa Suh* is used to bring the weight to the middle. Energy circulates in spirals from the hands toward the torso, following the Yang Metal meridians through the arms.

Both movements correspond to Lung, but the way each one is managed is different. The Yin movement is forward and the energy spirals follow the Yin Metal meridians in *Tan Shan Suh*; the Yang movement is upward in *Pu Ting Pu Pa Suh*.

As previously mentioned, with the *I Ching Hsi Ku Kung* the bones and tendons are stretched, just as with the *Shen Chin Pa Ku* (see p. 58). In *Shen Chin Pa Ku*, the stretching aims to make the tendons and muscles longer and to open the joints. In *I Ching Hsi Ku Kung* we study where the stretching starts and in which sense the energy is circulating according to its characteristics; we study which points must be stretched, where to start and which direction should be followed, and which is the direction of rotation. This is superior to *Shen Chin Pa Ku* because it requires knowing whether the circulation is inward or outward. The eight places of the body (see p. 59) also come into play, but in a specific order for each position, since for each position the energy is different and, consequently, the hexagram that represents it is also different.

The body contains blood, muscles, nerves, bones and marrow. *Shen Chin Pa Ku* only produces a linear lengthening and acts upon the outer part of the bones, while *I Ching Hsi Ku Kung* produces a radial extension as well. The latter is unmistakably more powerful and it can act upon the bones and the marrow. If the movements are properly executed, one can feel how the body expands. The linear lengthening only enables the energy to come out linearly, while being able to radially expand any part of the body makes one capable of applying energy in an explosive manner, in every direction, like a bomb.

Chapter 7

Master Su Yu-Chang's Philosophy of *Pachi Tanglang Chuan*

> Changing the body takes a lot of time, but no more than an instant is needed to acquire the spirit of a saint.

7.1 Energy, essence, spirit

The first step to be taken in the study of *Pachi Chuan* is achieving *Pien Hua Chi Tzu* 變化氣質. *Pien Hua* means change and development; *Chi* means energy; *Tzu* means structure of the organism.

Group of participants of an international seminar held in Venezuela, 1998

Tzu refers to the notion that the organism of every person is not only material, but it has essence (organs, bones, muscles, etc.) and spirit. The spirit component itself has two aspects, one constituted by what is inherited from our parents, and the other, that is configured at the moment of birth, is character, which corresponds to the original spirit. The organism also has the capacity of manifesting energy, *Chi*.

Master Su teaching acupuncture

Chi refers to the energy of the human being. It is the manifestation of the natural energy through the functioning of the organism. This energy is present in every living person, it is what enables us to carry out our actions. After death, it is no longer there. A person's *Chi* is changing, and it depends both on the essence and the spirit components of the organism. If health is good, the *Chi* will be strong; when ill, the *Chi* is weak.

This composite develops until a certain age when it starts to deteriorate. Both, the development and the degeneration, vary from person to person. People can be fat or slim, tall or short, strong or weak, etc. The same applies to the spirit: each person develops a mind and a spirit according to the possibilities offered by the education received and the environment, and the degeneration also takes place in different ways.

Our organism is constantly changing without us being able to control it. Chinese Martial Arts (Kung Fu) training makes people capable of controlling their organism. With this control it is possible to strengthen a weakened energy within a short time, just as it is possible to maintain and even strengthen more an already strong energy. Someone who is short and naturally not very strong, for whom a load of 10kg is already too much and who normally cannot defeat stronger opponents, can change his organism with the training of Kung Fu so to be able to manage 50kg or 100kg with the same constitution. Liu Yun-Chiao and Li Shu-Wen had both a weak constitution, just as Su Yu-Chang, but they proved that what is really used in *Pachi Chuan* is technique and not physical force.

Controlling the organism leads to the control of the energy, which itself gives the possibility of developing more endurance and of recovering from tiredness very fast.

The study of *Pachi Tanglang Chuan* starts with the practice of movements that clean and purify the body (essence) and consequently fortify health. Sick or deteriorated organs thus become healthy organs, the general degeneration is stabilized and aging is delayed. This is essential, because internal energy will otherwise be impure and may harm weak parts of the body when performing strong movements. The stronger the organic structure of the body, the stronger the energy can be, since the body will be able to bear it better. For example, the power of a car with a four cylinder engine is more limited than that of a car with an eight cylinder engine.

Book on Tai Chi Chuan written by Master Su

Once the movements have been mastered and one has a strong essence with a clean energy, one is able to commence the study of the control of the spirit to manage the internal energy. Thought, spirit, is very important because without giving thought to an aim, it will not receive the energy needed for its realization.

The use and the increase of the energy of the body depends as much on the appropriate management of the essence as on the influence of the spirit. Examples of this abound. Everyone knows that the energy produced by anger can damage the heart, the brain or the nerves. Similarly, a wrong movement of essence can damage the energy and weaken the body. So, a correct execution of the movements is necessary, as well as knowledge of the spirit, of the ideas that accompany each movement. Otherwise, energy will not emerge. Hence, a master should go beyond the teaching of the movements of the style, which are movements of essence, and also teach the thoughts that correspond to each movement so that our energy can reach where it should. Someone who has never thought about going to China, even if he wins flight tickets to go there, will not consider it as important as someone who has always dreamt about it. A bull and an ox are both strong and despite being of the same species, the former is wild because of its thought and cannot help the peasant. Similarly, a very strong person who only works as a peasant can do farm-work very well, but will not be very efficient in a combat, because his thought is not trained. Martial Arts require a strong body, capable of bearing with great efforts, and a spirit that makes known what the energy is for.

Book on the I Ching written by Master Su

This correlation between thought and movement, or between spirit and essence, is vital for obtaining results. Someone who trains weightlifting will be able to lift 100kg, while someone who trains wrestling will be able to bring down an opponent weighing 100kg. However, if roles are reversed, it is likely that the weightlifter will not be able to bring down an opponent weighing 100kg, and that the wrestler will not be able to lift 100kg weights. This is due to the fact that the thought behind each movement is different in each case.

The same happens in Martial Arts: someone who studies every day techniques to knock down a tree barehanded might achieve it and will surely be able to break someone's arm, but it is unlikely that he will be able to kill someone. On the other hand, someone who studies how to break an opponent's heart with energy will surely be able to kill with a simple touch, but will never be able to knock down a tree.

Every Martial Arts student must take care of the spirit and of the essence, because they are the source of energy. It is imperative that the spirit be filled with good thoughts and that movements of the essence (body) be correct.

Furthermore, a Martial Arts student must find a good master and a good style, one that is complete. The master should not only know Kung Fu, but also how to teach it. The style should be complete, otherwise the student will always remain at a low level. There are many people with the good physical conditions and the strong spirit required for learning, but by a lack of luck they never find a good master or a good style and hence never attain a superior level.

The study of *Pachi Tanglang Chuan* is very beneficial, but not only physically, since it increases the energy, it develops the mind intellectually and improves memory. The spirit acquires more focus, it becomes more joyful, and self-esteem and will for self-improvement are developed. All this is a consequence of the management of energy.

7.2 Internal energy

There are two types of internal energy: one involved in health and which helps in meditation to attain *Tao*, saintliness, wisdom; the other is to be exteriorized outside the body, affecting our environment (moving objects, killing, etc.). Both forms of energy are needed in Martial Arts. Younger people favor the study of the latter while older people favor the study of the former.

In *Pachi Tanglang Chuan*, as is the tradition in Martial Arts, the management of internal energy has several levels, some of which are superior and secret because the energy that comes out of the body can easily kill. The development of energy for meditation, on the other hand, is more openly taught because that risk is not present.

A good master will train a young *Pachi Tanglang Chuan* student, less than 15 years old, so that his body is filled with internal energy. Between the ages 15 and 25, thoughts become more focused and less dream-like, hence the unification of the spirit with the body is taught, so as to have internal energy. The period between the ages 25 and 35 is very important

Master Su during a class in Palma de Mallorca

for the continuation of the development of internal energy, and is decisive for the overcoming of the natural barriers of the body: the body is cleansed correcting what is "wrong", and a high level of skill and art are attained which is very difficult to reach later. The energy of students older than 35 years old should be gradually directed towards *Tao* meditation.

Both internal energies are necessary and very different. Both must be studied. If only the first one is studied, one will have a very good body and spirit, as a saint, but one will be incapable of exteriorizing the internal energy to affect the environment. If only the second one is studied, one will know how to cure and how to kill, but will not be able to meditate and will not attain the body and spirit of a saint.

7.3 Natural energy

One of the aims of the study of *Pachi Tanglang Chuan* is to be able to manage "Natural" Energy, both the one that is manifest in our body and the one that surrounds us. The natural energy of the Universe manifests itself in several ways, some but not all of which can be managed by our organism. The natural energy that reaches our body can be perceived and managed in three ways:

1. Through our individual perception

2. As the energy of our body is projected and unites with the external natural energy.

3. As the natural energy enters our organism.

Sensing natural energy within our body All our energy comes from the natural energy. The natural energy manifested in our body is converted into all types of activities, be they physical, mental or spiritual. This energy can be preserved and increased by exercising our body, so as to cleanse it from all illness and disease. Hence, our body will be constantly filled with energy and consequently very healthy. This makes us feel our energy become stronger and more united. Once this has been attained, we should try to make our energy circulate through the meridians so as to gain a body of *Tao* (become "wise").

The energy of our body is projected and unites with the external natural energy After studying *Pachi Tanglang Chuan* long enough, it is possible to project our energy outside of our body, either to help others when acting as a doctor, or to kill when acting as a Martial Artist.

It is also possible for the natural external energy to come into contact with our own. This sometimes happens spontaneously when visiting a very pleasant place, such as a mountain or a beach. In such occasions we may feel, even if only fleetingly, a pleasure that contrasts with what we may feel in everyday life. This is because in such situations, the energy of our body becomes very calm and open, and the external natural energy can merge with our own. This renews us and makes us feel stronger.

With the practice of *Pachi Tanglang Chuan* it is possible for the energy of our body to attain this tranquility and reach this communion with the external natural energy. When it does not happen spontaneously, we can prompt it by projecting our energy outside of our body and merge with the energies that surround us —that of plants, animals, mountains, etc.— so as to "capture" them and bring them back to us to be absorbed.

Cover of the *Wu Yi* magazine, 1998. Master Su performs a stance of the Earth group from the Chi Kung of the 12 meridians

The external natural energy enters our organism Cosmic energy acts upon us in different ways. There are two which are fundamental. One is Yin and corresponds to the magnetism of the Earth that determines the directions North and South. The other is Yang and corresponds to the sunlight and moonlight, governing the directions East and West.

Pachi Tanglang Chuan movements produce a friction that generates a current-like wave which enables us to synchronize ourselves with the natural energy. The magnetic current is very important during our lives. We must absorb this Yin energy for the benefit of our body.

The Yang solar energy is absorbed through the skin. This makes possible the generation of some nutrients that influence our *Chi*. Another reason why *Pachi Tanglang Chuan* movements are beneficial for our body is that they make our skin become pure energy and they open the pores of our skin to absorb this Yang energy.

7.4 Great Circle and Small Circle

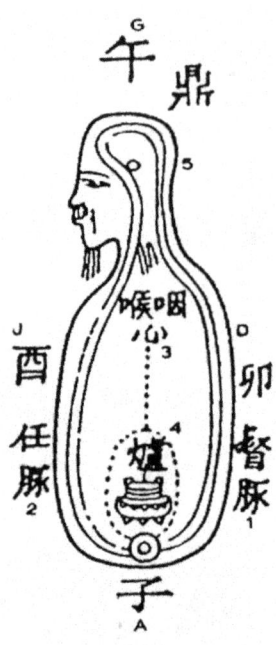

Small Celestial Circle

In the Chinese philosophical system, and hence in Kung Fu, there are channels for the circulation of energy throughout the body that have been defined for the purpose of identification. Within this network of channels, commonly known as meridians, there are two distinct circuits that correspond to the two types of energy mentioned in the previous paragraph. These two circuits are called "Great Celestial Circle" and "Small Celestial Circle."

The Small Celestial Circle is composed of the two meridians *Ren Mo* and *Tu Mo*, that go through the middle of the chest and the back. The Great Celestial Circle is a path that brings together in a line the other twelve meridians: starting in the middle of the abdomen (the lower *Tan Tien*) it rises through the left side of the chest; it goes along the inner part of the left arm to the fingers, and then it comes back through the outer part of the arm towards the shoulders; it then changes sides at the back of the neck and descends through the back towards the right kidney; it continues to the right side of the hip and then descends through the outer part of the right leg until the foot; finally, it rises through the inner part of the leg until the middle of the abdomen, from where the cycle starts symmetrically through the other side. It is because individual meridians cannot be felt at the beginning that a common path is set, grouping several of them into the Great Celestial Circle.

The Small Celestial Circle is for the vertical management of energy and for opening the third eye. We can connect with the energy of light through it, and it establishes a link with "the Natural", with God.

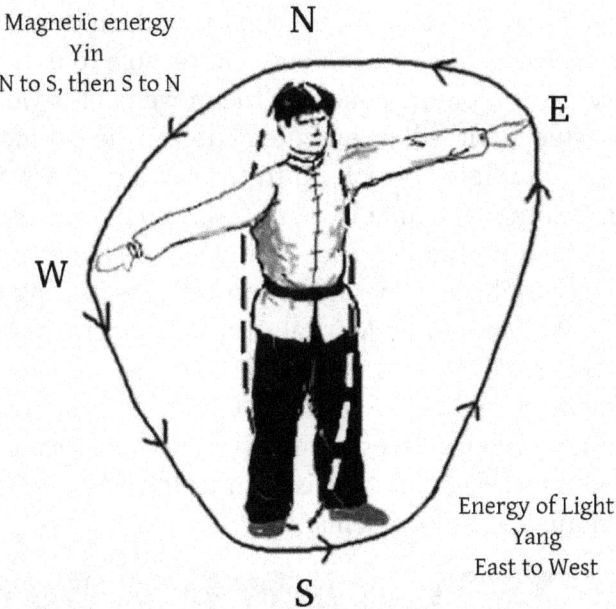

Master Su's teachings on the way the energy of the body is in contact with the natural Yin and Yang energies

The Great Celestial Circle is for the management of magnetic energy, and for us it represents the energy of the health of the body. The paths of energy covered by it are used to take energy throughout the body, to heal different parts of the body, to relieve pain, to help. The circuits of the Great Celestial Circle are the ones used to put energy into play in the practice of Kung Fu.

7.5 Spirit, thoughts

The thoughts of the spirit can be of two types. One is related to memories, it is Yin, and pertains the hidden, the past; the other is related to ideas, it is Yang, and concerns what is present, what is to be.

Memory is the warehouse of the brain. When we need the knowledge that is stored there, it is remembered naturally. For example, a beginner student will not have a movement such as *Pachi Tanglang Chuan*'s *Peng Chuei Pi Men Chiao* 崩捶閉門脚 well fixed in his memory. If attacked, the student will need to think of the different parts of the movement (the initial defense, the first strike, the kick) in order to be able to use it, making the execution very slow. If on the contrary, the movement is well fixed in the memory of the student, it will be executed naturally in the face of an attack and there will be no need to look up to the head or down to the legs of the opponent. Another example is that of a person who has been used to using the right hand repeatedly since childhood. As adult, this person will preferably use the right arm for any action because, having become fixed in the memory, it is natural. In Martial Arts, one same movement must be repeated one thousand times in the course of many years for it to become fixed in our memory and hence be available for a spontaneous use when it is required. Repetition is necessary in order to learn something well. For this reason, the basic forms are revised in every class and the advanced forms also contain basic movements.

Pachi Tanglang Chuan wins the trophy to the best school at the International Championship of Baltimore, USA, 1999

Regarding ideas, it is essential that the mind is focused on one single thing, discarding a hundred others. When in front of an object, one sees it differently when thoughts are focused solely on it or when thinking of several other things at the same time. For example, if you go shopping for a shirt, your decision might be different depending on whether you are alone or accompanied, as the suggestions of others can make you change your your mind.

The following story is told in China: A hunter in ancient times was out on a moonlit night when he saw a tiger seated some ten meters away. Frightened, he tensed his bow and with all his intent he let loose his arrow, because if he did not kill the tiger fast, the tiger would surely kill him. He hit the target and the arrow sank into the body of the animal, but strangely, it did not fall to the ground. So he waited until the sun came out and discovered to his surprise that the tiger was actually a rock, and that his arrow had gone halfway into it. He tried to repeat the feat, but his arrows never went into the rock.

This story shows that the spirit can enhance the capacity of the energy. This is why ideas must be guided by one thing at a time. For example, having thought focused on one master, one movement, one idea, is better than having one hundred masters, one hundred movements, or one hundred ideas at the same time.

The word "spirit" can have many meanings. It can refer to the brain, thought, sensations, dreams, fantasies. In Martial Arts it is necessary to know the two senses mentioned above: memory and idea.

◆

In Kung Fu, the spirit is used together with the movement of the body. This is how the energy is managed. Something basic that must be known in order to manage energy is the Yin and Yang aspects of the spirit that are involved in the execution of movements. It is very important to master the concepts of spirit, especially those that correspond to Yin and Yang. The spiral is Yin, while the straight line is Yang; not thinking of anything is Yang, while thinking of many things at the same time is Yin, etc. Movement needs Yin and Yang to help each other.

Regarding thought, there are two stages to the execution of a movement. If we want to do a movement, say, of Kidney, we first think. This is Yin. Then, we execute the movement with an empty mind. This is Yang. So, the Yin has given way to the Yang.

It is necessary to employ Yang and Yin thought, otherwise the movement is useless. In the Yin stage we think of spiral, we think of kidney; then, in the Yang stage, we do not think of the kidney nor of the spiral so that the body may have all the energy at its disposal. It is very important for a Martial Artist to know this, because without knowing how to execute movements with the interaction of Yin and Yang, movements are useless. There are three stages: first, the energy is concentrated, then the target and the type of energy are chosen (for example, Liver energy) and finally, only the fist is felt, the whole body has the energy of Liver without thinking about Liver.

7.6 The ultimate purpose of Kung Fu

What is the ultimate purpose of the practice of *Pachi Tanglang Chuan*?

We have explained in the previous sections that there are channels through which the energy circulates, and also that our individual energy comes from the natural energy. The connection between our own energy and the natural energy is established through 360 points that are distributed throughout these channels. When we are born, the circulation of energy is fluid and so is the connection with the natural energy, as it manifests itself freely in our body through these points. This is why a newborn is so soft and rosy, with that inexplicable charm.

These connecting points start closing at birth in order to make the natural energy available for use in our everyday activities. The first one, the navel, closes just as we are born. This sets off the functions of the body. Then the fontanel in the upper part of the head closes to allow the activities of the spirit. Later, during puberty, the *Huei Yin* (perineum) is closed. Before the flow through the Small Celestial Circle is cut due to the closing of the perineum, the energy circulates throughout the whole body as a gas. This type of energy does not allow for reproduction because procreation requires energy in a liquid form. Once the *Huei Yin* becomes closed, semen is produced in men, and women start menstruating. The energy can no longer complete the circle, so it goes to the kidney which transforms it into liquid and leads it downward. Therefore, if we want to have access to the natural energy, we need to open the *Huei Yin*, to restore the flow as it was when we were children.

Under normal conditions, the activities of our daily lives lead to the gradual closure of all the 360 points. When there are only one or two open points left, the "Five Natural Spirits" abandon the body through one of these, and death arrives. The location of the point through which the Five Natural Spirits leave the body is decisive in establishing the world where the next stage will take place. The more our lives have been attached to the activities of the "Seven Inherited Spirits", the less energy the Five Natural Spirits will have, and the less are the possibilities of having access to the superior energies.

If the point is in the head, one might be a saint, and may be able to stay in Heaven. This is because the type of frequency of the Five Natural Spirits is high. If the point is above the navel, one may be reborn as a human. If it is on the back of the body, one will be reborn as a boy, while if it is on the front of the body, one will be reborn as a girl. If the spirit leaves through a point at the height of the hip, one will reincarnate in a superior animal, such as a bear or a lion. If the point is even lower, reincarnation will be into an ant or a mouse. If the spirit leaves through the toes, into a devil.

Some might think, "if I am a human being, why would I be reborn as a dog?" There are human frequencies but there are also dog and other animal frequencies. There are different levels, and the higher ones are superior. If the spirit is very heavy when it leaves, because of attachments and because of not knowing the new realm where it is now moving, then it cannot rise to the human or superior levels and may reincarnate in an animal or other low being.

Having said that, the possibility of opening these points exists. However, the points cannot be opened from the outside, they are opened from within when we are alive, through the appropriate study and work. The practice of *Pachi Tanglang Chuan* allows for the opening of the points. This is the ultimate goal of the study of *Pachi Tanglang Chuan*, to clear all the points.

Having unblocked all the points means having gained a "Body of Saint". This is the most difficult step, because the transformation of the body requires a long time. Having a "Body of Saint" one has the capability of controlling the flow of natural energy through the body. This allows us to access the realm of the Energy of Light, and through it, reach other worlds as real as this one, but where there is no need of a body. Once we have this capacity, it is relatively easy to learn how to travel and get along in those worlds with the Five Natural Spirits. In this manner, the Five Natural Spirits acquire the energy and consciousness needed to act in immaterial realms at will and with conscience.

Buddha, Jesus, and other great saints such as Lao Tzu, got rid of all their debts and attachments, thus bringing about the unblocking of all the points. At the moment they decided to die, they opened all the points and

*Buddhism enables the adjustment of energy
for the understanding
of the doctrine of contemplation.
Taoism enables the movement of energy
for the discovery of the Truth.
Confucianism nurtures the energy,
thus allowing progress towards wisdom.
The result of all this is peace (靜).
And if peace can be guarded,
the* Tao *of* Pachi Chuan *can do it.*

Master Liu Yun-Chiao

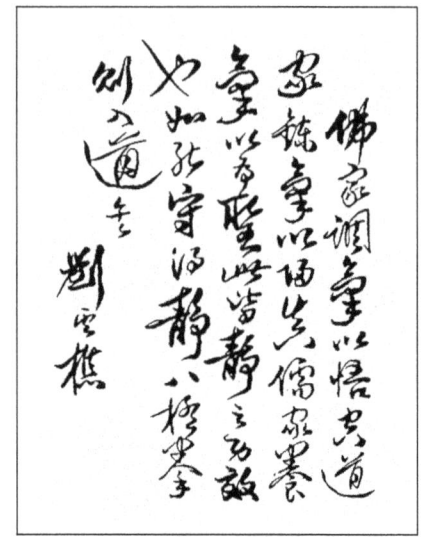

let light come in. The body then disappeared bathed in light, and the Five Natural Spirits, with all the energy and consciousness, ascended to Heaven.

♦

What is described here in a few lines could be studied for ten years without being grasped. Time is very important, and losing it is the greatest error a person can make. My students have the good fortune of having a good master that teaches them a good style, but I do not know if I will be fortunate enough to have a student who will reach the level that I have reached.

One must have faith and a strong heart, otherwise it is not possible to reach the higher levels. Following the teachings of Master Su, you can be sure to reach what is described here.

Chapter 8

Pikua Chuan

八極參劈掛
神鬼都害怕
劈掛參八極
英雄嘆莫及

Pachi together with *Pikua*, gods and demons are all terrified;
Pikua together with *Pachi*, heroes will sigh in despair.

The *Pikua Chuan* or *Pikua Chang* system is not a well-known Kung Fu style, neither in China nor abroad. The name of every Kung Fu style is usually a compound of two Chinese characters that define the style. In the case of *Pikua Chang*, these characters are *Pi* 劈 and *Kua* 掛. These two terms refer to the first two basic techniques of *Pikua Chang*. *Pi* 劈 means to chop, and refers to a way of striking with the palm and the arm that evokes the way a machete or an axe would chop. *Kua* 掛 means to hang and refers to the way the forearm "hangs" from the elbow in certain defensive movements.

8.1 *Pikua Chuan*. Chopping and hanging

Most about the origin of *Pikua Chang* is uncertain, but geographically its origins can be traced back to Tsang Zhou, Hou Pei province. The first evidence of the *Pikua Chang* system dates from the beginning of the Ming Dynasty, around the year 1400, in the form of a short document that mentions the system as an ancient style. However, it is not until the Qing Dynasty, around the year 1700, that we have historical records of its existence.

Traditionally, the study of *Pikua Chang* has been linked to that of *Pachi Chuan*. There is a saying that states: "*Pachi* together with *Pikua*, gods and demons are all terrified; *Pikua* together with *Pachi*, heroes will sigh in despair." In my lineage, these two systems are practically merged together.

Regarding *Pikua Chang*, the lineage starts with Li Yun-Piao, who initiated Huang Lin-Piao. Then, Li Shu-Wen was initiated by the latter. Liu Yun-Chiao learned and mastered *Pachi Chuan* and *Pikua Chang* under the guidance of Li Shu-Wen, and finally, I studied these styles from Master Liu Yun-Chiao.

The combat principles of *Pikua Chang* are similar to those of other styles such as *Tong Pei Chuan*. However, the authentic *Pikua Chang* is an ancient style that was always kept secret. Besides ordinary *Pikua Chang* there are other hybrid styles that were formed by bringing together some elements of *Pikua Chang* and some of other styles. This is how *Pikua Tong Pei Chuan* was born, combining *Pikua Chang* and *Tong Pei Chuan*. The *Tong Pei Chuan* style (long-arm monkey) uses the arms profusely, and the essence of *Pikua Chang* is added. There is a Chinese saying that expresses very clearly the character and certainty of these two styles: "*Tong Pei Chuan* and *Pikua Chang* are not afraid of immortals nor of ghosts." However, the greater part of the techniques in this hybrid style comes from *Tong Pei Chuan*.

The *Pikua Chang* style is also known in China for its broadsword techniques, both the single broadsword and the double broadsword. Since this weapon can be considered an extension of the arm, it is only natural that the techniques of *Pikua Chang*, were adapted to the use of the broadsword.

8.2 Techniques and study

Originally, *Pikua Chang* was studied independently, but *Pachi Chuan* masters adopted it to make their system more effective. Since then, *Pachi Chuan* and *Pikua Chang* have been studied simultaneously. Due to their complementarity, the combination of these two styles can take the practitioner to a superior level.

The aspects in which these two styles complement each other are many: *Pachi Chuan* includes soft techniques within its hard techniques, while *Pikua Chang* has powerful techniques within its light techniques; the techniques of the *Pachi Chuan* system consist mostly of linear movements, while in *Pikua Chang* the movements are predominantly circular; *Pachi Chuan* is characterized by its low stances and strait attacks, while *Pikua Chang* is characterized by its higher stances and multi-directional attacks. For all these reasons, *Pachi Chuan* is very well suited for short-range combat, while *Pikua Chang* is better for long-range combat. As we can see, bringing together the characteristics of these two styles produces a balance that makes their joint study very important.

The same can be concluded if we analyze the animals whose movements gave rise to these two styles. *Pikua Chang* took the movements of the eagle, the dragon, the snake and the long-arm monkey. *Pachi Chuan* took the movements of the bear, the tiger and the horse. Hence, the movements of *Pachi Chuan* are said to be like those of tigers coming down a mountain and like those of bears walking through the forest. In *Pikua Chang* the movements are those of eagles beating their wings and of snakes shaking their tail.

The movements of *Pikua Chang* are based on the wings and claws of the eagle as well as the arms of the long-arm monkey, and when the energy of the movements of these two animals is combined, the energy of dragon appears. *Pikua Chang* moves with the waist of the snake. The snake provides the Kidney energy and the waist mobility necessary for the twisting movements of *Pikua Chang*. The strikes are done with the arms of the eagle. The steps correspond to those of the long-arm monkey, and if several successive steps are to be taken, it will take the energy of the horse from *Pachi Chuan*. The horse provides the speed for advancing and the stability. The movements of the long-arm monkey are used for arm strikes and to twist the arms very quickly. The long-arm monkey reaches out, its arms are never tired. Because its lungs are very good, Lung energy is taken from it. The hand movements are taken from the eagle in the form of claws and they are used to immobilize and attack. Furthermore, the eagle has very powerful wings, which are controlled by the shoulder blades and the heart, so these energies are taken from this animal.

Both the arms of the monkey and the wings of the eagle move in circles, but their energy is different. The hands of the monkey have a powerful grip, but the hands must be relaxed, because a rigid hand cannot catch. The eagle has wings, but these do not need to be relaxed to be able to catch. Instead, they need a strong center to be beaten with energy and a soft exterior to be able to cut through the air. The energy of the monkey consists of using what is soft to generate the strong; from the soft core comes the hard exterior. The eagle is the opposite, it is soft at the outside but it must be very strong in the inside. These two animals are very important in *Pikua Chang*.

◆

Master Su Yu-Chang's Secret Poem

Move the arms rapidly,
like a shooting star flying to the Moon.
The back moves like a dragon,
unleashing a storm and infuriating the oceans.
Walk like a monkey to confuse the enemy.
Truth or lie, what is direct and what is indirect,
all must have the spirit of the idea and the energy of strength.

8.3 *Chang*. The palm

In *Pikua*, the term *Chang* 掌 indicates the use of the palm as a main feature of the style. The concept of palm does not only refer to the surface of one side of the hand, but rather it extends to the use of the whole arm. The palm may be likened to a drill-bit, and the arm together with the rest of the body would be the engine of the drill. This great weapon can be divided in three parts: the head is the palm, the middle part is the elbow, and the root is the shoulder. These three parts are combined in any Kung Fu technique.

To build greater strength, students sometimes use a punching bag made of dog skin to practice the palms. However, the proper study of *Pikua*

Chang, or of any other style, must lead to the adequate management of energy. In the case of *Pikua Chang*, the most important is to learn how to manage the energy for the movement of the arms. If this is not achieved, the punching bag may be used. The use of this type of equipment should not be over emphasized in any Kung Fu style. It is only a tool that in specific circumstances may contribute to the overall development of a student. In any case, free hand training is more important than any training equipment for acquiring the techniques of *Pikua Chang*.

8.4 Twelve characteristic movements

Pikua has twelve basic movements that specify its character. The first two give the style its name. These movements are accompanied by characteristic gestures.

劈 **Pi – To chop** This is the main attacking movement. The outer edge of the arm is used like a knife, in a circular movement, generally descending. There are many types of *Pi*.

掛 **Kua – To hang** This is the main defensive movement. The lateral or radial part of the arm and palm is used, swinging the forearm as if it was hanging from the elbow. There are two types of *Kua*, an upper one and a lower one. The upper one is performed by bending the elbow and swinging the arm upwards. The lower *Kua* swings the arm downward.

摔 **Suai – To knock-down** This is usually used together with *Pi*, its energy follows that of *Pi*. The back part of the hand and of the forearm are used to strike, swinging them in circles using the elbow as an axis. Generally, the circles are vertical, striking downward, but it can also be performed with horizontal circles, striking sideways with both arms.

滾 **Kun – To roll** The back part of the hand and the forearm are used in a spiraling movement. There is inner and outer *Kun*. For the inner *Kun*, the arm strikes downward, coming out from the inner part of the body, as if unrolling something. It ends by bending the elbow and the wrist with a strong downward jerk. For the outer one the arm goes spiraling forward as if drilling and ends with the arm extended.

撐 **Cheng – To prop** The tip of the fingers is used to strike. The arms come out horizontally or slightly slanted until they are completely extended with the palms facing down. The fingers should also be extended in the same line as the arms. It can be performed with both arms simultaneously, but in opposite directions; the arms can be placed to the sides or one in front and one in the back.

按 **An – To press down** The palm and the base of the hand are used in a pushing and pressing motion. There is a middle and a lower *An*. For the middle *An*, the arm draws a vertical circle, ending with the palm facing down. In the lower *An*, the forearm moves in a circle parallel to the torso with the elbow as the axis, starting outside and coming up and towards the body and then back down and out, pushing down and forward with the palm turned in such a way that the fingers are pointing to the ground.

輪 **Lun – To revolve** It is performed with extended arms, making them turn as if they were the blades of a mill, striking down at the end with the palm facing down. There is a straight *Lun* and a sloping *Lun*.

挾 **Hsia – To clasp** The arms come together and part from each other in an horizontal plane, similar to a swimming breaststroke. The arms turn as if separating something. There is an inner and an outer *Hsia*.

撲 **Pu – To pounce** *Pu* is of the same type as *An*, but in *Pu* one strikes the ground. The whole arm is used in a wide movement. *An*, on the other hand, being a smaller and faster movement, uses the elbow and the the wrist.

抱 **Pao – To embrace** The arms move very loosely in a horizontal plane. They are used to hug oneself in such a way that the hands reach the shoulder blades. They then bounce back horizontally in a circular motion as the body turns until the hands touch each other behind the back, with the shoulders brought back completely. Then the arms come back in a hug that strikes the back. When doing *Pao*, one must strike with *Pai Ta Kung* (see below, p.182). It can also be performed with "inward spiraling energy."

靠 **Kao – To lean** For performing *Kao*, we use horizontal movements of the arms similar to those of *Pao*, but in this case, what we use to attack is the shoulder or the hip.

挑 **Tiao – To heave** This technique strikes from below, with the inner edge of the arms. It is done with a small vertical circle, parallel to the torso. The arms strike the body to then bounce back opening, the one that will strike comes out and upward until it is horizontal and completely extended. The other arm opens downward with the elbow bent. The energy of the spine is essential.

8.5 Stances

The stances of *Pikua Chang* are practically the same as those of any other Kung Fu style. In section 5.2 we described the most important ones, so we will not repeat them here. However, in *Pikua Chang* basic stances are usually trained together with movements characteristic to the style, so that its basic movements are learned while the lower part of the body is being strengthened.

獨立式 **Tu Li Suh** — 馬式 **Ma Suh** We begin in *Tu Li Suh*, with both arms raised above our head. Then the raised leg is extended and lands into *Ma Suh* while we let the arms fall until they are horizontal at the height of the shoulders.

登山式 **Tan Shan Suh** — 馬式 **Ma Suh** We start in *Ma Suh*. The arms are made to swing around the body in horizontal circles that draw them towards the torso and then send them back away. Then, just as the arms are touching the torso, we make them come out using *Cheng* so as to form a cross with the direction of the legs, which now go into *Au Pu Tan Shan Suh* (*Tan Shan Suh* with the torso turned to one side).

8.6 Basic *Pikua* steps

The palm techniques are one of the most characteristic elements of the *Pikua* system. However, the footwork is also of great importance, the coordination of step and palm being essential to any attack or defense. In *Pikua* the step must be sprightly, making retreats and advances that constantly change direction, so that it is possible to go swiftly from protecting one's "door" to an attack through an opening in the opponent's "door". In general, the concept of "door" refers to an area of the body that is potentially vulnerable to an attack. In a combat situation one may choose to tempt the opponent by attacking his front "door" directly. The opponent will usually be able to close his front door, taking care not to give access to other more vulnerable inner doors. The natural response in this situation is to direct the attack to the sides.

Pikua Chang, as *Pakua Chang*, focuses on approaching the opponent through the side doors. In order to enter through the side doors it is necessary to manoeuvre by using the footwork to change the angle of approach.

8.7 *Pai Ta Kung*

Probably one of the most unusual characteristics of the *Pikua Chang* system is *Pai Ta Kung*, which means to hit oneself. In this technique, the arms swing freely in circles; they move away from the body and when they come back they strike against the torso producing a characteristic sound. In order to practice this technique correctly the arms and the whole body must be relaxed. This training method is convenient because it can be practiced alone.

There are other types of *Pai Ta Kung* where someone else strikes our body. Ideally in this case, it should be a master who strikes, so that he can carefully develop the student's potential. Students can help each other in training, but unlike a master, they do not have complete control of the force of their strikes, and may even take advantage to hurt a rival student deliberately. A traditional alternative for this type of training was to have children strike the student. This is safer, as children do not have the strength to damage and are more easy to control.

Pai Ta Kung improves the capacity to withstand attacks and it develops endurance, as the strikes on every part of the body help in the conditioning of the muscles and tendons. This, however, is not the only aim of *Pai Ta Kung*, as it also favors the development of *Chi*, to be able to respond automatically to an attack. By means of *Pai Ta Kung*, the spontaneous defense mechanisms of the body are developed, triggering the automatic response against an attack.

The inclusion of *Pai Ta Kung* in *Pikua Chang* also serves to establish one of the combat principles of the style. In the training of many Kung Fu styles the practitioner will have a fixed target he aims to strike, but *Pikua* aims to go beyond the target, completely destroying the opponent. The execution of *Pai Ta Kung* enables the complete development of energy through the arms, which makes the strikes in a real combat situation to reach the target and beyond. If the target is missed, the arm continues its path until it strikes our own body and bounces back. As soon as the impact of the arm against the body is felt, the palm is immediately projected in the opposite direction responding to *Pai Ta Kung*. This new attack will have gained the power of the entire body's coordinated movement.

A common criticism of *Pikua Chang* is that although its techniques are very powerful, they are too wide and leave the doors open, which gives the enemy possibilities of attack. These comments show a lack of understanding of the use of the palms and of the concept of door. In real combat, it is not only the palm but the whole arm that is used, having a greater surface with which to defend or attack. Furthermore, *Pikua Chang* has a very effective footwork that enables the martial artist to enter and get out of the combat zone with ease. This is a way of approaching the open doors of the opponent without compromising our own safety.

8.8 The practice of *Pikua*

In general, Martial Arts training puts an emphasis on the use of the stronger energy from the start, relying on force and speed to execute techniques. Later, with practice, the form and the techniques are softened as we reach higher levels of study.

The character of *Pikua Chang* is the opposite. Total relaxation is stressed from the start. This does not mean that movements should be sluggish or weak, rather that power should be cultivated without using unnecessary force, thus allowing the muscles, bones, and joints, to move in a flexible and effective manner.

Nien Ching, sticking energy, and *Ting Ching*, listening energy, are two principles behind the techniques of *Pikua Chang*. The martial artist should stick to (*Nien*) the opponent, maintaining contact so as to listen (*Ting*) or feel his intentions and always be able to adjust to the situation. This enables us to protect our door effectively and to feel when there is an opportunity to open a door of the opponent and use a *Pikua Chang* technique.

Traditionally, the training of forms is preceded by an extensive basic training which develops a strong foundation of the style. Subsequently, the practice of forms is divided into three levels designed to progressively develop the potential of the student. The first level introduces the basic movements, footwork and strikes with the palms. The second level is more complex and advanced in terms of technique usage, elaborating on the content and essence of the first form. Tempo and rhythm are also explored, and the *Pai Ta Kung* training is added. In the third level, the application of the movements is emphasized more than the form. Thus, on the third level, the potential of the student is not hindered, and the master has the possibility of helping him bring to surface his own special talents. Movements may appear simple, but they contain many high-level techniques.

Pikua Chang training is comparable to the construction of a building. Firstly, the foundations are laid as the student is shaped by means of the basic elements of the style. If the basis is not deep or strong enough, it will only support a small building, but if the student develops a solid basis and has the guidance of a good master, he will be able to progressively build a skyscraper, reaching the highest levels of *Pikua Chang*.

In *Pikua*, the movement is studied first, and then the energy. It is better to study *Pikua* while still young because if you start too late you might not be able to make the energy surface. The eagle dies if it can not fly far; the eagle dies not because it is sick, but because of hunger, being unable to go far enough in search of food.

Rotation is fundamental in *Pikua*. There are three circles in the arm, centered on the wrist, the elbow and the shoulder. There are three in the torso, centered on the middle of the neck, the waist and the coccyx. There are three in the legs, centered on the head of the femur, the knee and the ankle. Everything turns. Of particular importance are the movements centered on the neck, waist and coccyx.

Rotations occur not only in one sense; they should be reversed after a certain point. A ball that only rolls in one direction is useless. Both Yang and Yin turning are needed.

8.9 Chi Kung

The *Chi Kung* of *Pikua Chang* is called *Nei Kung,* and there are two classes, one of which has movement while the other does not. The first one is commonly known as *Chi Kung*. The second one is taught at a later learning stage and includes stretching. *Pikua Chang* also has *Shen Chin Pa Ku* and is called *Shen Chu Kung* 伸缩功, stretching meridians and tendons.

A term used in the *Pikua Chang* system is *Chio Pan Chin* 九盤架. *Chio* means the number nine. *Pan* may mean a disc or a rounded thing. *Chin* is a term that refers to the movements of the joints. The term as a whole refers to the axes that make circular movements possible throughout the body. There are nine (*Chio*) circular movements (*Pan*) possible through the joints of the body (*Chin*). In the torso there are three: an upper one that corresponds to Heaven – *Tien* 天 – and is located in the *Ta Tsuei* point (below the prominence of the 7th cervical vertebra); a middle one that corresponds to People – *Ren* 人 – and is located in the waist, between the kidneys, in the *Ming Men* point (between the second and third lumbar vertebrae); and a lower one that corresponds to Earth – *Ti* 地 – and is located around coccyx and hips. In the arms we have shoulder, elbow, and wrist. In the lower part of the body – *Hsia Pan* 下盤 – we have the joint at the head of the femur, the knee, and the ankle. By considering both arms as a unit, and both legs as a unit, we get the "nine discs."

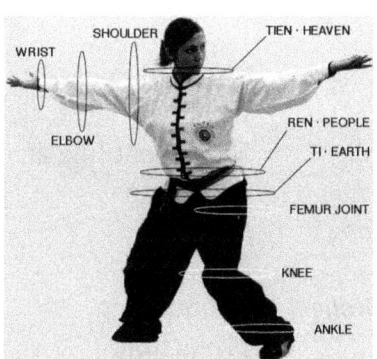

Secret teaching of Master Su Yu-Chang
of *Chio Pan Chin* in Pikua Chuan theory

劈掛十八動透勁功 Pikua Shih Pa Tong Tou Ching Kong
18 Grinding Movements to Deepen the Energy of Pikua

1.	風擺功 Fong Pai Kong	The wind rocks	Head, brain
2.	撥水功 Poh Shuei Kong	To splash the water	Kidney and back
3.	游水功 You Shuei Kong	To swim	Middle *Tan Tien*
4.	推浪功 Tuei Lan Kong	To push the waves	Tendons and muscles
5.	攪浪功 Chio Lan Kong	To stir the waves	Hips
6.	踢浪功 Ti Lan Kong	To kick the waves	Lower *Tan Tien*
7.	伏地功 Puh Ti Kong	To crouch towards the ground	Stomach
8.	挾身功 Hsia Shen Kong	To pinch the body	Five Elements
9.	抱身功 Pao Shen Kong	To embrace the body	Five Elements, *Tien Pan* and *Ti Pan*
10.	車輪功 Lun Kong	To roll	Strengthening the waist
11.	拍打功 Pai Ta Kong	To strike the body	Nerves of the skin
12.	撐身功 Cheng Shen Kong	To stretch the body	Exchanging the left and right energies through the spine
13.	飛翔功 Fuei Hsiang Kong	To fly with wings	Lower *Tan Tien* and *Hsia Pan Chin*
14.	揚鞭功 Yang Pen Kong	To shake the whip	*San Pan Chin* of the arms
15.	展翅功 Chang I Kong	The bird opens its wings	*Tu Mo* meridian
16.	開屏功 Kai Pin Kong	Movement like an accordion	Body balance, cerebellum
17.	爬行功 Pa Hsin Kong	To crawl	Body strength and endurance
18.	彈勁功 Tan Chin Kong	Rebounding projection	Energy projection (*Fa Ching*)

Traditionally, these 18 movements are attributed the property of assuring longevity. As stated above, there are three animals that play an important role in *Pikua*, the long-arm monkey, the eagle, and the snake or dragon. All these are long-lived animals.

The monkey, for example, has a way of breathing that helps it stay healthy. It rarely falls ill, so it has a long life.

In the eagle spirit and body are united. When it wants to achieve something, it focuses all its attention on its goal. If it rests, the entire body and the spirit rest. It does not waste any energy.

The snake and the dragon move in a special way. Once the movement starts, the whole body is set in motion. Yin and Yang are always balanced and the body is relaxed, without tension.

Group of Pachi Tanglang Chuan students, Caracas, Venezuela.

8.10 Basic movements of *Pikua Chuan*

• 1 • 泰山壓頂 *Tai Shan Ya Ting*. The weight of the Tai mountain.

Tiao 1

Tiao 2

Tiao 3

7   Pu 1   8   Pu 2

Two-man set of the first movement

1

2

3

4

5

6

• 2 • 蓋天伏地 *Kai Tien Hu Ti*. Cover the sky and fall to the ground.

1

2 Kua 1

3 Kua 2

4 Kua 3

5 Kua 4

6

7 Suai 1

8 Suai 2   9 Suai 3
10 An 1   11 An 2

• 3 • 烏龍盤打 *Wu Long Pan Ta*. The black dragon coils and whips.

1 Lun 1   2 Lun 2
3 Lun 3   4 Lun 4

Lun 5

Lun 6

Lun 7

Lun 8

Lun 9

11

• 4 • 流星趕月 *Liu Hsing Kan Yue*. The shooting star darts to the moon.

1
2
3
4
5 Pi 1
6 Pi 2
7 Pi 3
8

• 5 • 金龍梱珠 *Jin Long Kun Chu*. The golden dragon embraces the pearl.

Chia 1

Chia 2

Chia 3

9 Chia 4   10 Kao 1

11 Kao 2

• 6 • 飛燕穿林 *Fei Yen Chuan Lin*. The swallow flies through the forest.

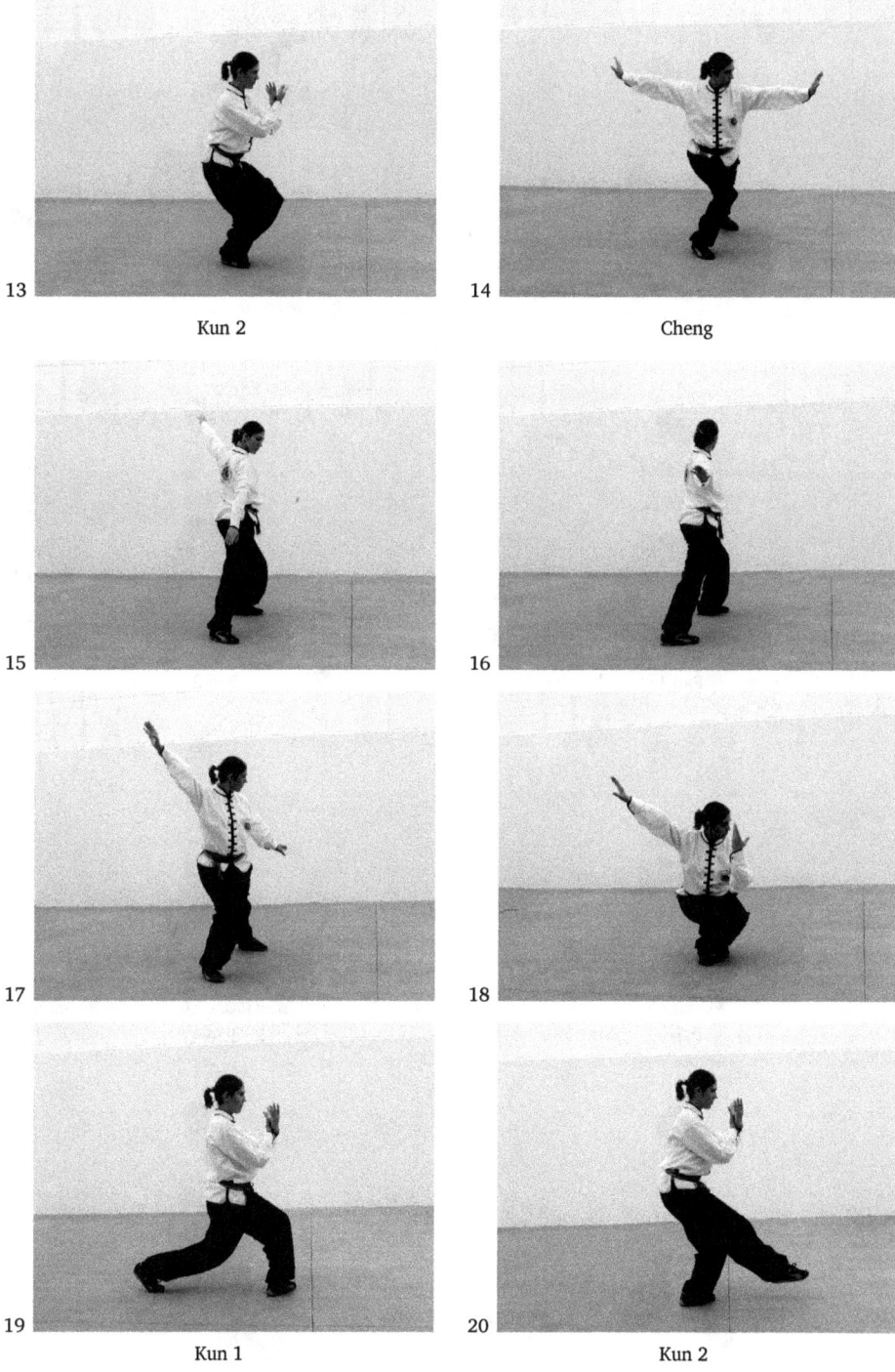

13 Kun 2

14 Cheng

15

16

17

18

19 Kun 1

20 Kun 2

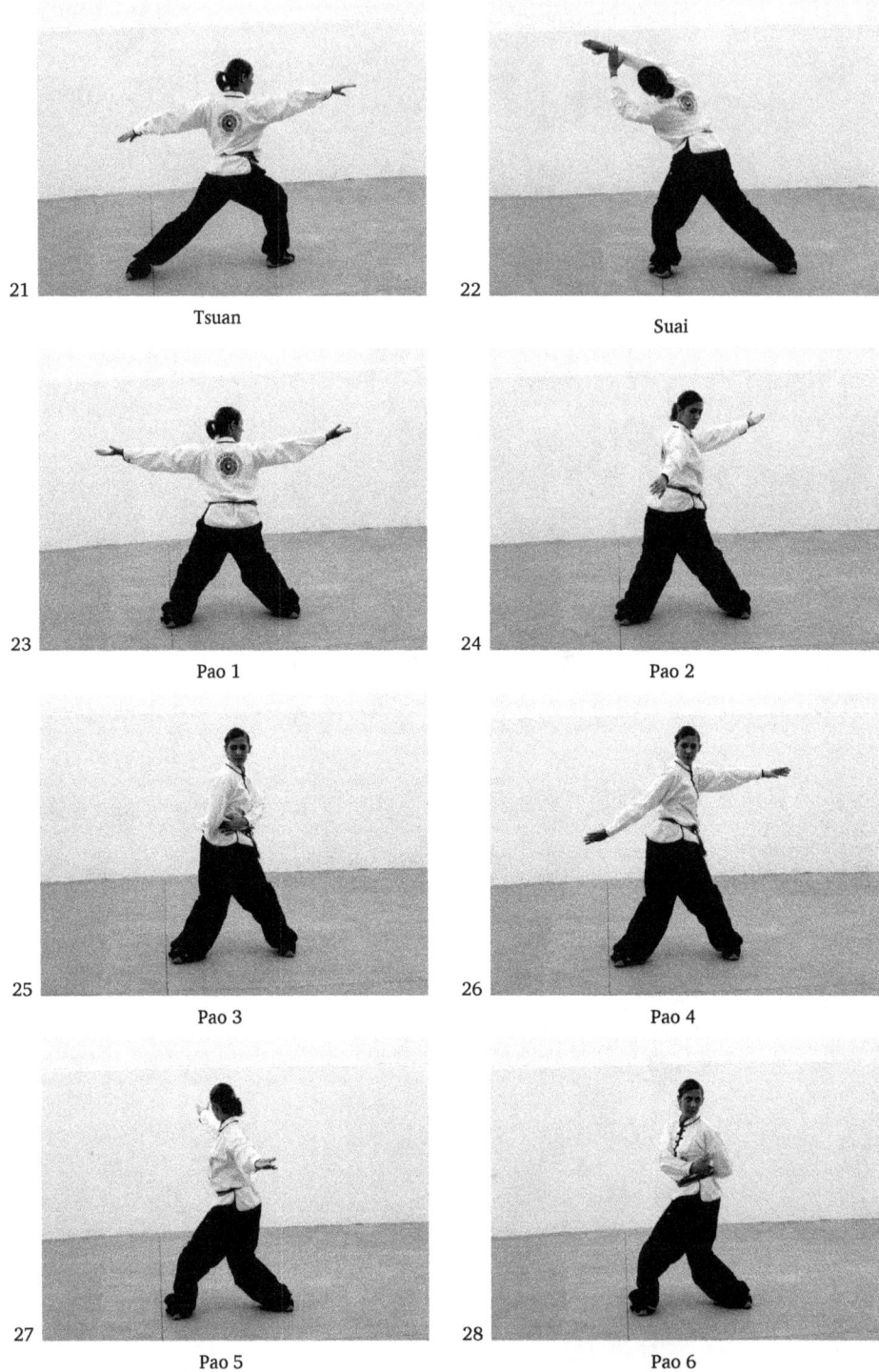

Pao 7

Pao 8

Chapter 9

Tanglang Chuan

> Someone who studies *Tai Chi Chuan* for ten years may reach the door. Someone who studies Praying Mantis for one day can leave the house.

The *Tanglang Chuan* (Praying Mantis) style originates from Shandong province. For thousands of years, this province has been renowned in China as the cradle of great sages, and not without reason, as two of the most important contributors to the development of Chinese thought were natives of Shandong: Confucius and Lao Tzu. It is not surprising then to see the special wit that martial artists from Shandong had for the creation of martial movements. This is apparent in the Praying Mantis style, with its very elaborate, unpredictable and effective movements. Praying Mantis has a great variety of movements: fast, slow, long, short. They are movements that require the coordination of the entire body, not just the hands or feet, and are consequently very difficult to execute, but at the same time make Praying Mantis a very special style. For this reason, it is said that an intelligent person studying Praying Mantis will learn the movements very fast and will become proficient, while an unintelligent person will become smarter.

9.1 Praying Mantis: variety, speed, and change

For three hundred years the Praying Mantis style developed inside Taoist monasteries or inside the houses of rich people, and was never taught outside these circles. Only over the last hundred years has it started to spread beyond Shandong. For this reason, Shandong province has become known as the cradle of superior and little known Martial Arts.

The Praying Mantis style is based on the movements of two animals: the praying mantis and the monkey. The praying mantis is a six-legged insect with wings, but when hunting it does not chase after its prey, because its capacity to move about is inferior to that of its victims. Instead, it keeps its legs and wings still and uses only its waist and front legs or "arms". For this reason only the movements of the waist and of the "arms" of the praying mantis are adopted; for the purposes of Martial Arts, it is considered that the praying mantis does not move its legs.

In contrast, the legs of the monkey are more skilled than its arms. The arms execute relatively simple movements, such as scratching or embracing, that rely mainly on the wrist. We could say that the arms of the monkey lack force and mobility. But this is compensated by great skill in their legs: they can walk and change position very quickly and with great precision; they can jump very high and even hold objects with their feet. The monkey, just like the praying mantis, uses the waist to execute these movements. The Praying Mantis style uses the arms of the praying mantis and the legs of the monkey, and to be able to unify and coordinate the movements of the arms and the legs, the waist is of vital importance. Hence the waist has a privileged place in the study of the Praying Mantis style.

Praying Mantis in a combat stance
Drawing by Master Su

This basis, outlined above, made the integration of eighteen Kung Fu styles possible to give birth to the Praying Mantis style. A great number of Martial Art techniques were incorporated and they were provided with very skilled arms, fast and versatile legs, and an elastic and relaxed waist. This clever combination gave birth to a style with such a speed of movement that it is possible to strike up to five times in a single breath, and with changes of position so fast that make it possible to carry out three, or even four attacks in one second.

The spirit of the Praying Mantis style is the absence of spirit. In other words, the mind is empty. When attacking, there should be absolutely no thoughts. This state of the mind helps in the learning of movements through repetition.

The earlier the student begins his study of Praying Mantis, the greater his possibilities of attaining the superior levels of the art, since this style has five levels of study, and each one may require up to ten years of practice. Reaching the higher levels of Praying Mantis is very difficult, because as the fruit of the combination of eighteen styles, it has a great number and variety of components, and details are very important.

I have dedicated myself to the study of all Praying Mantis styles for almost thirty years, reuniting them for the first time in three hundred years.

9.2 Origins of *Tanglang Chuan*. Wang Lang

As stated in an earlier chapter, the first document to mention this style, the *Lio Tao*, dates to the beginning of the Zhou dynasty, more than 3000 years ago. It is a book that mentions *Tanglang Wusu* 螳螂武士, Praying Mantis

Warrior Knights, as being the personal guard of the emperor. Since this was an official book, it is a trustworthy source.

The earliest information we have of known masters of the style dates back to the end of the Ming dynasty (1368–1644 AD). Since then, Wang Lang has been recognized as the founder of the modern version of this style. However, the Praying Mantis style existed before him, without it being talked about. Wang Lang was the first to make it known, and therefore he is considered the founder of the style.

Wang Lang was born in Chi Mo, Shandong province, into a wealthy and influential family during the Ming dynasty. He studied until his twenties under his father, Wang Mang Tang, who was a general of the Ming dynasty renowned as a martial artist.

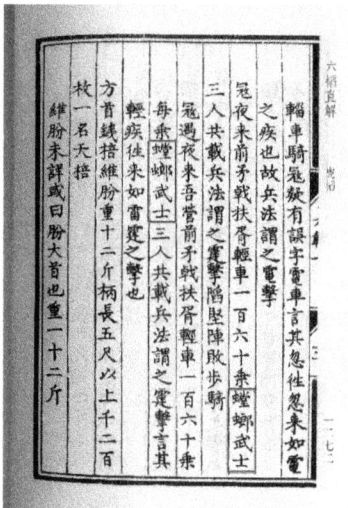

A fragment of the *Liu Tao* mentioning Praying Mantis soldiers, about 11th century BC

Then came the decline of the Ming dynasty and the Manchu invasion, which brought the persecution of the Han ethnic group in general, and in particular of the supporters of the Ming. Since Wang Lang's father was ethnically Han and a well-known Ming general, he became one of the first targets. The Manchu army under the command of general Tang Tung devastated Wang Lang's town, they destroyed his house and killed his family. He bravely confronted Tang Tung to defend his family, but the invaders were too many and they chased him until he fell off a cliff and was given up for dead. While half-dead, he swore that one day he would finish the one responsible for all that destruction. Heaven took pity on him and he was picked up by a passing Shaolin monk called Tung Chang, who took him to the temple to be cured and taken care of.

While he was recovering, the young Wang Lang observed the training of the monks and thought of his vengeance. Wanting to further his Martial Arts knowledge, as soon as he had recovered he asked the monks to teach him. The monks agreed, and Wang Lang spent several years studying Shaolin Kung Fu fervently.

Until relatively recently, it was common in China for great warriors to retire to monasteries towards the end of their lives. Also, for those having conflicts with the government, a monastery would be a safe haven. The arrival of the Manchu dynasty had led to the gathering of many important Kung Fu experts related to the Han government in the Shaolin Temple. Hence, Wang Lang had access to many different styles of Kung Fu, and being the martial artist that he was, he was able to assimilate all this knowledge.

This presence of Martial Arts masters and of opponents of the Manchu establishment was the reason for the attack and ransacking of the Shaolin temple by the Manchu in the year 1650. Many were killed in the bloody battle, but some managed to escape. Wang Lang fought against the invaders but had to flee, after which he went back to his native land in Shandong. There he took refuge in *Lao Shan* 崂山 (Lao Mountain).

That second escape was for him the last straw. Certain that he had waited long enough, he went after the one responsible for the destruction of his town. Tang Tung was an important military man, so accordingly, he lived protected by great security measures. This made it impossible for Wang Lang to reach him. So instead, he decided to learn as many techniques as possible from the best Martial Arts masters he could find, and then he went back to his mountain. He continued his training and a year later he came back from the mountain. This time he managed to enter Tang Tung's fortress, but despite his skill, he was not able to reach his target, because of the numerous guards, and had to flee. Disheartened, he went back to the mountain and promised to himself that he would find a way to finish off the Manchu general.

Time went by, and on a hot summer day as he thought about how to improve his Kung Fu, he sat under the shade of a tree to take shelter from the oppressing heat. Then and there he saw the strangest combat he had ever seen: a praying mantis was trying to catch a cicada. Wang Lang noticed the fast and peculiar way the praying mantis moved its front legs: being firmly grounded it would stretch them to deliver powerful blows and would retrieve them immediately in the form of hooks. In the blink of a eye, it had captured the cicada and made a good meal out of it.

Wang Lang decided to study the strange insect. He captured a few and started to attack them with small twigs while observing their defense and attack movements. For several months he put all his time into the analysis of the movements of the insect, certain that he would be able to learn its techniques. He developed the use of his hands as strong claws or as hooks and the way to duck by moving his waist. Soon, his perseverance and training made him an expert on the movements of the hands of the praying mantis.

One day, he went to a river to refresh himself after a long practice. He left his clothes on the river bank and immersed himself in the clear waters next to a waterfall. He had not gone very far when a monkey appeared and shamelessly took his clothes and ran away. Wang Lang came out of the water and went running after it, but the monkey evaded him once and again with its agile steps. After climbing a tree, the monkey mockingly threw the clothes at Wang Lang's feet.

This made Wang Lang ask himself how he, being a Kung Fu expert, was unable to capture a small monkey. So he reconstructed the movements of the monkey by studying the tracks it had left in the sand, and from that day on, he started following monkeys, observing them and trying to reproduce their steps in detail. He trained himself following this method until he was able to assimilate the wonderful mystery of the monkey feet. This is how he developed the step techniques.

He then combined the steps of the monkey with the claws of the praying mantis, and further added the best techniques of the seventeen styles he already knew. Then, once again, he set out to look for Tang Tung. He entered the fortress and one by one he got rid of all the guards in his way. Finally, when he found Tang Tung, he challenged him to fight. At the first contact of hands, Tang Tung was thrown back a good distance away. Surprised, Tang Tung charged towards Wang Lang but found himself unable to touch his opponent, due to his fast and strange movements, and was instead thrown an even longer distance away.

Then Tang Tung furiously asked:

"What Kung Fu style is that?"

"*Tanglang Chuan*," replied Wang Lang.

"That style hasn't been heard of in four thousand years!" said Tang Tung roaring with laughter, and in a desperate move he attacked with all his might. But Wang Lang used the praying mantis hands to break his head with an accurate movement, thus ending the fight. Having fulfilled his promise, he went back to *Lao Shan* with Tang's head as proof. From then on, Wang Lang stayed in the *San Chin Kong* temple, where he taught the style to the Taoist monks and others. From *Lao Shan* he also organized clandestine combat groups and actions against the Manchu, in an attempt to restore the Ming regime. It is said that Wang Lang died in *Lao Shan* leaving several students behind, the most famous of which was Li Ping-Hsiao, who being a Taoist monk was also known by his Taoist name Shen Hsiao Tao Ren.

The name *Shaolin Chuan* ceased being used for a long time and it was not until 1912 that this name reappeared. In the meantime, Kung Fu practitioners called it the style of the Tiger, of the Dragon, of the Black Panther, etc., according to the movements of the animal which was foremost in their practice. Sometimes the surname of the master or the name of the place where the style was practiced was used to name it. This is the case of *Kun Lun*, which was born in the eponymous mountain. Among the many styles derived from Shaolin, Praying Mantis is the one that has preserved more of its original features.

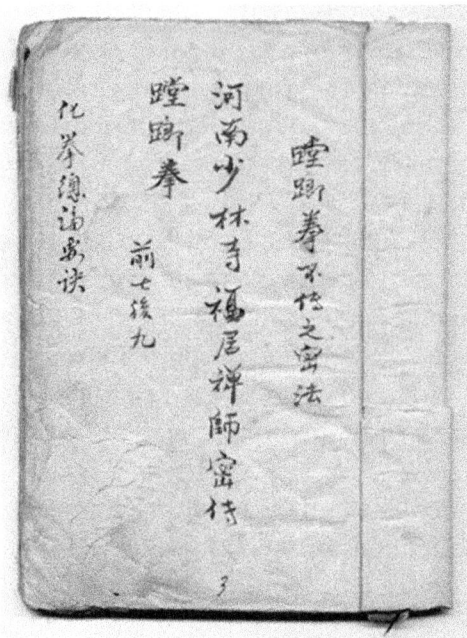

Secret Praying Mantis book, more than 300 years old. Handwritten and illustrated, it contains restricted explanations about the style. It is currently in the care of Master Su.

Nowadays Praying Mantis is one of the styles with more forms among Chinese Martial Arts: it has 108 forms and 360 different fundamental movements. The Praying Mantis style is the result of the combination of seventeen ancient Chinese Martial Arts with an additional new one. Praying Mantis is a reunion of Shaolin styles.

9.3 Modern Masters

Wang Lang taught *Tanglang Chuan* according to the capacity of the student, and because of this, many variants came about. From the very beginning two types of Praying Mantis could be distinguished, one soft and the other hard. Within the first category there is *Liohoe Tanglang Chuan* (Six unions), and among those called hard stand out *Chihsing Tanglang Chuan* (Seven Stars) and *Meihua Tanglang Chuan* (Plum Flower). These three are the oldest sub-styles and the closest to the original Praying Mantis. The other sub-styles arose from these. Wang Lang transmitted his knowledge to several students, the most important ones being, as we said before, Li Ping-Hsiao and Shen Hsiao Tao Ren.

In the following, we will list the most well-known Praying Mantis masters of the last hundred years, about whom information is more accessible.

Li Kuen-Shan was the greatest representative of the styles *Chihsing Tanglang Chuan* and *Meihua Tanglang Chuan* in modern times. As a disciple of Chiang Hua-Long, he was heir to the earliest knowledge of Praying Mantis. Among his students, those to receive the true knowledge of this style were his son Li Teng-Wu, his adopted son Tzui Chih-Ko, Su Yu-Chang, Adam Hsu, and Ma Chin-Shan.

Liu Tzu-Yuan was another of the great representatives of *Meihua Tanglang Chuan*. Song Chu-Long was his most representative student.

Chang Hsiang-Shan is the most important *Liohoe Tanglang Chuan* master who settled in Taiwan. This is one of the styles that has been better preserved to date. Chang Hsiang-Shan studied under Ting Tzu-Cheng and his most outstanding students were Tai She-Che, Chang Hsiang-San and Chen Wei-Shan.

Liu Yun-Chiao is better known for other styles, but he studied *Liohoe Tanglang Chuan* with Ting Tzu-Cheng. His most outstanding students are Adam Hsu, Su Yu-Chang, Liang Chi-Tsu and Chen Kuo-Chin.

Chang Te-Kuei was the most representative master of *Pimen Tanglang Chuan* in modern times. The most prominent disciples of Master Chang are Su Yu-Chang and Li Ching-Shiong.

Master Chang Te-Kuei (1902–1990) performing the "Lurking Mantis" stance of Pimen Tanlang.

Praying Mantis master Chiang Hua-Long, together with *Tong Pei Chuan* master Chen Shan-To and *Hsing-I* and *Pakua* master Wang Chong-Chen, decided to unite these four styles to create *Papu Tanglang Chuan*. Feng Huan-I was the heir of this new style. Master Feng had very few students, and among these, only Wei Hsiao-Tang learned the whole style, thus becoming the greatest modern representative of *Papu Tanglang Chuan*. The most outstanding students of Master Wei were Su Yu-Chang, Chen Kuo-Chin and Wang Chiu-Hsiung.

Wang Song-Ting was a master of a superior technical level. He knew several Kung Fu styles of the North besides *Chihsing* and *Meihua Tanglang*. He was specialized in Kung Fu weapons. His most important students are Chen Chun-Chan and Huang Tien-Pa. I studied under master Wang during the three final years of his life, but I did not become an initiated disciple (*Paisu*). Therefore I do not include him in my lineage.

In Taiwan, I had the opportunity to study all the Praying Mantis styles from masters that had fled to the island after the 1949 coup in China. I studied *Pimen Tanglang Chuan* with Master Chang Te-Kuei; *Chihsing* and *Meihua Tanglang Chuan* with Master Li Kuen-Shan; *Papu Tanglang Chuan* with Master Wei Hsiao-Tang; and *Liohoe Tanglang Chuan* with Master Liu Yun-Chiao. Thus, for the first time in 300 years, all the Praying Mantis styles were reunited in one person. To all this, I added elements of the energy of *Pachi Chuan*, and this is how the style now known as *Pachi Tanglang Chuan*, Eight Ultimate Praying Mantis, came to be.

9.4 The *Tanglang Chuan* of Master Su Yu-Chang. His masters

I was born in Tong Shan, in Tainan, Taiwan, a village with a strong tradition in Martial Arts. When I was seven years old I was a sickly and small child, partly due to the fact that I was born during the Second World War, when food was scarce. So my father took me to learn Martial Arts with the hope to improve my health.

The village had several temples that received contributions in exchange for teaching calligraphy, music, embroidery, Martial Arts, etc. In the temple closest to my house there was a master called Su Fu (Rock Tiger) who taught Kung Fu from the South, such as *Taitzu Chang Chuan, Pai Hou, Wing*

Chun and *Hou Chuan*. He also taught *Song Jiang Zhen*, weapon manoeuvers for groups of 36 or 108 people, like in a military platoon.

The neighboring villages had the tradition of organizing tournaments two or three times per year, usually as part of the celebrations for the patron saint of the village. Naturally, the winner of these contests would feel very happy.

After the Communist Revolution in China, in 1949, many Martial Arts masters and military servicemen fled from all Chinese provinces to Taiwan. Many people from Shandong came to settle in Tong Shan, and one of them was a man called Chang Te-Kuei.

Chang Te-Kuei earned his livelihood selling firewood that he collected in the mountains. He had to walk on narrow and winding paths, carrying very heavy loads of up to 100kg, for as much as five hours each way.

Master Su next to Master Chang Te-Kuei, Taiwan

On these journeys, he always crossed paths with a very tall man renowned in the town for his strength and mastery of Martial Arts. The trails were so narrow that two men could not pass past each other, especially when carrying large burdens. This provoked repeated disputes regarding the right to pass first because although Chang Te-Kuei was older, the tall man refused to give way.

One day, they met close to the village, by a ravine some four meters wide. Chang Te-Kuei tried to pass first, but the man pushed him aside and made Chang Te-Kuei lose his firewood. The locals who where there laughed about this, but Chang Te-Kuei had had enough and responded by knocking down the man's load. Without a word, the man threw a punch, which Chang Te-Kuei intercepted and then used a lock that made the man scream in pain. The people who saw this could not believe their eyes because the man was indeed very strong. Then Chang Te-Kuei "flew" to the other side of the ravine carrying the man, left him there, jumped back and told him: "If you want to fight, come here." From then on, Master Chang Te-Kuei acquired a lot of prestige among the people of the village.

Later a group of eight people from the village put together some money and asked the master to teach them. On the first day of class, many people went to look and observed many unusual things. Firstly, Master Chang Te-Kuei spoke Mandarin Chinese which was very uncommon in the area at the time, when everyone spoke Taiwanese Chinese. Then, his movements were very different to those of southern styles: the footwork did not seem very firm, but rather weak and unstable, with many winding steps; they noticed a very narrow *Chi Ma Suh* (horse-riding stance), since in the South the stance is broader than in the North; the steps were shorter and there were more movements. All this seemed amusing to the villagers.

After an hour, the Master told the public he would do a demonstration.

He drank a glass of liquor and went to an appropriate place. He saluted and executed a series of very fast movements with his hands and feet, moving as fast as a bicycle. To finish, he performed a double kick in the air, and without anyone noticing how, he suddenly appeared on the roof of a nearby house, more than three meters high. He then asked: "Am I qualified to teach you or not?"

Master Wei Hsiao-Tang (1905–1984) performing the Kua Hu Su stance of Pa Pu Tanglang

Although most were very frightened, they gradually joined the group of students.

During this period, I studied *Pi-men Tanglang Chuan* (Secret Door Praying Mantis) and *Mitzong Chuan* (Hiding or Labyrinth Fist). Also during that time, at the age of 14, I took part in a national tournament, winning first place in forms and sixth in combat. Combat categories were quite loose those days: 45–65kg, 66–85kg, and more than 85kg. I was included in the 45–65kg category, even though I weighed only 35kg.

In 1960, I left the village and went to live in Taipei, where I studied with Masters Wei Hsiao-Tang and Li Kuen-Shan.

Master Wei Hsiao-Tang arrived at Taiwan relatively late. Before, he had spent a few years in Korea, where he got into a fight with a local who was an expert in a Korean Martial Art. Master Wei killed him with a single punch, and so moved to Taiwan to avoid the police. I was fortunate to study with him right from the first classes he taught in Taipei. From Wei Hsiao-Tang I learned *Papu Tanglang Chuan* (Eight-step Praying Mantis) and *Wu Chia Tai Chi Chuan* (Wu style Tai Chi Chuan).

Master Li Kuen-Shan
(1895–1980)

Among the Martial Arts masters in Taiwan at the time, Li Kuen-Shan was the oldest and the highest in hierarchy too. In 1933, he won the first place in weapon combat in the first National Martial Arts Tournament in Nanking. Master Li Kuen-Shan studied Martial Arts the old-school way, that prepared candidates who wanted to qualify for top military positions. These examinations were first carried out at the town level, then those selected would go to the province-level examination in the following year. Finally, in the third year, those who succeeded would go to a national level examination. The candidate would be given a position according to how far they succeeded in the selection process, and could even become a general or a minister.

Master Li lived in Chi Lung, a city two or three hours drive away from Taipei. I would visit him two or three times per week. At that time, Master Li Kuen-Shan was 65 years old, but he punched a 200kg punching bag every day. I learned *Chihsing Tanglang Chuan* (Seven Star Praying Mantis), *Meihua Tanglang Chuan* (Plum Flower Praying Mantis), *Ti Kung* (ground combat), and all types of weapons.

Master Liu Yun-Chiao (1909–1992)

I then studied with Master Liu Yun-Chiao, starting in 1963. With him I studied the styles *Pachi Chuan, Pikua Chuan, Pakua Chang, Chen Tai*

Chi Chuan and *Liohoe Tanglang Chuan* (Six Harmonies Praying Mantis). I spent more than ten years studying with each of my masters, completely assimilating their respective styles.

In 1965, I started teaching at Taiwan University, but only Praying Mantis. At the time, there were no other universities where this style was taught. Gradually, through public performances and tournaments, the Praying Mantis style became better known and eventually I found myself teaching at eight different universities.

Tsuankong Chiao. Master Su Yu-Chang

In 1968, Taiwan sent for the first time a delegation to an international Martial Arts competition. I was one of a team of eight. From then on, people from different parts of the country would come to study with me every year. The art was thus disseminated. I even participated in several films as a Martial Arts director.

In 1976, I moved to in Venezuela, where I also started teaching Praying Mantis. This style is nowadays very well known in this country.

Having returned to Taiwan, I still teach in many countries around the world, such as Venezuela, Japan, Spain, USA and the Netherlands.

Over the past 300 years, the different Praying Mantis styles have been preserved and looked after separately. When the communists took power in China, most good Kung Fu masters fled to Taiwan, which led to a concentration of Kung Fu masters unique in history. I spent almost thirty years looking for and studying all the Praying Mantis styles, until I managed to bring them together in one person once again. Someone wanting to study with me can learn all the Praying Mantis styles. Long years of study are necessary for reaching the superior levels, but it is possible to reach an acceptable and efficient grasp of its techniques in a relatively short time.

Chapter 10

Tanglang Chuan Styles

The first steps in *Tanglang Chuan* are to be taken slowly. One must follow the master. The student must not create, he should not change the form taught by the master. Later, the student will be able to choose what he likes best within the whole of Praying Mantis.

Initially, there was only one Praying Mantis style, but when Wang Lang started teaching, he found himself with so many students that he could not teach all of them the same. This led to the formation of two characteristic branches in the style, hard Praying Mantis and soft Praying Mantis.

He taught a faster and harder Praying Mantis (*Ing Tanglang*) to his younger students. In this branch we find Seven Star (*Chihsing*), Plum Flower (*Meihua*), Eight-step (*Papu*) and Secret Door (*Pimen*). To those who already knew other styles or who were older in age, he taught the soft styles of Praying Mantis (*Rou Tanglang*): Six Harmonies (*Liohoe*), Whip Hand (*Suaishou*) and Monkey (*Mahou*).

10.1 *Ing Tanglang*. Hard Praying Mantis

The *Ing Tanglang* styles have fast steps, like that of the monkey; it has both long and short range attacks; it is strong without being tense; it is soft but not slack; it is fast and precise; when it stops it does not break the stance; it is firm but not still; it spreads without weakening. What is important in the *Ing Tanglang* styles is to be able to strike five times with a single energy. This is called *Lien Wu Chuei* 連五捶, and it could be described as striking five times in a single breath, like five petals blossom in a flower. The most characteristic styles of this branch are *Chihsing Tanglang* and *Meihua Tanglang*.

10.1.1 *Chihsing Tanglang Chuan*. Seven Star Praying Mantis

Chihsing Tanglang has both long and short range attacks, but the latter are more common. A great number of these are to be done in a very short time. With each attack comes a series of strikes, not just one; there are high and low strikes. Changes of direction are quick and with long steps, be it towards the front, the back, or sideways. Movements are deceptive, creating false impressions in the adversary. The steps are taken from the monkey, and the most characteristic stance is *Chihsing Suh*, which gives its name to the style. This name comes from the fact that in this stance the body has seven vertices or supporting points. These are located in the wrists, elbows, shoulders, hips, knees, ankles and the lumbar region. Note that the first six points are to be counted in pairs while the last one is single. The lumbar region has a special role in the transmission of energy between the upper and lower parts of the body. Six of the seven points have a grappling function while the seventh is for chopping and for finishing off the attack.

The most characteristic seven vertex stances are *Chihsing Suh* (Seven Star stance), *Ruhuan Suh* and *Yuhuan Suh*.

Master Su executes a characteristic stance of the *Chihsing Tanglang* style: The praying mantis bends down to drink, *Tanglang Chi Shuei*. Two characteristic elements of the Praying Mantis style can be appreciated, the stance *Chihsing Pu* and the Praying Mantis hands.

10.1.2 *Meihua Tanglang*. Plum Flower Praying Mantis

In *Meihua Tanglang* long range attacks are more frequent, specially in the form of sequentially ordered techniques. Changes of direction are not so common and are somewhat slower than in *Chihsing Tanglang*. It is a more settled style, with less steps. However, transitions between stances are very fast. It is characterized by the use of hand techniques in sequences of four or five strikes.

In contrast to *Chihsing Tanglang*, the name of *Meihua Tanglang* is not related to stances but to movements. As just mentioned, the sequences of strikes and attacks are very characteristic, usually in sets of five, combining attacks high and low, left and right, thus suggesting the five-petalled shape of a plum flower.

Pei Ho Chuei Pao, search for the genitals at the back. A characteristic stance of the *Meihua Tanglang* style.

For example, the attack called *Lienhuan Wuchuei Suh* 連環五捶式, that combines high and low attacks, is executed as follows. First the right fist strikes the abdomen, then the left one strikes the area of the nose and mouth. The third strike hits the heart, the fourth goes to the forehead and the fifth is a kick to the groin. Although very different from each other, all these strikes are on the same vertical plane.

An example of an attack in a left-right orientation is one called *Wu Ta Lienhuan Pi* 五打連環劈, which is executed as follows. The wrist is raised to hit the chin, then the palm strikes the heart and two strikes to the sides follow, one to the left ear and one to the right temple. Finally, the fifth strike is done with the edge of the hand vertically to the middle of the face. These five strikes are to be done with one hand.

10.1.3 *Pimen Tanglang*. Secret Door Praying Mantis

Tanglang Huan Sen Pu Tang, the praying mantis turns around to catch the cicada. A *Pimen Tanglang* stance.

Pimen Tanglang (Secret Door Praying Mantis) was born from the union of *Chihsing Tanglang* and *Meihua Tanglang*. It is similar to the ancient Praying Mantis, with the difference that it contains secret forms such as *Pimen Choyao* 秘門摘要, and *Fun Shun Patuan Chuan* 分身八短拳. Today, this last form is only present in the *Pimen Tanglang* style. *Pimen Tanglang* was conceived to fight and defeat other Praying Mantis styles. It takes advantage of the weak points of the Praying Mantis system and for this reason it is a secret style.

In the oldest Praying Mantis book there is a set of ninety techniques called *Mi Shou* (Secret Hands), from which *Pimen Tanglang* is believed to have originated. These techniques also appear in an even older document.

In *Pimen Tanglang*, almost all the movements are short range, with tight stances and narrow arm movements. The adversary is approached rapidly and the aim is to defeat him in the first encounter.

10.1.4 *Suaishou Tanglang*. Shake-off Praying Mantis

The *Suaishou Tanglang* style (Shake-off Hand Praying Mantis) is a combination of *Chihsing Tanglang* and some movements of *Liohoe Tanglang*. It tends to use wide circular arm movements, and fewer direct punches.

10.1.5 *Papu Tanglang*. Eight Step Praying Mantis

Papu Tanglang (8 Step Praying Mantis) is the result of introducing some elements of *Pakua Chang, Hsing-I Chuan* and *Tong Pei Chuan* into *Chihsing Tanglang*. This style develops combat skills in the shortest time.

This Praying Mantis style is the most recent of the traditional styles. Later styles should not really be called traditional. This style appeared for practical reasons when, at the turn of the 20th century, Chinese martial artists started having contact with those of other countries. *Tanglang Chuan* fighting techniques took for granted that the opponent would be wearing long-sleeved traditional dress, with the possibility of grabbing the clothes rather than directly the arms. Furthermore, the fighting system was not limited to a ring or a tatami, instead its movements were conceived to allow for the unfolding of combat without boundaries. For these reasons, when the first foreign opponents were confronted, it became apparent that some changes needed

Tanglang Pu Tang, the praying mantis catches the cicada. *Papu Tanglang* stance.

to be introduced for the sake of effectiveness under the new combat rules and circumstances.

In 1912, the greatest Praying Mantis specialist was Master Chiang Hua-Long, the master of one of my masters. He, together with two friends of his who were also Martial Arts masters, worked during two years on the best *Tanglang Chuan* styles, *Chihsing Tanglang* and *Meihua Tanglang*, adding elements from *Hsing-I Chuan, Pakua Chang* and *Tong Pei Chuan*. New forms were created where speed was combined with grappling techniques that allowed for more efficient ways of fighting in a ring with the upper body naked. High jumps and kicks were eliminated and speed of steps and long range attacks were emphasized. Once they had completed the new style, they taught it to Master Feng Huan-I. The latter fought against opponents from other countries, reaping many victories. Feng Huan-I taught my master, Wei Hsiao-Tang.

When the communists came to power in China, Wei Hsiao-Tang fled to Korea. One day he was in a restaurant of a friend in Seoul when a drunkard tried to assault his friend. Wei defended his friend and gave the drunkard a beating. As a response, a group or Koreans came to the restaurant some time later with the intention to destroy the restaurant and to punish Master Wei. However, Master Wei confronted them using *Papu Tanglang* techniques and killed three of them. The Korean police then tried to arrest him, but the Taiwanese government, knowing his quality as a martial artist, intervened on his behalf and made it possible for him to travel to Taiwan. That is when I met him and studied with him.

The fighting philosophy of *Papu Tanglang* says: "forward rapidly and backwards rapidly, so much so that people cannot know where you are moving." Movements are discrete and effective, avoiding the spectacular: "if you see a punch coming from the left, the strike will come from the right." The character of the forms and their linkage make the practitioner acquire long lasting energy that builds the capacity of enduring long combat.

10.2 *Rou Tanglang*. Soft Praying Mantis

In *Rou Tanglang* (Soft Praying Mantis) styles, the movements are soft and continuous, reaching their end without interruptions. Heart with thought, thought with energy, energy with the force of the movement; this is called the union of the three internals. The hands with the feet, the elbows with the knees, the shoulders with the hips; this is the union of the three externals. The three internals are joined to the three externals in a continuous rotating motion, such that the opponent will not know where the attack is coming from.

Yunu Chuansuo, the beautiful maiden weaving. A *Liohoe Tanglang* stance.

10.2.1 *Liohoe Tanglang*. Six Harmonies Praying Mantis

Liohoe Tanglang (Six Harmonies Praying Mantis) is the most representative style of *Rou Tanglang*. This style demands the connection of the internal (spirit, energy and essence) with the external (hands, feet and torso). The aim is to maintain continuous contact with the opponent until he has been defeated, without breaks between techniques. The greater part of the movements are done in continuous circles. In the rare cases where a linear movement is done, for example a forward, upward or downward movement, as soon as the energy reaches a certain point, a new energy is produced immediately that makes the movement continuous. This gives the feeling that the energy has not stopped, an effect similar to that of the circular movement. The steps in *Liohoe Tanglang* are akin to those of a big ape walking in every direction, with characteristic steps and very few jumps. For this reason *Liohoe Tanglang* is sometimes also called *Mahou Tanglang* (Big Monkey Praying Mantis).

10.2.2 *Kuangpan Tanglang.*
Shining Board Praying Mantis

Kuangpan Tanglang Chuan (Shining Board Praying Mantis) has its origin in *Liohoe Tanglang* and was derived from the teachings of a prominent master called Wei San who had a congenital malformation of the fingers of his left hand that did not allow him to separate them. This style came about when his students started imitating him, thinking that the hand movements should be performed as with a "*Kuangpan*", a shining board. The movements of this style are similar to those of *Liohoe Tanglang* with the difference that the fingers are never separated.

10.3 Praying Mantis of the 21st century.
Pachi Tanglang Chuan

Pachi Tanglang Chuan is not really a distinct Kung Fu style, because there are no forms or movements that belong to a style with such a name. Instead, *Pachi Tanglang Chuan* is a fighting capacity that results from studying and practicing the teachings of Master Su Yu-Chang. These teachings include five Praying Mantis styles (*Chihsing*, *Meihua*, *Pimen*, *Papu* and *Liohoe*) and *Pachi–Pikua Chuan*, *Pakua Chang*, *Hsing-I Chuan* and *Tai Chi Chuan*. All of these styles are studied independently, in accordance with tradition, but once they have been assimilated, this combination provides great speed of movement together with very powerful energy projection. Often, with speed some force is lost and vice-versa, when movements are executed with a lot of power the transition from one stance to another requires a short pause. However, this is not the case in *Pachi Tanglang Chuan* because these transitions are extremely fast. *Pachi Tanglang* is both fast and powerful.

Pachi Tanglang may be likened to an authentic Chinese banquet where 10 or 12 dishes will be presented. Each plate has its particular taste and all are excellent. When we finish eating, we do not know which one was the best, but what we do know is that the food was magnificent. It might be the case that nowadays *Pachi Tanglang* is the only style that preserves the techniques of *Fa Ching* (energy projection).

Chapter 11

Tanglang Chuan Techniques

> Every Praying Mantis hand technique carries *Chinna* energy, that is, it works as a lock.

11.1 *Kou Shou*: Praying Mantis hook

The "Praying Mantis hand" is of fundamental importance in this style. *Kou Shou* 鉤手 is the name given to the hand in the shape of a hook like a Praying Mantis claw. This hand position is unique to the style. It is formed by placing the fingers in a specific way. First the little finger and the ring finger are bent toward the center of the hand. Then, the index and the middle finger are joined to the thumb, and the wrist is bent down. It is important for these last three fingers to be touching each other, otherwise the attack will not be effective. These three fingers perform *Chin* 擒, clutching, and the other two perform *Na* 拿, locking. For this

reason, every Praying Mantis hand technique carries *Chinna* energy, that is, it works as a lock.

There are many ways of using the Praying Mantis hand. Generally, it is used for attacking, although it can also be applied to catch the arm of the opponent using the thumb, the index and middle finger to hold it while the ring finger and little finger put pressure on the *Shenmen* point 神門, in the lower part of the wrist. It is also possible to poke the eyes of the opponent while pushing the nose cartilage from below with the thumb.

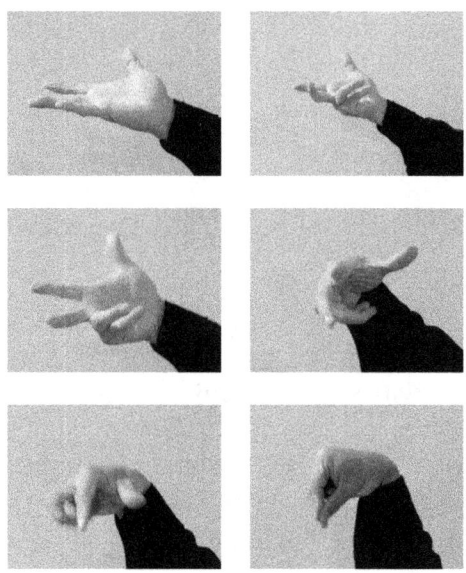

The forearm also plays a very important role in the use of the Praying Mantis hand. It is used not only to block, but also to follow the action until breaking the guard of the opponent. Well used, it can close your own guard completely, like magic, making it very difficult for someone to hit you; but you must know how to use it. The arm should move like a screw, spirally, both to defend and to attack. When the use of the forearm has been mastered, it is called *Tie Chi* 铁齿, iron tooth.

11.2 Chia Suh 架式. Stances

The stances in Praying Mantis are the same as in most other Kung Fu styles. However, some have special names within the system despite being the same as those of other styles. Here, we will only list them, referring the interested reader to section 5.2, to my book *The Invisible Web*[1] or to my instructional videos for a more detailed description.

1. *Chi Ma Suh*
Horse-riding stance

2. *Tan Shan Suh*
Mountain-climbing stance

3. *Ruhuan Suh*
Door-shutting stance

4. *Tuli Suh*
One-leg stance

5. *Yuhuan Suh*
Jade ring stance

6. *Chihsing Suh*
Seven-stars stance

7. *Tsopan Suh*
Sitting on the basis stance

8. *Shi Suh*
Empty stance

9. *Putingpupa Suh*
Weight-centering stance, also *Yuenho Pu*, monkey stance

---

[1] Asociación Europea Pachi Tanglang Chuan y Tao, Mallorca, 1998.

10. *Putuei Suh*
Body-lowering stance

11. *Pai Suh*
Defeated stance

12. *Panma Suh*
Half *Chi Ma Suh* stance

13. *Kuahu Suh*
Hip-guarding stance

14. *Dengta Suh*
Crushing step stance

15. *Hanchi Suh*
Cold rooster stance

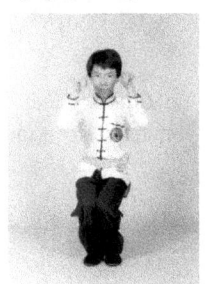
16. *Pentun Suh*
Joint feet low stance

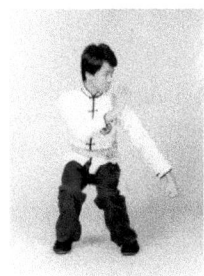
17. *Tsongtun Suh*
Centered low stance

18. *Tsongping Suh*
Center balance stance

19. *Penli Suh*

11.3 Basic leg techniques

11.3.1 Kicks

In *Tanglang Chuan* there are eighteen technical series of kicks. In order to master them, it is necessary to first learn the basic kicks of the style. In a future book, dedicated exclusively to the Praying Mantis style, we will explain the eighteen series in detail. In the following, the basic kicks of the Praying Mantis style are presented.

1. *Liaoyin Chiao*   2. *Gaoti Chiao*   3a. *Pentsuan Chiao*

3b. *Gao Pentsuan Chiao*   4. *Furen Chiao*   5. *Tsuai Chiao*

6. *Pimen Chiao*   7. *Teng Chiao*

8a. *Chiao Tuei*  8b  9a. *Huwei Chiao*  9b

10. *Chuanhsing Chiao*  11. *Kuamen Chiao*  12a. *Pailen Chiao*  12b

13. *Chensao Tuei* 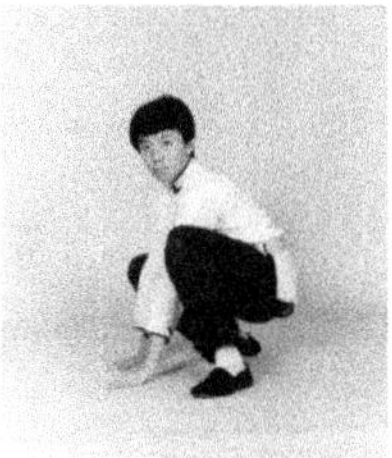 14a. *Housao Tuei*  14b  14c

15a. *Shenfong Chiao*  15b

16a. *Ohyi Tsoshin Chiao* 16b

17. *Tsuanten Chiao* 18a. *Itai Erhti Chiao* 18b

19a. *Tsan Pai Chiao* 19b 19c

20a. *Tsou Tuei* 20b 20c 20d

| 21a. *Fantenyun Chiao* | 21b | 21c | 22. *Tsuankong Chiao* |

11.3.2 Steps

The most characteristic steps of the Praying Mantis style are taken from the monkey, but there are other steps common to other styles as well. The four most characteristic steps are the following:

1. *Hou Pu* 猴步 is the usual monkey step. It is performed in the *Pu Ting Pu Pa* stance. When going forward, the front foot goes first and the rear one follows without overtaking the first one. If going backwards, the rear foot is moved first and the front foot follows.

2. *San Tsai Pu* 三才步 is a diagonal step that changes from *Tan Shan Pu* into *Shi Pu* 虛步. *San Tsai Pu* can be performed towards the front or towards the back. There is also a variation of it called *Fan San Tsai Pu* 反三才步 (see the photographs of the *Chan* technique, p. 256).

3. *Ting Pu* 丁步 advances with the rear foot half a step, so that it reaches the front foot. It does so with a strong stomp to take another step into *Tan Shan Pu* moving the other foot forward. This step may be performed forward or backward.

4. In *Kai Pu* 開步 the rear foot overtakes the front one to land in *Yuhuan Pu*. This step can be done in any direction.

Pa Pu and *Tsontiao Pu* are two similar long-reach steps, the former goes backward and the latter forward. To execute *Tsontiao Pu* we start in *Tan Shan Pu*, with the left leg in front. First, we lift the left knee to gain momentum, putting it back down with the intention of going forward.

Immediately after, the right knee is lifted and brought forward in a jump that makes us lift the left knee again. The right foot lands first followed by the left, ending in *Tan Shan Pu* once more, with the left foot in front as at the start. This step can also be performed starting in *Tan Shan Pu* with the right foot in front.

Pa Pu follows a similar principle but moves backward. We start in *Shi Pu* with the right foot in front. We move back the left foot a little before the right knee is lifted and the whole leg is brought back above and past the left knee in a jump. During the jump, the left foot reaches up so as to tap the buttocks. The right foot lands first, and when the left one arrives we use the waist to turn and face forward again. The study of these steps in Praying Mantis aims to make the practitioner able to advance four or five meters rapidly, using *Tsontiao Pu*, or to retreat a similar distance using *Pa Pu*.

As mentioned above, the steps in Praying Mantis come from the monkey. Monkeys move with great agility, strength and speed through the trees; they need this skill to be able to jump from tree to tree. In Praying Mantis there is a secret step of a very high level. It is called *Papu Kanchan* 八步趕蟬, eight steps to pursue the cicada. The principle behind this step is the following: we see a cicada at a distance of eight steps (*papu*), as we notice that the cicada is about to fly away, we charge towards the insect covering the distance of eight steps catching it before it can escape. Master Wei Hsiao-Tang was the only one to know and to be able to execute this technique. Today, there are only two people able to execute it, Master Chen Kuo-Chin and myself.

11.3.3 Knees

There are twelve knee techniques in Praying Mantis. Among these, only three are basic:

1. *Ting Ti* 頂膝 is an upward knee attack. It is aimed at the center of the opponent.

2. *She Ting Ti* 側提膝 is a sideways knee attack. The knee comes from behind following an arched path.

3. *Kuei Ti* 跨膝 is used when the opponent is on the ground. The rear knee pushes downward until it reaches the ground.

1. *Ting Ti*   2. *She Ting Ti*   3. *Kuei Ti*

11.4 Basic arm techniques

When we speak about arm techniques in the Praying Mantis style, we divide them into techniques of the shoulder, elbow, wrist, fist, palm and fingers. There are plenty of these techniques and they are very sophisticated. Once again, here we will only give a short introduction, leaving an in-depth discussion for a future book dedicated exclusively to *Tanglang Chuan*.

11.4.1 Shoulders

There are three basic uses of the shoulder. These are *Ting* 頂 lift, *Tzuan* 鑽 strike, and *Ti* 提 push. In the photographs below, you can see one application of the shoulder.

11.4.2 Elbows

Elbow techniques in Chinese Martial Arts are very secret. This is why in any style the forms that study the different elbows are always taught at the very end. This is the case with *Fun Shun Pa Tuan Chuan* 分身八短拳 in *Tanglang Chuan*, *Liu Chou Toh Chuan* 六肘頭拳 in *Pachi Chuan*, *Chenkun Shi Er Chuanchou Chuan* 乾坤十二轉肘拳 in *Pakua Chang*, *Sansan Chuan* 三三拳 in *Tai Chi Chuan* and *Shi Er Hong Chuei Chuan* 十二橫捶拳 in *Hsing-I Chuan*. Most of these forms have the word *Chou* 肘, which means elbow, as part of their name. I have taught for over fifty years and until now I have only taught the form *Funshin Pachou Chuan* to less than a dozen of my students. This shows that students must practice with perseverance and patience.

In the following pages we show twelve basic elbow techniques of the Praying Mantis style.

1a. *Chong Chou*
1b
2a. *Ting Chou*
2b

3a. *Ti Chou*
3b
4a. *Teh Chou*
4b

5a. *Tenfun She Chou* 5b 6a. *Pan Chou* 6b

7a. *Kuai Chou* 7b 8. *Ya Chou*

9a. *Tso Chou* 9b

10a. *Lienhuan Chong Chou* 10b 10c

11a. *Lienhuan Tiao Chou* 11b 11c 11d

12a. *Lienhuan Ya Chou* 12b 12c 12d

11.4.3 Wrists

Wrist techniques in Praying Mantis are called *Kou* 鉤. They are also known as *Tanglang Shou*, Praying Mantis hands. We need to apply the hand and the

1. *Tanglang Chishuei*
The praying mantis drinks water

2. *Yunu Chuansoh*
The beautiful maiden weaving

forearm in order to use *Kou*. The hand is used as the Praying Mantis hand, tucking the little finger and the ring finger inside the palm, joining the middle finger, the index and the thumb, and finally, bending the wrist. The forearm should have a spiraling motion, *Chan Suh Ching* 纏絲勁. It is the first to make contact with the opponent, dispersing attacks and blocking the entrance. This is what gives it the name *Tie Chi*, iron tooth. Below, we show two of the 24 *Kou* movements existing in Praying Mantis.

11.4.4 Fists

Fists are a common feature of all Chinese Martial Arts. In Praying Mantis, there are 36 different fists. They are sometimes called *Chuan* 拳 and sometimes *Chuei* 捶, but the principle is the same. In general, direct punches are called *Chuan*, while fist techniques that require the help of the other arm are called *Chuei*.

Eight basic fist techniques are shown below.

1. *Ping (Fu) Chuan* 2. *Ou (Ying) Chuan* 3. *Tsu (Suh) Chuan*

4a. *Chuan Chuan* 4b 5. *Png Chuan*

6-1a. *Chong Chuan* 6-1b 6-2

7a. *Chuan Chuei* 7b 7c

8a. *Tsa Chuei* 8b 8c 8d

11.4.5 Palms

When we speak about the palm, we may refer to several different uses. One or both hands may be used, one may strike with the middle of the palm or with the edge. This is why there are twenty-four different palm techniques. Towards the end of this chapter you may see how the palms are used in the Praying Mantis style by looking at the applications photographs.

11.4.6 Fingers

In the Praying Mantis style, the fingers are called *Tanglang Zhua* 螳螂抓, Praying Mantis rake. We have already described the use of *Tanglang Shou*, where the thumb, index and middle finger are used to apply *Chin* while the ring finger and the little finger apply *Na*. The fingers can be used to catch, to strike or to press. Some of the Praying Mantis techniques that use the fingers are *Paiyuen Toutao Shou* 白猿偷桃手, the white monkey steals the peach; *Tanglang Tenting Shou* 螳螂頂手, which is a technique to pluck out the eyes; *Hsienren Hsienhua* 仙人献花, the sage pulls off the hair; *Chokuei Shou* 摘盔手, hand that tears away the helmet; *Chasuh Shou* ?嗉手, technique directed at the throat, pressing Adam's apple; *Pichi Shou* 閉氣手, block the wind; *Choku Shou* 折骨手, break the bones; *Funchin Shou* 分筋手, Displace the tendons; and *Tienhsue Shou* 奌穴手, pressure points that may leave someone unconscious or even kill. Some of these techniques are shown in the photographs at the end of this chapter.

11.5 Combat: energy, force and speed

When we throw a punch it should reach its target as fast as possible. However, speed in Martial Arts is defined somewhat differently to what is generally understood as speed. Speed in *Pachi Tanglang* is not only the result of the physical aspects related to the mechanics of the body, rather it requires taking into account physiology and spirit as well. In other words, besides the velocity that may be developed due to purely mechanic training, it is possible to develop speed through the appropriate use of the energy of the body by executing specific movements with a particular disposition of the spirit or the mind.

We may distinguish three levels of practice for the development of these techniques. The effects of the training depend on the skill of the practitioner. In these three levels we deal successively with knowledge related to the body or essence, reflected in the movements; to the management and projection of energy; and finally, to those techniques that concern only the spirit. There are two other superior levels, very difficult to achieve, and which are mastered by very few people today. The fifth in particular is only known to myself and a handful of others.

Movement The first level concerns the execution of movements and pays special attention to breathing. Beyond the knowledge of the mechanics of the movements, it is necessary to master the breathing that corresponds to each type of movement. The speed of the strikes in Martial Arts is directly proportional to the amount of strikes we are able to execute in one breath. For untrained people, one strike per breath is the norm, but in *Pachi Tanglang* the aim is to strike five times in one breath.

Energy Projection Strong strikes require energy. However, in Kung Fu in general and in *Tanglang* in particular, in addition to mere physical energy, which we may call muscular, the energy of the organism is activated and transmitted through the tendons. This energy can be applied not only where the strike arrives, but it can be transmitted through liquid and electric components of the organism.

For a strike to be really destructive, the energy should have several effects. The first effect of energy is to make the brain register pain through the nervous system, but the same strike should also have a second effect, penetrating the body and generating an impact wave through the blood, muscles, bones, etc. This wave spreads through the body to ultimately reach the heart and other vital organs. The very same strike should finally have a third energetic effect: to dissolve or pulverize organic structures.

Techniques pertaining to spirit.
I-Hsing Huan Ying Shu *I-hsing Huan Ying Shu* 移形換影術, spirit that shifts the body and changes the position of the shadow, is a secret technique that is easily misunderstood by people who have not reached a high level. They may even regard it as being a fantasy or magic. To give an idea I will only mention that he who has attained this level can capture and control the mind or spirit of the adversary. It is possible for him to change the intention of the strike of the opponent or to distort the perception of his own strike.

Mastering this technique implies the capacity to influence the perception of the opponent. For example, with this technique we may throw a punch to the face but change the perception of the adversary so that he thinks the strike is going towards the stomach, or that the strike comes from ten different places at the same time, thus not knowing what to expect.

Thought is quicker than the movement of the body. Usually, there is a delay between the thought and the movement, but when we have arrived at the level we are talking about, this delay disappears and in combat the techniques are executed with the thought. Regardless of what the opponent might do, we have the certainty that before his strike touches us, the right technique will come about to finish him. Similarly, it suffices to think for our punch to come out. Since fights are always settled in short range combat, this level of technique is very effective because it eliminates the time gap between thought and movement.

11.5.1 Phases of combat

Any fighting encounter occurs in three phases. The first is before there is physical contact, the second is at the moment of the initial contact, and the third is when the force of the strike is transmitted. We explain each of these phases below.

Before physical contact There are only two possibilities, either attack first or wait for the attack of the opponent. Here we should see with the eye of a saint, *Shen Yen* 神眼. This is a glance that involves all the attention. Usually, when we see we focus 80% of our attention to only one point, but with *Shen Yen* the totality of our field of vision is observed with attention and in detail, including the periphery. This way of observing allows us to know the situation and to have the whole field of action under control.

If we decide to attack first, the first movement should be a feint or a deceiving movement. By doing this, we must capture all the attention and "nerves" of the adversary, making him leave the rest of his body "empty" and unguarded . The definitive strike will then be directed towards any of these unguarded areas, producing a devastating effect. For example, if someone is grabbing us with both hands, all his attention is likely to be focused on his hands. Under these circumstances it will be difficult to free ourselves struggling with his hands. Instead, a better tactic would be to stomp on his feet, diverting his attention from the arms so that we can break free.

In *Pachi Tanglang Chuan* this first step is basic and automatic. For example, we might do a feint toward the upper area followed by an effective downward strike, or we might deceive with the right hand and strike with the left, etc. Another type of trick is called *So Shen Fa* 縮身法, which means renouncing oneself, sacrificing our life for a cause. It pretends to surrender in order to provoke a full-on attack from the opponent. When this happens and it is already too late for him to retreat, we change our attitude and attack.

The other possibility for this initial phase is to wait for the attack of the opponent. In this case it should be kept in mind that there is only one place in our body that is really in danger and this is where the opponent will direct his strike. Hence, we only need to take care of that small place. When his strike attempt reveals our weak point, it is relatively easy to avoid the strike and respond by striking at the "empty", vulnerable areas that will have become apparent in the opponent.

In the Praying Mantis style it is rare that only one strike is thrown. In general, one throws from three to five. In contrast, continuing the energy of a single strike until it reaches the target is characteristic for *Pachi Chuan*.

The initial contact At this moment it is important to use *Ting Ching*, "listening to the energy". If *Ting Ching* is mastered, all the body and all the energy of the opponent will be perceived with the first contact. In an instant, all this information arrives as quick as lighting.

Immediately after *Ting Ching* it is necessary to apply *Hua Ching*, "dissolving energy projection". The force directed against us must be dispersed, diluted, melted away in order to avoid the possible harm of the attack.

Melting away the energy of the opponent also serves the purpose of getting rid of obstacles to our strike and for striking without giving any clues about the aim of our strike so that the opponent feels as if he is being attacked in the dark.

The strike It is necessary to know how to project energy, *Fa Ching*, to be able to adequately apply energy according to the harm we want to inflict at the moment our strike reaches its target. It may affect just the essence of the opponent (muscle, tendons, bone, etc.) or, if our energy is stronger, it may affect the blood or the nerves. Finally, it may "break" the energy or spirit, producing different types of harm or even death.

♦

Master Su performing the *Pan* technique, one of the few in which both fists are used together

Confrontation in Martial Arts always follows these phases, even though in each style there will be different approaches to each phase. *Ting Ching* and *Fa Ching* should always be studied during practice, either in two-man sets or in forms.

The level of a school or of a person can be assessed by looking at the three stages of combat. Nowadays there are many "masters" who say they have attained high levels in their art, but most have actually not finished their studies. These are low quality "masters". It is unlikely that someone following their teachings will get very far.

11.6 Basic combat applications

Different parts of the body are used to strike in combat. In Praying Mantis the parts used to attack are called *Chi Chang Pa Tuan*, which may be translated as The Seven Long and Eight Short. The Seven Long are the head, the two hands, the coccyx, the two feet and the step. The Eight Short are the two shoulders, the elbows, the hips and the knees. Below we show some representative examples of *Chi Chang Pa Tuan*, out of the 360 combat techniques of Praying Mantis.

Head

Chin

Shoulder

A

B

Elbow

Forearm

A

B

Fist

A. Pang

B. Upward

C. Downward

Wrist

Palm

A

B

Fingers

Back

Coccyx

Hip

Knee

Foot

A

B

11.7 Special techniques

11.7.1 *Ti Kung*. Ground combat

Ground combat is used in cases of emergency or as a deception strategy, to escape the fighting area when being attacked by multiple opponents. Emergency situations are for example when we are knocked over or we have fallen and we must be able to get up rapidly, or know how to fight taking advantage of our position. It is also important to know how to fall without hurting oneself. In an attack by multiple opponents it is convenient to reduce our size to diminish the possibilities of being hurt. Additionally, by throwing ourselves to the ground we may cover a greater distance in an instant; all this is comprised in *Ti Kung* techniques.

There are three forms that contain these techniques: *Tzuei Pai Hou Chuan*, Drunk White Monkey Form; *Tzuei Tanglang Chuan*, Drunk Praying Mantis Form; and *Chaikuei Chuan*, Tear the Helmet Form.

11.7.2 *Chie Mo Tsu* 截脉穴. Steel tooth

This is a secret and special technique of the Praying Mantis style. Almost every Martial Arts style includes some form of *Chinna*, a set of locking and dislocation techniques. *Chinna* basically means firmly grabbing the opponent and, without letting him go, executing some type of joint lock to produce intense pain or a dislocation in order to immobilize the adversary. In the Praying Mantis style, *Chinna* is very important and is of a superior level, with special characteristics.

If we observe a praying mantis, we will see that when it catches its prey it holds it in such a way that it is impossible for it to escape. This is thanks to the spikes it has in its arms, which sink in the body of the prey.

As humans, we do not have such spikes on our arms, but nevertheless, the Praying Mantis style has developed a technique that allows for the use of energy in such a way that it would seem as if we did indeed have them. The Praying Mantis *Chinna* is the only one to have this technique, making it the most special and effective.

The name of these techniques is *Han Chin Chie Mo Tsu*. *Han Chin* is to tear tendons and *Chie Mo* produces such a force that it may interrupt the blood flow, the flow of energy and the transmission of nerve impulses. This secret technique is difficult to perform and can be used to rapidly paralyse the opponent or, if necessary, to produce some type of harm or even to kill. In the past, it was common that when meeting a Praying Mantis master one would keep a distance out of fear of coming into contact with his forearms, since this might have implied not being able to disengage without suffering some harm.

We will narrate an anecdote as an example. Once Master Su was in a restaurant with some of his students when a drunkard tumbled upon him. The students did not realize in time and only saw Master Su do a small movement that made the drunkard fall to the ground. When they went to pick him up they were astonished to find the man with half of his body paralyzed. Frightened, they told Master Su, but he reassured them and left the place. Several days later the man was taken by some friends to Master Su's office in a wheel chair. They apologized and begged him to help the man. Master Su agreed, and after three weeks of acupuncture treatment the man recovered. The students then asked Master Su what had happened and he explained that it had been *Han Chin Chie Mo Tsu*; he had used energy to paralyze by blocking a part of the brain.

Chapter 12

Praying Mantis Techniques and Forms

> Form practice leads to mastery of technique sequences and of energy linkage, so as to be able to put them into practice intuitively.

12.1 Characteristic techniques

Every Kung Fu style has basic techniques that characterize it. Basic techniques condense the foundations of a style, and when combined properly are then part of the forms.

Photograph taken in Kaohsiung. Master Su is accompanied by his first Paisu students, as well as other Paisu students from Taiwan, Japan, Venezuela and Spain.

Tanglang Chuan has twelve internal and twelve external techniques. The twelve external are *Kou* 鉤 to hook, *Lou* 摟 to embrace, *Tsai* 採 to pluck, *Kua* 掛 to hang, *Tiao* 刁 to bend, *Chan* 纏 to knead, *Peng* 崩 to rebound, *Tza* 砸 to smash, *Tsan* 粘 to attach, *Nien* 黏 to adhere, *Pang* 幫 to row and *Tie* 貼 to paste (also known as *Kao* 靠, to lean). It is extremely important to study these techniques in order to progress and properly learn the system.

The twelve internal are: *Ti* 提 to lift, *Na* 拿 to grab, *Fong* 封 to cover, *Pi* 閉 to lock, *Nien* 黏 to adhere, *Tsan* 粘 to attach, *Pang* 幫 to row, *Tie* 貼 to paste, *Lai* 來 to come, *Chiao* 叫 to call, *Shun* 順 to follow and *Song* 送 to offer.

鉤 **Kou – To hook** The forearm is used to block, followed by the Praying Mantis hand that grabs as a hook and pulls. Both hands may be used. It is important for the practice of the Praying Mantis hand. Liver energy is used.

1

2

3

4

摟 **Lou – To embrace** The forearm is used to block and is swung down using Kidney palm. It may be used from the outside or from the inside. It should be performed toward the inside of the guard of the opponent. The strike is weaker when blocked from the inside, because it has not yet gathered momentum.

採 **Tsai – To pluck** In this technique the arms are swung vertically drawing circles to push with the forearms. The circles may be vertical or horizontal. The hand starts closed in a fist at the height of the nose, then it opens, wraps and returns as if plucking out something, all the while using the forearm. Both arms may be used. *Tsai* is performed using monkey feet and praying mantis hands. It is a *Chi Kung* for the five organs, Liver, Heart, Lung, Kidney and Stomach.

掛 **Kua – To hang** The forearms are used to defend at every level and every direction: upper level, middle level and lower level, and also to the sides. Heart energy is used.

1

2

3

4

5

6

勺 **Tiao – To bend** This movement evokes an excavating motion with the hand, deflecting upwards. The strike of the opponent is blocked with the forearm from the outside and then his arm is hooked with the wrist using an upward movement of the elbow. It is important to use the outer part of the wrist turning it as we lift the elbow, as if digging. This movement requires a twist of the waist. Lung and Shoulder Blades energy is used.

PACHI TANGLANG CHUAN

5

6

7

8

9

10

11

纏 **Chan – To knead** Both hands are used. The strike of the opponent is deflected with one hand while the other is used to control his elbow. There is a high version and a lower version. Kidney and Lung energies are used. It is important to make use of the diaphragm and the Stomach.

1

2

3

4

5

6

7

崩 **Peng – To rebound** *Peng* extends the arm with the inside up. The strike arrives and comes back as a rebound. There are two uses for this movement, an upper and a lower one. The energies used are those of Kidney, Heart and Stomach.

1

2

3

4

5

6

7

8

9

10

砸 **Tza – To smash** Two successive downward strikes are performed. The arms draw vertical circles towards the back, then forward. It can be used to break the arm of the opponent. The energy goes from Heart to Lung to Kidney.

粘 **Tsan – To attach** It is used after the opponent has blocked our attack. We should press on with the movement until completion, not letting go, non stop.

7

8

黏 **Nien – To adhere** *Nien* means to adhere and to stick to the opponent, closing in on him ever more so that he can not escape.

1

2

3

4

幫 **Pang – To row** The important points of the body for this technique are the forearms and the elbows, which are used in a rowing motion to enter the guard of the opponent. Then the strike follows using both hands. This is a very important movement in the Praying Mantis style because there are very few techniques that use the energy of both hands together in a single point.

貼 **Tie – To paste (also known as Kao 靠, to lean)** This is the first part of *Tie* (*Kao*). We block by closing in on the opponent and using the the whole body, and then we apply *Tie* (*Kao*). Shoulders or hips may be used to thrust. This a close range combat technique.

12.2 The forms

At a basic level all the Praying Mantis styles use the same techniques. Consequently, there is a set of forms that is common to all the sub-styles, with the aim to develop the essential elements. Among the basic forms of *Ing Tanglang* we find *Lipi Chuan* (Strong Diagonal Strike Form), *Hsiao Huyuan Chuan* (Small Tiger Swallow Form) and *Tanglang Shou Chuan* (Praying Mantis Hands Form).

In the intermediate level the styles begin to differentiate their techniques from each other more clearly. The forms to be taught differ according to the characteristics of the student and the place where they are to be practiced.

The forms of *Meihua Tanglang* have the same names as in *Chihsing Tanglang* and the movements are very similar, with only slight differences.

12.2.1 *Hsiao Huyuan Chuan*

Hsiao Huyuan Chuan was created by Wang Lang. It was a very hot day and he was sitting in the shade of the temple *San Chin Kong*. Wanting to take a rest, he leaned against a pillar and looked up towards the paintings covering the ceiling of the temple. They depicted the *Fong Shen Chuan* (*Book of the Investiture of the Gods*), a novel set in the Shang dynasty. One of the figures was of a saint riding a winged tiger. When he saw this, Wang Lang thought that if a form could be as strong as a tiger and as agile as a swallow at the same time, it would be a very powerful form. Having studied at the Shaolin Temple, Wang Lang used many of the movements that he learned there to create this form.

The *Hsiao Huyuan* form consists of arm movements such as linear punches (*Chong* 衝), rebound strikes (*Peng* 崩), chopping strikes (*Pi* 劈), crushing movements (*Tza* 砸), pushes (*Tuei* 推), defenses (*Kua* 掛) and penetrating actions (*Tsa* 插). Regarding feet and legs, it contains heel kick, instep kick, descending kick, chopping kick, scissor kick and stomping. By studying *Hsiao Huyuan Chuan* it is possible to keep the energy constantly in the *Tan Tien* so that it is not lost. There are no limits in energy and the body is able to make very fast changes of movement, upward and downward. When learning how to fight at the basic level the student will learn one to one combat, but with the techniques of *Hsiao Huyuan Chuan* one learns to fight one against three. This makes this form very important. It develops the capacity to be strong like a tiger and as light as a swallow.

12.2.2 *Hsiao Huyuan Chuan* two man form

• 1 • Greeting

• 2 • 開門見山式 *Kaimen Chien Shan Suh.* Open the door to see the mountain

1

• 3 • 大鵬展翅式 *Ta Peng Chan Chih Suh.* The great Roc opens its wings

1

2

3

4

5

6

- 4 • 馬式左密肘 *Ma Shin Tzuo Mi Chou*. Strike with the back part of the left wrist in Horseback riding stance

1

2

3

- 5 - 馬式右衝捶 *Ma Suh You Chong Chuei*. Punch with the right arm in Horseback riding stance

- 6 - 右左連環劈 *You Tzuo Lienhuan Pi*. Continuous sequence of diagonal strikes

3

4

5

• 7 • 馬式十字劈 *Ma Suh Shih Tzu Pi*. Diagonal strike in a cross, in Horseback riding stance

1

2

• 8 • 仆腿下身式 *Pu Tuei Hsia Shen Suh*. Low leg with lowered body

PACHI TANGLANG CHUAN

• 9 • 拗步右直捶 *Ao Pu You Chih Chuei.* Traverse step and straight right arm punch

• 10 • 十字彈腿式 *Shih Tzu Tan Chiao Suh.* Crossed rebound kick

- 11 - 馬式蓋頂劈 *Ma Shi Kai Ting Pi.* Diagonal strike to the top in Horseback riding stance

- 12 - 右旋風腳法 *You Hsuan Feng Chiao Fa.* Wind mill kick with the right leg

• 13 • 馬式右衝捶 *Ma Suh You Chong Chuei*. Strike with the right arm advancing in Horseback riding stance

- 14 • 捆封連環拳 *Kuen Feng Lienhuan Chuan.* Wrap and close in a continuous sequence of punches

- 15 • 回身連環劈 *Huei Shen Lienhuan Pi.* Continuous sequence of diagonal strikes

1

2

- 16 • 虛步破骨手 *Hsu Pu Po Ku Shou.* Empty step and break the bone of the hand

1

- 17 - 左右虎抱頭 *Tzuo You Hu Pao Tou.* The tiger covers its head on both sides

1

2

3

4

5

6

• 18 • 右勾摟採手 *You Kou Lou Tsai Shou*. *Kou, Lou, Tsai* with the right arm

- 19 • 順風掃葉式 *Shuen Feng Sho Ye Suh.* Sweep the leaves following the direction of the wind

1

2

3

4

5

6

- 20 - 採手鎖口捶 *Tsai Shou Suo Kou Chuei.* Pluck the arm and lock the mouth fist

• 21 • 閉截手崩捶 *Pi Chie Shou Peng Chuei.* Closing that chops and rebound strike

1

2

3

4

5

- 22 - 偷手漏進捶 *Tou Shou Lou Chin Chuei.* Hidden hand and sneaking fist

- 23 - 崩捶左頂膝 *Peng Chuei Tzuo Ting Hsi.* Rebound fist and left upward knee

2

3

• 24 • 白猿偷桃式 *Pai Yuan tou Tao Suh.* White monkey steals the peach

1

2

3

4

- 25 - 摟手拗步捶 *Lou Shou Ao Pu Chuei*. Embracing hand and traverse step punch

- 26 - 封手二起腳 *Feng Shou Er Chi Chiao*. Hands clap, double kick in the air.

1

2

3

4

5

6

- 27 - 仆腿下身式 *Pu Tuei Hsiao Shen Suh.* Low feet with lowered body

- 28 - 登山雙叫掌 *Tang Shan Shuang Chiao Chang.* Mountain climbing step with double calling hand

- 29 • 右後掃膛腳 *You Hou Sao Tang Chiao*. Back sweeping kick with right leg

- 30 • 雙綑左坐肘 *Shuang Kuen Tzuo Tzuo Chou.* Double tie and sitting elbow strike

- 31 • 回身閉接手 *Huei Shen Pi Chie Shou.* Turn with *Pi Chie* hand

- 32 - 轆轤偷心捶 *Lu Lu Tou Hsin Chuei*. Winch arm and punch that hides the heart

• 33 • 崩捶偷心捶 *Peng Chuei Tou Hsin Chuei*. Rebound strike and punch that hides the heart

7

- 34 • 雙封腰斬式 *Shuan Feng Yao Chan Suh*. Double closing and cut the waist

1

2

3

3 Front view

7 Front view

• 35 • 前後拗步捶 *Chien Hou Ao Pu Chuei.* Traverse step fist toward the front and the back

1

2

3

4

5

6

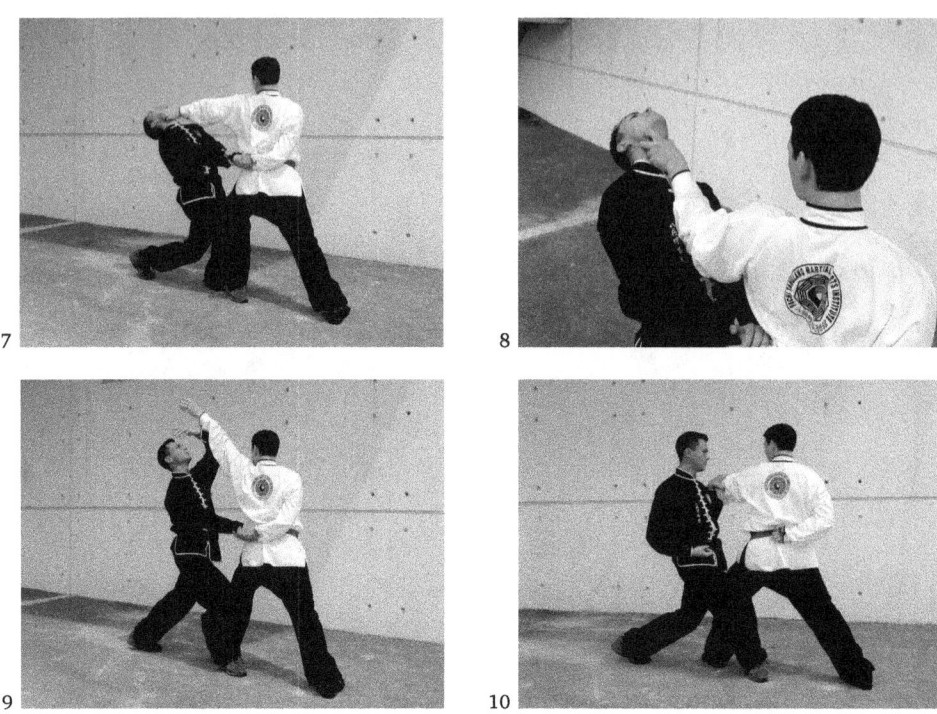

• 36 • 纏絲連環腿 *Chan Si Lienhuan Tuei*. Continuous sequence of silk reeling kick

• 37 • 背後虎尾腳 *Pei Hou Hu Wei Chiao*. Backward tiger tail kick

- 38 • 寒雞式蓋捶 *Han Chi Suh Kai Chuei.* Cold Rooster stance and covering fist

- 39 • 退步跨虎式 *Tuei Pu Kua Hu Suh.* Retreat a step to mount the tiger (protect the hip)

- **40** • 退步停身式 *Tuei Pu Tin Shen Suh*. Retreat a step and finish with both hands and collect the energy

3

4

5

6

Epilogue

In this book we have sketched the foundations of *Tanglang Chuan* and *Pachi–Pikua Chuan*. Each of these styles would deserve at least one whole book in its own right. I might write them one day. In order to write a book we must be knowledgeable in what we intend to write about. Knowing only a basic form does not give us the capacity to write a whole book about the form and its implications. With this I am referring to the book on the *Miaotao* edited by Mr Carlos García García (21/12/68).

In the *Pachi Tanglang Martial Arts Institute* I teach the following double hand sword forms: *Miaotao Chipen Si Lu, Chirin Miaotao* and *Chimen Shuang Shou Chien*.

Master Su performs *Chi Men Shuang Shou Chien*.

Group of students at the 2005-2006 international seminar held in Palma de Mallorca, where Master Su taught the form *Chi Men Shuang Shou Chien*.

Pachi-Pikua Curriculum

黃色 YELLOW (10–9 chi)

拳譜 FORMS

1. 三盤架法 SAN PAN CHIA HUA
   Stance Practice (*Pachi Chuan*)

2. 三肘法 SAN CHOU HUA
   Three Basic Elbows (*Pachi Chuan*)

3. 丁字八式拳 TING TZU PA SU CHUAN
   Eight Forms to generate Energy in a Triangle (*Pachi Chuan*)

器械 WEAPONS

4. 劈掛基本十二刀法 PIKUA CHIPEN SHIH ERH TAO HUA
   Twelve Basic Broadsword Techniques of *Pikua*

氣功 CHI KUNG

5. 劈掛十八動透勁功 PIKUA SHIH PA TONG TOU CHING KONG (1–5)
   18 Grinding Movements to Deepen the Energy of *Pikua*

6. 養生還原法 YANG SUN YEN HUAN HUA
   Techniques to Maintain Health and Recover Youth

橙色 ORANGE (8–7 CHI)

拳譜 FORMS

7. 開門拳（對練領招） KAIMEN CHUAN (TUEIREN)
   Opening the Door Form, two-man set (*Pachi Chuan*)

8. 金剛八式拳 CHIN KAN PA SU CHUAN
   Eight Directions like a Diamond Form (*Pachi Chuan*)

9. 劈掛基本六路 PIKUA CHIPEN LIU LU
   Six Basic Lines of *Pikua*

器械 WEAPONS

10. 劈掛基本十二刀法 PIKUA CHIPEN SHIH ERH TAO HUA
    Twelve Basic Broadsword Techniques of *Pikua*

氣功 CHI KUNG

11. 劈掛十八動透勁功 PIKUA SHIH PA TONG TOU CHING KONG (6–10)
    18 Grinding Movements to Deepen the Energy of *Pikua*

綠色 GREEN (6–5 CHI)

拳譜 FORMS

12. 金剛拳（對練領招） CHINKAN CHUAN (TUEIREN)
    Diamond Form, two-man set (*Pachi Chuan*)

13. 劈掛基本六路對練領招 *Pikua Chipen Liu Lu Tueiren*
    Two-man set of the Six Basic Lines of *Pikua*

器械 WEAPONS

14. 基本十劍法 CHIPEN SHIH CHIEN HUA
    Ten Basic Straight Sword Techniques

氣功 CHI KUNG

15. 劈掛十八動透勁功 PIKUA SHIH PA TONG TOU CHING KONG (11–15)
    18 Grinding Movements to Deepen the Energy of *Pikua*

蓝色 BLUE (4–3 CHI)

拳譜 FORMS

16. 小八極拳第一套 HSIAO PACHI CHUAN TI I TAO
    Small *Pachi* Form, First Level

17. 風磨掌拳 FONG MO CHANG CHUAN
    Wind Mill Arms (*Pikua Chang*)

器械 WEAPONS

18. 基本十劍法 CHIPEN SHIH CHIEN HUA
    Ten Basic Straight Sword Techniques

氣功 CHI KUNG

19. 劈掛十八動透勁功 PIKUA SHIH PA TONG TOU CHING KONG (16–18)
    18 Grinding Movements to Deepen the Energy of *Pikua*

紅色 RED (2–1 CHI)

拳譜 FORMS

20. 小八極拳 第二套 HSIAO PACHI CHUAN TI ERH TAO
    Small *Pachi* Form, Second Level

21. 風磨掌拳對練領招 FONG MO CHANG CHUAN TUEIREN
    Two-man set of the Wind Mill Arms (*Pikua Chang*)

器械 WEAPONS

22. 基本十劍法 CHIPEN SHIH CHIEN HUA
    Ten Basic Straight Sword Techniques

氣功 CHI KUNG

23. 劈掛十八動透勁功 PIKUA SHIH PA TONG TOU CHING KONG (1–18)
    18 Grinding Movements to Deepen the Energy of *Pikua*

黑色 BLACK 1 TUAN

拳譜 FORMS

24. 大八極拳 第一套（對練） TA PACHI CHUAN TI I TAO (TUEIREN)
    Great Pachi Form, First Level (two-man set)

25. 劈掛第一路 PIKUA TI I LU
    First Form of *Pikua*

器械 WEAPONS

26. 昆吾劍 KUN WU CHIEN
    Kun Wu Straight Sword

27. 劈掛單刀 PIKUA TANTAO
    Pikua Broadsword

氣功 CHI KUNG

28. 八趟伸筋滲骨功 PA TANG SHEN CHIN TO KU KONG (1–2)
    Eight lines of techniques to stretch the tendons and let the energy enter the bones.

黑色 BLACK 2 TUAN

拳譜 FORMS

29. 大八極拳 第二套 TA PACHI CHUAN TI ERH TAO
    Great *Pachi* Form, Second Level

30. 劈掛第二路 PIKUA TI ERH LU
    Second Form of *Pikua*

器械 WEAPONS

31. 夜戰刀 YEH TSAN TAO
    Nocturnal Fighting Broadsword

32. 劈掛風磨雙刀 PIKUA FONG MO SHUANG TAO
    Wind Mill Double Broadsword of *Pikua*

氣功 CHI KUNG

33. 八趟伸筋滲骨功 PA TANG SHEN CHIN TO KU KONG (3–4)
    Eight lines of techniques to stretch the tendons and let the energy enter the bones.

黑色 BLACK 3 TUAN

拳譜 FORMS

34. 六大開拳 LIU TA KAI CHUAN
    Six Great Openings Form (*Pachi Chuan*)

35. 六大連招拳（對練） LIU TA LIEN TSAO CHUAN (TUEIREN)
    Combined Form of the Six Great Openings, two-man set (*Pachi Chuan*)

36. 劈掛第三路 PIKUA TI SAN LU
    Third Form of *Pikua*

器械 WEAPONS

37. 八極劍 PACHI CHIEN
    Pachi Straight Sword

38. 六合大槍 LIU HOE TA CHIANG
    Six Harmonies Long Spear

39. 劈掛風磨棍 PIKUA FONG MO KUN
    Pikua Wind Mill Staff

氣功 CHI KUNG

40. 八趟伸筋滲骨功 PA TANG SHEN CHIN TO KU KONG (5–6)
    Eight lines of techniques to stretch the tendons and let the energy enter the bones.

黑色 BLACK 4 TUAN

拳譜 FORMS

41. 六大硬架拳 LIU TA IN CHA CHUAN
    Six Great Defences Form (*Pachi Chuan*)

42. 熊虎合一拳 SHIONG HU HO I CHUAN
    Uniting the Bear and Tiger Form (*Pachi Chuan*)

43. 劈掛滲八極拳（拆招對擊） PIKUA CHAAN PACHI CHUAN
    Pikua United with *Pachi* Form (Individual Techniques for combat)

44. 小八極拳 第三套 HSIAO PACHI CHUAN TI SAN TAO
    Small *Pachi* Form, Third Level

器械 WEAPONS

45. 八極劍 PACHI CHIEN
    Pachi Straight Sword

46. 六合大槍 LIU HOE TA CHIANG
    Six Harmonies Long Spear

47. 劈掛摔手棍 PIKUA SHUAI SHOU KUN
    Pikua Throwing Down Arms Staff

氣功 CHI KUNG

48. 八趟伸筋滲骨功 PA TANG SHEN CHIN TO KU KONG (7–8)

黑色 BLACK 5 TUAN

拳譜 FORMS

49. 八極連環拳母架式（對練）
    PACHI LIEN HUAN CHUAN MU CHIA SU (TUEIREN)
    Pachi Chuan Linking Form Mother Form (two-man set)

器械 WEAPONS

50. 八極劍 PACHI CHIEN
    Pachi Straight Sword

51. 六合大槍 LIU HOE TA CHIANG
    Six Harmonies Long Spear

氣功 CHI KUNG

52. 十四經絡流注導氣法 SHIH SHU CHING LU LIO TSU TAO CHI HUA
    Techniques to Circulate the Energy through the 14 Meridians

黑色 BLACK 6 TUAN

拳譜 FORMS

53. 連環屬性拳 LIENHUAN SUH SHING CHUAN
    Projection of Energy Techniques of the 5 Elements (one person studies one energy)
    金功 CHIN KONG Metal Technique · 水功 SHUEI KONG Water Technique · 木功 MU KONG Wood Technique · 火功 HUO KONG Fire Technique · 土功 TU KONG Earth Technique

器械 WEAPONS

54. 六合大槍 LIU HOE TA CHIANG
    Six Harmonies Long Spear

氣功 CHI KUNG

55. 十四經絡流注導氣法 SHIH SHU CHING LU LIO TSU TAO CHI HUA
    Techniques to Circulate the Energy through the 14 Meridians

黑色 BLACK 7 TUAN

拳譜 FORMS

56. 六肘頭拳（對練） LIU CHOU TOH CHUAN (TUEIREN)
    Six Short Elbows Form (two-man set)

器械 WEAPONS

57. 六合大槍 LIU HOE TA CHIANG
    Six Harmonies Long Spear

氣功 CHI KUNG

58. 十四經絡流注導氣法 SHIH SHU CHING LU LIO TSU TAO CHI HUA
    Techniques to Circulate the Energy through the 14 Meridians

59. 八極拳八方位六十四掌秘圖
    PACHI CHUAN PA FANG HUEI LIO SHIH SU CHANG MI TU
    Secret map of 64 hand tecniques in 8 directions of *Pachi Chuan*

黑色 BLACK 8 TUAN

拳譜 FORMS

60. 蘇式八趟應手拳 SU SUH PA TANG ING SHOU CHUAN
    Su Style Eight Lines of *Ing Shou* (*Pachi Chuan*)

器械 WEAPONS

61. 六合大槍 LIU HOE TA CHIANG
    Six Harmonies Long Spear

氣功 CHI KUNG

62. 十四經絡流注導氣法 SHIH SHU CHING LU LIO TSU TAO CHI HUA
    Techniques to Circulate the Energy through the 14 Meridians

63. 八極拳八方位六十四掌秘圖
    PACHI CHUAN PA FANG HUEI LIO SHIH SU CHANG MI TU
    Secret map of 64 hand tecniques in 8 directions of *Pachi Chuan*

黑色 BLACK 9 TUAN

拳譜 FORMS

64. 八大招式(個人各別八種絕招) PA TA CHAO SUH
    Eight Great Techniques Form. The Master will teach the student eight unique combat techniques.

器械 WEAPONS

65. 六合大槍 LIU HOE TA CHIANG
    Six Harmonies Long Spear

氣功 CHI KUNG

66. 十四經絡流注導氣法 SHIH SHU CHING LU LIO TSU TAO CHI HUA
    Techniques to Circulate the Energy through the 14 Meridians

67. 八極拳八方位六十四掌秘圖
    PACHI CHUAN PA FANG HUEI LIO SHIH SU CHANG MI TU
    Secret map of 64 hand tecniques in 8 directions of *Pachi Chuan*

Genealogy of *Pachi-Pikua Chuan*

Kuan Tsun-Tzi — Practiced a Kung Fu system with characteristics very similar to *Pachi Chuan*.

Huang Ti (2697 – 2599 BC) — Conceived techniques which he called *Pa Men Hsiong Chang Chuan* and taught them to his army. Huang Ti was the first emperor of China.

Pang Tsu (? – 2333 BC) — Practiced *Pa Tze Chuan*, the ancient name of *Pachi Chuan*.

Chou Tong (? – 1120 AD) — Monk who taught *Pachi Chuan* to the young Yueh Fei.

Yueh Fei (1103 – 1142 AD) — He created *Hsing-I Chuan* based on his *Pachi Chuan* knowledge and later taught it to his army.

Chi Chi-Kuan (1528 – 1587 BC) — Wrote an official military treatise, the *Chi Hsiao Hsin Shu*, where he mentions the systems *Pachi Chuan*, *Pikua Chuan*, and *Tanglang Chuan*.

Until here, the genealogy is not very clear. However, names and facts are taken from military or historic documents.

PIKUA CHUAN

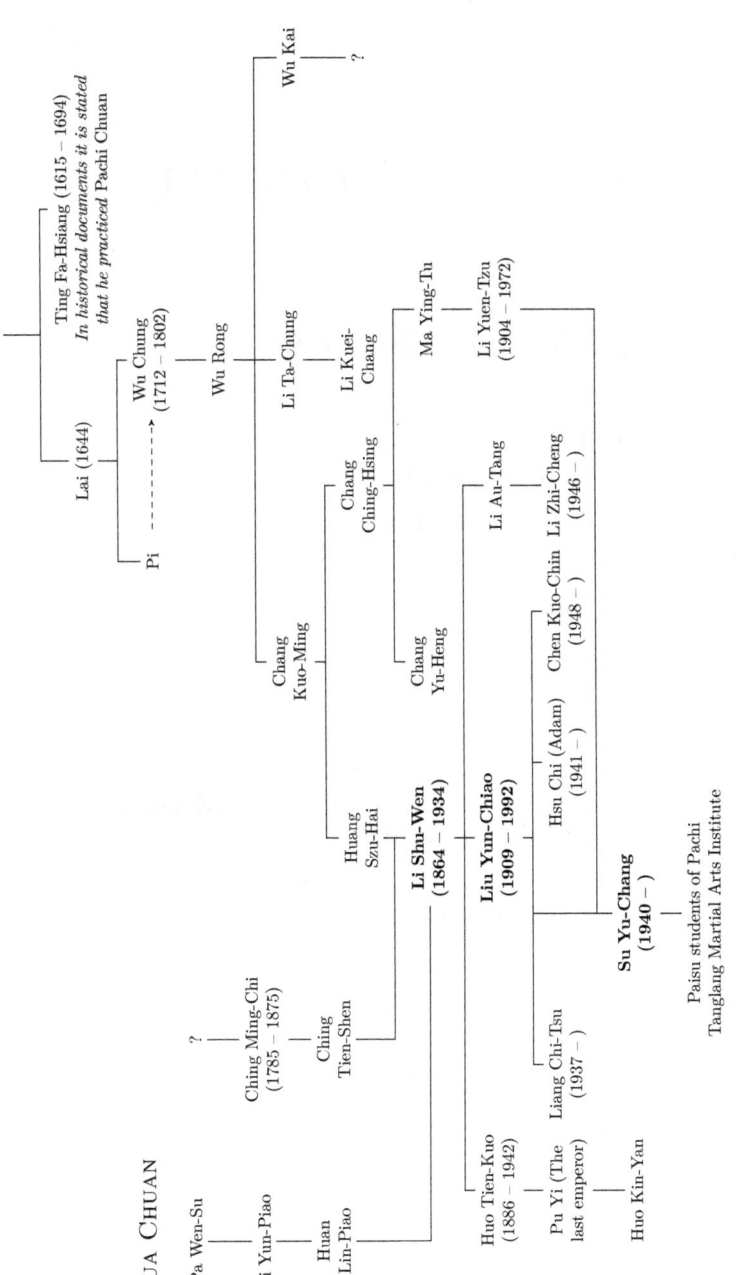

Praying Mantis Curriculum

黃色 Yellow (10–9 chi)

拳譜 Forms

1. 十二字訣 Shih Er Tzu Chie
   12 Fundamental techniques (two-man set)

2. 基本十二路拳（對練）Chipen Shih Er Lu Chuan (Tueiren)
   Twelve Basic Lines (two-man set)

   (a) *Chishing/Meihua*: 12 Basics

   (b) *Papu*: 12 Basics

   (c) *Liohoe*: 12 Basics

   (d) *Pimen*: 12 Basics

   Beginners will only learn a basic mix of all five styles; black belt students will study others for a deeper study of a given style.

3. 螳螂出洞（對練）Tanglang Tsu Dong (Tueiren)
   Linking form and two-man set of the basic lines.

4. 力劈拳（對練）Lipi Chuan (Tueiren)
   Strong Strikes form, two-man set (*Papu Tanglang*)

氣功 Chi Kung

5. 五勢舒氣法 Wu Su Shu Chi Hua
   Five Ways to Relax the Energy (*Chihsing Tanglang*)

6. 輕功提縱術 Chin Kong Ti Tong Su
   Light Body to Jump High (*Pimen Tanglang*)

橙色 ORANGE (8–7 chi)

拳譜 FORMS

7. 小虎燕拳（對練）Hsiao Huyuen Chuan (Tueiren)
   Small Tiger Swallow (two-man set). There are three levels, Small, Middle and Big. All are to be studied here (*Chihsing Tanglang*).

8. 小番車拳 Hsiao Fan Che Chuan
   Small Windmill Form (*Papu Tanglang*)

器械 WEAPONS

9. 苗刀基本四路（對練）Miao Tao Chipen Suh Lu (Tueiren)
   Sprout Sword four basic lines, two-man set (*Pimen Tanglang*)

氣功 CHI KUNG

10. 神勇八段錦 Shen Yung Pa Tuen Chin
    Eight Movements of Chikung of the Powerful Saint
    (*Pimen Tanglang/Chihsing Tanglang*)

綠色 GREEN (6–5 chi) (Intermediate)

拳譜 FORMS

11. 插捶拳 Chachuei Chuan
    Penetrating Fist (*Chihsing Tanglang*)

12. 崩步拳（對練）Peng Pu Chuan (Tueiren)
    Demolishing Step, two-man set (*Chihsing Tanglang/Pimen Tanglang*)

器械 WEAPONS

13. 十八單刀法 Shih Pa Tantao Hua
    Eighteen Broadsword Techniques (*Pimen Tanglang*)

14. 五虎攔門刀 Wu Hu Lan Men Tao
    Five Tigers Guarding the Gate Broadsword (*Pimen Tanglang*)

15. 單刀破單刀（十八單刀法對練）
    Tantao Po Tantao (Shih Pa Tantao Hua Tueiren)
    Broadsword against Broadsword (*Chihsing Tanglang*)

16. 瘋魔棍 Hong Mo Kun
    Crazy Devil Staff (*Chihsing Tanglang*)

17. 短梢子棍（雙節棍）Tuan Sao Tsu Kun (Shuang Che Kun)
    Short Sprout Sticks [Two-Section Staff/Nunchakus] (*Chihsing Tanglang*)

氣功 CHI KUNG

18. 排打淨身功 PAI TA CHING SHEN KONG
    Strike to Clean the Body (*Papu Tanglang/Pimen Tanglang*)

19. 三回九轉還陽法 SAN HUEI CHIO TUAN HAI YANG HUA
    Three Returns and Nine Circles to come back to the Yang Place
    (*Chihsing Tanglang/Papu Tanglang*)

藍色 BLUE (4–3 chi)

拳譜 FORMS

20. 螳螂手拳（分三段） TANGLANG SHOU CHUAN (FUN SAN TUAN)
    Mantis Hands Form (There are three levels) (*Pimen Tanglang*)

21. 摘盔拳 CHAIKUEI CHUAN
    To Rip Off the Helmet (*Chihsing Tanglang*)

22. 白猿出洞拳 PAI YUEN TSU TONG CHUAN
    The White Monkey Exits the Cave (*Chihsing Tanglang*)

23. 八剛拳法 PA KANG CHUAN HUA
    Eight hard fighting techniques (*Chihsing Tanglang*)

器械 WEAPONS

24. 空手奪單刀 KONG SHOU TUO TAN TAO
    Empty Hand against Broadsword (*Chihsing Tanglang*)

25. 黑虎槍 HEI HU CHIANG
    Black Tiger Spear (*Chihsing Tanglang*)

26. 棍對棍 KUN TUEI KUN
    Basic lines of staff against staff (*Chihsing Tanglang/Papu Tanglang/Pimen Tanglang*)

27. 六合單刀 LIOHOE TANTAO
    Liohoe Broadsword (*Liohoe Tanglang*)

28. 六合雙刀 LIOHOE SHUANG TAO
    Liohoe Double Broadsword (*Liohoe Tanglang*)

29. 擒猿短棒 CHIA YUEN TUN PAN
    Short Staff Catches the Monkey (*Pimen Tanglang*)

30. 螳螂青鋒劍 TANGLANG CHING FONG CHIEN
    Praying Mantis Green Rays Straight Sword (*Pimen Tanglang*)

紅色 RED (2–1 chi)

拳譜 FORMS

31. 大番車拳 TA FAN CHE CHUAN
    Big Windmill Form (*Papu Tanglang*)

32. 四路奔打拳 SUH LU PENTA CHUAN
    Rapid Strikes in all directions (*Chihsing Tanglang*)

33. 梅花落拳 MEIHUA LO CHUAN
    Falling Plum Flower (*Meihua Tanglang*)

34. 擒拿對打 CHIN NA TUEI TA
    Joint locks, two-man set (*Pimen Tanglang*)

35. 總敵拳（對練）TSONG TI CHUAN (TUEIREN)
    Against any enemy (*Chihsing Tanglang*)

36. 十二路拍按（破案）連手 SHIH ER LU PAIAN (POAN) LIEN SHOU
    12 Lines of Poan (two-man). 1–6 up to red belt (*Papu Tanglang*)

37. 十二柔手法 SHIH ER ROU SHOU HUA
    Twelve soft fighting techniques (*Chihsing Tanglang*)

器械 WEAPONS

38. 單刀破花槍 TANTAO PO HUA CHIANG
    Broadsword against Spear (*Pimen Tanglang*)

39. 逍遙鐵扇 HSIAO YAO TE SAN
    "Hsiao Yao" Iron Fan (*Chihsing Tanglang*)

氣功 CHI KUNG

40. 十八羅漢功 SHIH PA LOHAN KONG
    Eighteen Lohan Saints Chikung (*Pimen Tanglang/Chihsing Tanglang*)

黑色 BLACK 1 Tuan (Advanced)

拳譜 FORMS

41. 八步摘要第一路拳 PAPU CHOYAO TI I LU CHUAN
    First Summary Form of Eight Step Praying Mantis

42. 攔截拳 LAN CHIE CHUAN
    Block and Intercept (*Chihsing Tanglang/Pimen Tanglang*)

43. 鐵齒拳 TIE CHI CHUAN
    Iron Teeth Form (*Liohoe Tanglang*)

44. 十二路拍按（破案）連手 SHIH ER LU PAIAN (POAN) LIEN SHOU
    12 Lines of Poan, two-man sets. 7–12 from black belt onwards (*Papu Tanglang*)

器械 WEAPONS

45. 雁翎刀 YEN LING TAO
    Goose Feather Broadsword (*Liohoe Tanglang*)

46. 滾趟雙刀 KUN TANG SHUANG TAO
    Double Broadsword Comes in Contact with the Ground (*Chihsing Tanglang*)

47. 十八大槍法 SHIH PA TA CHIANG HUA
    Eighteen Long-Spear Techniques (*Chihsing Tanglang*)

48. 斷門槍 TUAN MEN CHIANG
    Spear that Blocks the Way Like a Door (*Pimen Tanglang*)

49. 螳螂劍 TANGLANG CHIEN
    Mantis Straight Sword (*Chihsing Tanglang*)

50. 三節棍 SAN CHE KUN
    Three Sectioned Staff (*Chihsing Tanglang*)

黑色 BLACK 2 Tuan

拳譜 FORMS

51. 八步摘要第二路拳 PAPU CHOYAO TI ER LU CHUAN
    Second Summary Form of Eight Step Praying Mantis

52. 七星摘要第一路拳 CHIHSING CHOYAO TI I LU CHUAN
    First Summary Form of Seven Star Praying Mantis

53. 六合短捶拳（對練） LIOHOE TUAN CHUEI CHUAN (TUEIREN)
    Short Distance Strikes Form of Six Harmonies Praying Mantis, two-man set

54. 秘門摘要第一路拳 PIMEN CHOYAO TI I LU CHUAN
    First Summary Form of Secret Door Praying Mantis

55. 醉羅漢拳 TSUEI LOHAN CHUAN
    Drunken Lohan Saint (*Chihsing Tanglang/Pimen Tanglang*)

器械 WEAPONS

56. 九節鞭 CHIO CHE PEN
    Basics of Nine Sectioned Whip (*Chihsing Tanglang*)

57. 螳螂扒棍 TANGLANG PA KUN
    Short Mantis Staffs (*Pimen Tanglang*)

58. 楊家槍 YANG CHIA CHIANG
    Yang Style Spear (*Chihsing Tanglang*)

59. 八仙劍 PA SHEN CHIEN
    Eight Saints Straight Sword (*Papu Tanglang*)

60. 雙刀破槍 SHUANG TAO PO CHIANG
    Double Broadsword against Spear (*Chihsing Tanglang*)

61. 三節棍對花槍 SAN CHE KUN TUEI HUA CHIANG
    Three Sectioned Staff Against Spear (*Chihsing Tanglang*)

黑色 BLACK 3 Tuan

拳譜 FORMS

62. 八步摘要第三路拳 PAPU CHOYAO TI SAN LU CHUAN
    Third Summary Form of Eight Step Praying Mantis

63. 螳螂八肘第一路拳 TANGLANG PA CHOU TI I LU CHUAN
    First Form of the Eight Elbows (*Chihsing Tanglang*)

64. 善手奔拳 SAN SHOU PEN CHUAN
    Hand Techniques to Reach (*Liohoe Tanglang*)

65. 八打八不打秘法 PA TA PA BU TA MI HUA
    Eight Attacks and Eight Secret Attacks (*Chihsing Tanglang*)

器械 WEAPONS

66. 二十四趟單刀對擊法 ER SHIH SUH TANG TANTAO TUEI CHI HUA
    Two-man set of the Twenty Four Lines of Broadsword. Advanced techniques (*Chihsing Tanglang*)

67. 白猿棍 PAI YUEN KUN
    White Monkey Staff (*Papu Tanglang*)

68. 純陽劍 SUN YANG CHIEN
    Purely Yang Straight Sword (*Liohoe Tanglang*)

69. 暗器飛鏢 ANCHI FEI PIAO
    Hidden throwing weapons (*Pimen Tanglang*)

70. 蝴蝶雙劍 HU TEH SHUANG CHIEN
    Butterfly Double Straight Sword (*Chihsing Tanglang*)

71. 繩鏢 SHENG PIAO
    Dart on a String (*Chihsing Tanglang*)

黑色 BLACK 4 Tuan

拳譜 FORMS

72. 八步摘要第四路拳 PAPU CHOYAO TI SUH LU CHUAN
    Fourth Summary Form of Eight Step Praying Mantis

73. 七星摘要第二路拳 CHIHSING CHOYAO TI ER LU CHUAN
    Second Summary Form of Seven Star Praying Mantis

74. 秘門摘要第二路拳 Pimen Choyao Ti Er Lu Chuan
    Second Summary Form of Secret Door Praying Mantis

器械 Weapons

75. 黎花槍 Li Hua Chiang
    Pear Flower Spear (*Liohoe Tanglang*)
76. 驚虹九節鞭 Chin Hong Chio Che Pen
    Rainbow Nine sectioned Whip (*Pimen Tanglang*)
77. 九節鞭擒刀 Chio Che Pen Chin Tao
    Nine Sectioned Whip Removes the Broadsword (*Pimen Tanglang*)
78. 空手入白刃 Kong Shou Ru Pai Ren
    Empty Hand against Knife (*Papu Tanglang*)

黑色 BLACK 5 Tuan

拳譜 Forms

79. 八步摘要第五路拳 Papu Choyao Ti Wu Lu Chuan
    Fifth Summary Form of Eight Step Praying Mantis
80. 七星摘要第三路拳 Chihsing Choyao Ti San Lu Chuan
    Third Summary Form of Seven Star Praying Mantis
81. 鏡裡藏花拳 Chin Li Tsang Hua Chuan
    Hidden Flowers in the Sleeve Form (*Liohoe Tanglang*)

器械 Weapons

82. 六會棍 Liohoe Kun
    Six Harmonies Staff (*Liohoe Tanglang*)
83. 雙飛短劍 Shuang Hue Tuan Chien
    Double Short Throwing Straight Swords (*Chihsing Tanglang*)
84. 麒麟苗刀 Chilin Miao Tao
    Chilin (Unicorn) Sprout Sword (*Pimen Tanglang*)

黑色 BLACK 6 Tuan

拳譜 Forms

85. 八步摘要第六路拳 Papu Choyao Ti Lio Lu Chuan
    Sixth Summary Form of Eight Step Praying Mantis
86. 七星摘要第四路拳 Chihsing Choyao Ti Suh Lu Chuan
    Fourth Summary Form of Seven Star Praying Mantis
87. 秘門摘要第三路拳 Pimen Choyao Ti San Lu Chuan
    Third Summary Form of Secret Door Praying Mantis

器械 WEAPONS

88. 奇門雙手劍 CHI MEN SHUANG SHOU CHIEN
    Double Handed *Chi Men* Long Sword (*Pimen Tanglang*)

89. 摔手棍 SHUAI SHOU KUN
    Shaking Hands Staff (*Papu Tanglang*)

氣功 CHI KUNG

90. 六底仙十四動功 LIO TI SHEN SHIH SUH TONG KONG
    Fourteen Movements of Six Saints Chikung (*Chihsing Tanglang*)

黑色 BLACK 7 Tuan

拳譜 FORMS

91. 七星摘要第五路拳 CHIHSING CHOYAO TI WU LU CHUAN
    Fifth Summary Form of Seven Star Praying Mantis

92. 螳螂八肘第二路拳 TANGLANG PA CHOU TI ER LU CHUAN
    Second Form of the Eight Elbows (*Chihsing Tanglang*)

93. 截手圈拳 CHIE SHOU CHUAN CHUAN
    Circle Intercepting Hands (Putting on the Bracelet) (*Liohoe Tanglang*)

94. 秘手九十式手法 MI SHOU CHIO SHIH SUH SHOU HUA
    Ninety Secret Hand Techniques (first part) (*Pimen Tanglang*)

器械 WEAPONS

95. 燕青單刀 YEN CHING TANTAO
    Swallow Broadsword (*Chihsing Tanglang*)

96. 六合槍 LIOHOE CHIANG
    Six Harmony Spear (*Liohoe Tanglang/Chihsing Tanglang*)

97. 暗器袖裏箭 ANCHI HSIU LI CHIEN
    Hidden Weapon, Arrow Inside the Sleeve (*Pimen Tanglang*)

黑色 BLACK 8 Tuan

拳譜 FORMS

98. 七星摘要第六路拳 CHIHSING CHOYAO TI LIO LU CHUAN
    Sixth Summary Form of Seven Star Praying Mantis

99. 螳螂八肘第三路拳 TANGLANG PA CHOU TI SAN LU CHUAN
    Third Form of the Eight Elbows (*Chihsing Tanglang*)

100. 葉底藏花拳（照面燈拳）Ye Ti Chang Hua Chuan (Chao Mien Tang Chuan)
    Flower Hidden Under the Leaves
    (Using the Lantern to Illuminate the Face) (*Liohoe Tanglang*)

101. 秘手九十式手法 Mi Shou Chio Shih Suh Shou Hua
    Ninety Secret Hand Techniques (second part) (*Pimen Tanglang*)

器械 WEAPONS

102. 夜戰單刀對練 Ye Tsan Tantao Tueiren
    Nocturnal Broadsword, two-man set (*Chihsing Tanglang*)

氣功 CHI KUNG

103. 禪坐道功法 Chan Cho Tao Kong Hua
    Seated Meditation with Taoist Techniques (*Papu Tanglang*)

黑色 BLACK 9 Tuan

拳譜 FORMS

104. 秘手九十式手法 Mi Shou Chio Shih Suh Shou Hua
    Ninety Secret Hand Techniques (third part) (*Pimen Tanglang*)

105. 七星摘要第七路拳 Chihsing Choyao Ti Chi Tuan Chuan
    Seventh Summary Form of Seven Star Praying Mantis

106. 分身八短拳 Fun Shun Pa Tuan Chuan
    Eight Strikes to Hit Separate Bodies [First, Second and Third] (*Chihsing Tanglang*)
    密肘藏手拳 Mi Chou Chan Shou Chuan
    Repetitive Elbows Hide the Hand (*Pimen Tanglang*)
    —These two are in fact the same form but with different names in each style.

107. 雙封拳 Shuang Fong Chuan
    Double Lock Form (*Liohoe Tanglang*)

器械 WEAPONS

108. 梅花暗器 Meihua Anchi
    Plum Flower hidden weapon (*Meihua Tanglang*)

氣功 CHI KUNG

109. 三清真人成仙術 San Chin Tsun Ren Cheng Shen Su
    Three Taoist Wise Men teach how to become a Saint (*Chihsing Tanglang*)

氣功 SPECIAL

110. 錯骨截脈術 Tso Ku Chi Me Su
    Open the Joints to Stop Blood Circulation (*Pimen Tanglang*)

Genealogy of Tanglang Chuan

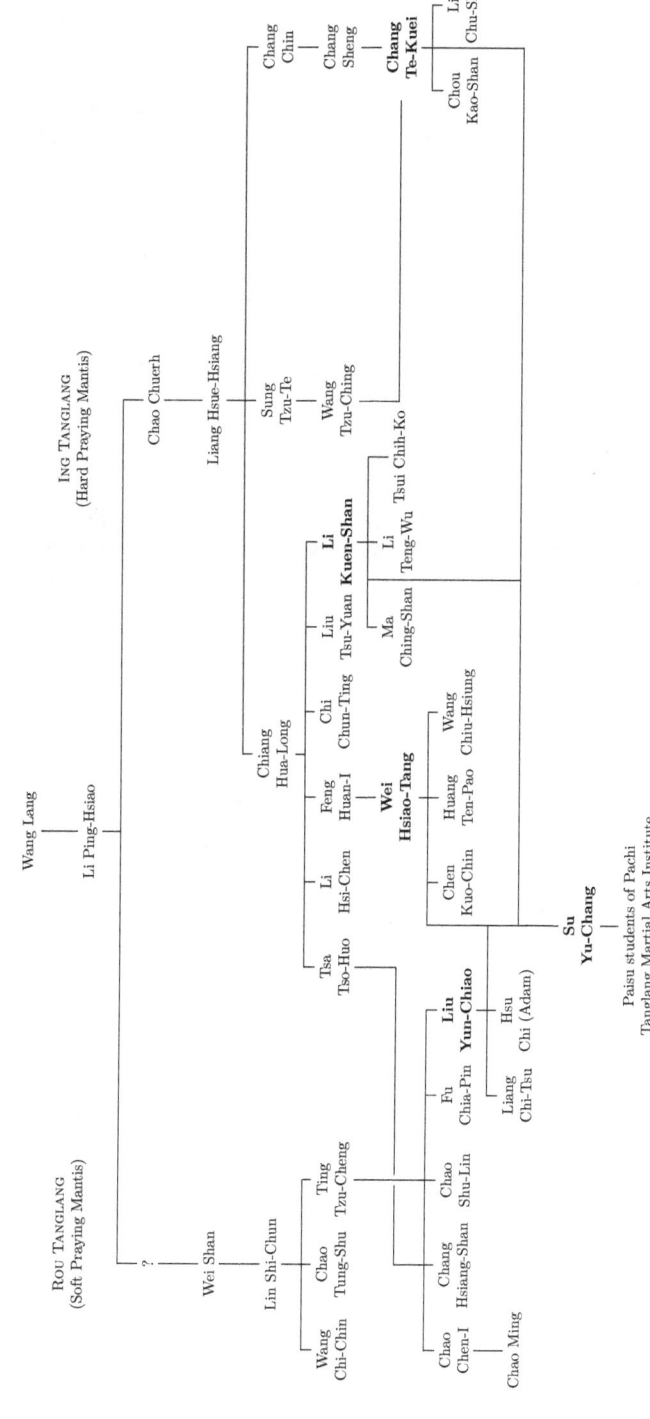

Paisu Students of Pachi Tanglang Martial Arts Institute

European Group

Francisco Orejudo, Monica Florit, Pere Mayol, Rita Lliteras, Tomeu Cloquell, Catalina Trobat, Baltasar Martínez, Remedios Artacho, Jaume Cloquell, Sebastian Cloquell, Juan Manuel Cano, Manuel Vega, José Antonio Bonilla, Eva Ocaña, Miguel García, Zaidah Bellod, Iraima Orejudo, Guillermo Arroyo, Rubens Cano, I-Ting Su, Marit Ramberg, María Isidora Santiago, José Antonio De Paz, Pedro Mayol Bauza, Marian Lemmen, Roland Smit, Robbert De Bruin, Jan Harteveld, Juan Acevedo.

USA and Canada

Jason Tsou, Kurt Wong, Tony Yang, John Hum, Wei-Jen Su, Yasushi Kanetake, Chi-Kai Shum, Cary Wei Kung, Daisaku Nagumo.

South America

Roberto Orozco, Elsa Fernández, Gladys Morando, Getulio Aguilera, Marisol Calzadillas, Daisy Pellicer, Eduardo Ng, Juan Goncalves, Tse Pok-Man, Manuel Bárcenas, Alejandro Bárcenas, Cristóbal Rodríguez.

♦

Asian students will appear when the book is published in their respective countries.

Glossary

We hope that the following glossary, including the pinyin transcription and the traditional Chinese characters of the most important terms and names, will be of help to the readers in more than one way.

Adam Hsu	Xú Jì	徐纪	*Pakua Chang*, *Pachi Chuan* and *Pikua Chuan* master. Liu Yun-Chiao's disciple.
An Ching	Àn Jìng	暗勁	Technique that strikes when the fist is already in contact with the opponent.
Cha Chuan	Chá Quán	查拳	Islamic Long Fist, Martial Arts style.
Chan	Chán	禪	Buddhist school founded by Bodhidharma. In Japan, *Zen*.
Chan Suh Ching	Chán Sī Jìng	纏絲勁	Spiraling energy, "silk reeling".
Chang Chi-Chiang	Zhāng Zhī Jiāng	張之江	Founder of the Nanking Central Kuoshu Institute.
Chang Ching-Hsing	Zhāng Jǐngxīng	張景星	*Pachi Chuan* master, Chang Kuo-Ming's son.
Chang Chuan	Cháng Quán	長拳	Long Fist, Martial Arts style.
Chang Fei	Zhāng Fēi	張飛	Kuan Yu's sworn brother. Represented in black.

Chang Hsiang-Shan	Zhāng Xiángsān	張詳三	*Liohoe Tanglang Chuan* Master.
Chang Hsiang-Wu	Zhāng Xiāngwǔ	張驤伍	Army general, Li Shu-Wen's student.
Chang Kuo-Ming	Zhāng Kèmíng	張克明	*Pachi Chuan* master, initiated by Wu Rong.
Chang Tai Kong	Jiāng Tàigōng	姜太公	Chou Wen Wang's Prime Minister. Studied different combat systems.
Chang Te-Kuei	Zhāng Dékuí	張德奎	*Pimen Tanglang Chuan* Master.
Chang Yao-Ting	Zhāng Yàotíng	張燿庭	*Mitzong Chuan* and *Taitzu Chuan* Master.
Chang Yu-Heng	Zhāng Yùhéng	張玉衡	*Pachi Chuan* master, Chang Ching-Hsing's son.
Chao Ti	Jiǎo Dǐ	角抵	Ancient hunting techniques for knocking down an animal; later used in combat.
Chen Kuo-Chin	Chén Guóqīn	陳國欽	*Pachi Chuan* master, Liu Yun-Chiao's disciple.
Chen Shan-To	Chén Shàndé	陳善德	*Tong Pei Chuan* master, co-founder of *Papu Tanglang Chuan*.
Chen Sui Ching	Shēn Zhuì Jìng	沈墜勁	Sinking energy
Chen Tai Chi Chuan	Chénjiā Tàijí Quán	陳家太極拳	Tai Chi Chuan of the Chen family.
Chen Yu-Shan	Chén Yùshān	陳玉山	*Mitzong Chuan* master
Chi	Qì	氣	Steam, vapor, internal energy.
Chi Chang Pa Tuan	Qī Zhǎng Bā Duǎn	七長八短	The Seven Long and Eight Short.
Chi Chi-Kuan	Qī Jìguāng	戚繼光	Army general from the Ming Dynasty.
Chi Ho	Qì Hé	氣合	Group combat system of Huang Ti's time.

Chi Hsiao Hsin Shu	Jì Xiào Xīn Shū	紀效新書	*New Book Recording Effective Techniques*; military treatise.
Chi Hsing Pu Hua	Qī Xīng Bù Fǎ	七星步法	Seven Stars Step
Chi Kung	Qì Gōng	氣功	"Energy work", revitalizing exercises.
Chi Mo	Jí Mò	即墨	City in Shandong province, were Wang Lang was born.
Chi Pei To	Jí Běi Tóu	集北頭	Liu Yun-Chiao's place of birth.
Chiang Hua-Long	Jiāng Huàlóng	姜化龍	*Chihsing-Meihua Tanglang Chuan* master.
Chihsing Suh	Qīxīng Shì	七星式	Seven Star stance
Chihsing Tanglang Chuan	Qīxīng Tángláng Quán	七星螳螂拳	Seven Star Praying Mantis, Martial Arts style.
Chin Kong	Qīng Gōng	輕功	Technique for very high jumping.
Chin Ming-Chi	Jīn Míngqí	金鳴琦	*Pachi Chuan* master from the *Chin Pachi Chuan* lineage.
Chin Pachi Chuan	Jīn Bājí Quán	金八極拳	A branch of the *Pachi Chuan* lineage.
Chin Shu-Huang	Qín Shǐ Huáng	秦始皇	Founder of the Qin dynasty and uniter of China.
Chin Tien-Shen	Jīn Diànshēng	金殿陞	Chin Ming-Chi's initiated student and Li Shu-Wen's master.
Chin Tuei Lien-huan Pu	Jìn Tuì Liánhuán Bù	進退連環步	Forward and backward linked steps.
Ching	Jīng	精	Essence
Chinkan Ti	Jīngāng Tī	金剛體	Body and mind as strong as a diamond.
Chinna	Qín Ná	擒拿	Clutching and locking techniques.
Chou Tong	Zhōu Tóng	周侗	Monk who taught *Pachi Chuan* to Yuei Fei.

Chou Wen Wang	Zhōu Wén Wáng	周文王	King and compiler of the *I Ching*.
Chou Wu Wang	Zhōu Wǔ Wáng	周武王	Founder of the Zhou dynasty.
Choy Lee Fat	Cài Lǐ Fó	蔡李佛	Martial Arts style. Its name is the surnames Choy and Lee, and the chinese name for Buddha.
Chuan	Quán	拳	Fist. Refers to a Martial Arts form or style.
Chuan Chiao	Chuān Jiǎo	穿腳	Piercing step
Chuan Tao	Quán Tào	拳套	Form exhibition
Fa Ching	Fā Jìng	發勁	Energy projection
Feng Huan-I	Féng Huányì	馮環義	*Papu Tanglang Chuan* master, disciple of Chiang Hua-Long.
Fong Shen Chuan	Fēng Shén Bǎng	封神榜	Book of the investiture of the gods.
Fua Shen	Huàshēn	化身	Embodiment. Third version in which a *Pachi Chuan* form is practiced.
Han	Hànzú	漢族	Majority ethnic group of China.
Han Chi Suh	Hán Jī Shì	寒雞式	Cold Rooster stance
Hou Chuan	Hóu Quán	猴拳	Monkey Fist, Martial Arts style.
Hou Pei	Héběi	河北	Chinese province
Hou Tien Ching	Hòudiān Jīng	后天勁	Non-natural energy of the body.
Houyi	Hòuyì	后羿	Warrior from the Xia dynasty, invented archery.
Hsia Tan Tien	Xià Dāntián	下丹田	Lower Tan Tien. Focal point of energy of essence, located in the lower abdomen.
Hsiao Chi	Xiǎo Jí	小集	Town of Tsang county

Hsiao Pa Wang	Xiǎo Bà Wáng	小霸王	Small Tyrant King
Hsiao Un Ti	Xiào Wén Dì	孝文帝	King who founded the Shaolin monastery.
Hsing-I Chuan	Xíng Yì Quán	形意拳	Mind fist
Hsiong Chang	Xióng Zhǎng	熊掌	Weapon devised by Huang Ti using bear claws.
Hsiong Pu	Xióng Bù	熊步	Bear Step. *Pachi Chuan* step.
Hsu Lan-Cho	Xǔ Lánzhōu	許蘭洲	Army general, employer of Li Shu-Wen.
Hua Ching	Huà Jìng	化勁	Continuity of force and energy.
Hua To	Huá Tuó	華佗	Famous physician who treated Kuan Yu for a poisoned arrow.
Huang Hsian	Huáng Xiàn	黃縣	Huang county, in Shandong province, now called Longkou county.
Huang Lin-Piao	Huáng Línbiāo	黃林彪	*Pikua Chuan* master
Huang Szu-Hai	Huáng Sìhǎi	黃四海	*Pachi Chuan* master, initiated by Chang Kuo-Ming.
Huang Tien-Pa	Huáng Tiānbà	黃天霸	Disciple of Wang Song-Ting.
Huei Yin	Huì Yīn	會陰	Point in the perineum
Hui	Huízú	回族	Sino-Islamic ethnic minority.
Hung Gar Kuan	Hóng Jiā Quán	洪家拳	Hung Family Fist, Martial Arts style.
Huo Pachi	Huó Bājí	活八極	"Alive Pachi". Second version in which a *Pachi Chuan* form is practiced.
Huo Tien-Kuo	Huò Diàngé	霍殿閣	Li Shu-Wen's first disciple.
I-hsing Huan Ying Shu	Yí xíng huàn yǐng shù	移形換影術	Spirit that shifts the body and changes the position of the shadow.

Ing Tanglang	Yìng Tángláng	硬螳螂	Hard Praying Mantis
Kaimen Chuan	Kāimén Quán	開門拳	Opening the door form. First *Pachi Chuan* form.
Kan Pai Hsia Fong	Gānbài xiàfēng	甘拜下风	Traditional way of expressing desire to become someone's disciple.
Kan Rou Shiang Chi	Gāng Róu Xiāngjǐ	剛柔相濟	Union of hardness and softness.
Ke Hung	Gě Hóng	葛洪	Famous Taoist and alchemist, founder of the Wu Tang Shan temple.
Kendo	Jiàndào	劍道	Modern Japanese sword-fighting Martial Art.
Kou Shou	Gōu Shǒu	鉤手	Hook hand, Praying Mantis hand.
Kuan Yu	Guān Yǔ	關羽	Father of Chinese Martial Arts, also known as Kuan Kong or Kuan Ti. Represented in red.
Kuangpan Tanglang Chuan	Guāngbǎn Tángláng Quán	光板螳螂拳	Shining Board Praying Mantis.
Kun Lun	Kūnlún Shān	崑崙山	Martial Arts style. Mountains in Shandong province.
Kung Fu	Gōng Fū	功夫	Cultivated skill
Kung Li	Gōng Lì	功力	Skill developed by intense training.
Kung Pao-Tien	Gōng Bǎotián	宮寶田	*Pakua Chang* Master
Kuoshu	Guóshù	國術	National Art
Lai	Lài	癩	Taoist monk, *Pachi Chuan* Master.
Lai Kuei Yuen	Lái Kuí Yuán	來魁元	Army general who turned into a monk and taught the long spear.

Li Chen-Wu	Lǐ Jiànwú	李健吾	Li Shu-Wen's disciple and Mao Tse Tung's bodyguard.
Li Ching-Lin	Lǐ Jǐnglín	李景林	Government official, employer of Li Shu-Wen.
Li Chuan	Lì Quán	立拳	A position of the fist
Li Kuen-Shan	Lǐ Kūnshān	李崑山	*Chihsing Tanglang Chuan* master.
Li Ping-Hsiao	Lǐ Bǐngxiāo	李炳霄	A disciple of Wang Lang.
Li Shu-Wen	Lǐ Shūwén	李書文	*Pachi Chuan* and *Pikua Chuan* master.
Li Teng-Wu	Lǐ Dēngwǔ	李登五	*Chihsing-Meihua Tanglang Chuan* master, son of Li Kuen-Shan.
Li Yuen-Tzu	Lǐ Yuánzhì	李元智	*Mitzong Chuan* and *Pachi Chuan* master.
Li Yun-Piao	Lǐ Yúnbiǎo	李雲表	*Pikua Chang* master
Li Zhi-Cheng	Lǐ Zhìchéng	李志成	*Pachi Chuan* master, Li Shu-Wen's grandson.
Liang Chi-Tsu	Liáng Jìcí	梁紀慈	*Pachi Chuan* master, disciple of Liu Yun-Chiao. *Meihua Tanglang* master, disciple of Liu Tzu-Yuan.
Lien Wu Chuei	Lián Wǔ Chuí	連五捶	Five strikes with a sigle energy.
Lio Hoe Ta Chiang	Liù Hé Dà Qiāng	六合大槍	Six Unions long spear
Lio Tao	Liù Tāo	六韜	*Six Secret Teachings*, the first Chinese Martial Arts book.
Liohoe Chuan	Liù Hé Quán	六合拳	Six Harmonies Fist, Martial Arts style.
Liohoe Tanglang Chuan	Liù Hé Tángláng Quán	六合螳螂拳	Six Harmonies Praying Mantis Fist, Martial Arts style.

Liu Pei	Liú Bèi	劉備	Founder of the Kingdom of Shu and Kuan Yu's sworn brother. Represented in white.
Liu Tzu-Yuan	Liú Zǔyuǎn	劉祖遠	*Meihua Tanglang Chuan* master, disciple of Chiang Hua-Long.
Liu Yun-Chiao	Liú Yúnqiáo	劉雲樵	*Pachi Chuan*, *Pikua Chuan* and *Pakua Chang* master.
Lo Han Chuan	Luóhàn Quán	羅漢拳	Lohan Fist, Martial Arts style.
Lohan	Luóhàn	羅漢	Saint who has attained enlightenment.
Lun Pei	Lún Bì	倫臂	Strike in circular motion.
Luo Tong	Luó Tuǎn	羅疃	Village of Tsang Zhou County.
Ma Chin-Shan	Mǎ Zhènshān	馬振山	*Chihsing-Meihua Tanglang Chuan* master, disciple of Li Kuen-Shan.
Ma Fong-Tu	Mǎ Fèngtú	馬鳳圖	Li Shu-Wen's disciple
Ma Pu / Ma Suh	Mǎ Bù / Mǎ Shì	馬步 / 馬式	Horse-riding step/stance. Also known as *Chi Ma Pu/ Suh*.
Ma Shu Pachi Chuan	Mǎ Shì Bājí Quán	馬氏八極拳	*Pachi Chuan* of Ma
Ma Shu Shuang Chong Chang	Mǎ Shì Shuāng Chēng Zhǎng	馬式雙撐掌	Horse stance double palm.
Ma Shuang Tao	Mǎ Shuāng Daō	馬雙刀	Ma Double-Broadsword
Ma Ying-Tu	Mǎ Yīngtú	馬英圖	Li Shu-Wen's disciple
Mafeisan	Máfèisǎn	麻沸散	Drug mixture of hemp and strong wine used as anaesthetic in traditional Chinese medicine.
Mahou Tanglang	Mǎhóu Tángláng	馬猴螳螂	Big Monkey Praying Mantis.

Man Ching	Mǎnqīng	滿清	Qing dynasty's ethnic group.
Mang	Mèng	孟	Village of Tsang Zhou County.
Meihua Tanglang Chuan	Méihuā Tángláng Quán	梅花螳螂拳	Plum Flower Praying Mantis, Martial Arts style.
Men	Mén	門	School. Refers to Martial Arts school.
Mi Shou	Mìshǒu	秘手	Secret Hands
Miao Tao	Miáo Dāo	苗刀	Sprout Saber
Ming Men	Mìng Mén	命門	Point in the lower back, between the second and third lumbar vertebra.
Mitzong Chuan	Mízhōng Quán	迷蹤拳	Labyrinth Fist, Martial Arts style.
Mo Nien Shi Rong	Mò niàn shī róng	默念師容	To see your Master in your thought.
Mo Pan Pu	Mò Pán Bù	磨盤步	Grinding step
Mou Cha Kuan	Mò Jiā Quán	莫家拳	Mou family Fist, Martial Arts style.
Nan Liang	Nán Liáng	南良	Name of the village where Li Shu-Wen was born.
Nanking Central Kuoshu Institute	Nánjīng Zhōng Yāng Kuóshù Guǎn	南京中央國術館	Important Martial Arts center of study, established in 1928.
Nei Ching	Nèi Jìng	內勁	Internal energy
Nei Kung	Nèi Gōng	內功	Internal work
Nien Ching	Nián Jìng	黏勁	Sticking energy
Nien Pu	Niǎn Bù	撵步	Deployment step
Pa Ku Wun	Bāguwén	八股文	Eight-legged style of writing used during the Ming and Qing Dynasties.

Pa Men Hsiong Chang	Bā Miàn Xióng Zhǎng	八面熊掌	Sequence of movements developed by Huang Ti for using Hsiong Chan.
Pa Ta Chao Su	Bā Dà Zhāoshì	八大招式	Last form to be learned in *Pachi Chuan*.
Pa Tze Chuan	Pázi Quán	耙子拳	Rake Fist
Pachi Chuan	Bājí Quán	八極拳	Eight Ultimate Fist, Martial Arts style.
Pachi Ta Chang	Bājí Dà Cháng	八極大槍	Eight strong points of the body.
Pachi Tanglang Chuan	Bājí Tángláng Quán	八極螳螂拳	Eight Ultimate Praying Mantis Fist, Martial Arts school created by Master Su Yu-Chang.
Pai	Pài	派	Sect. Refers to Martial Arts school.
Pai Hou	Bái Hè	白鶴	White Crane, Martial Arts style.
Pai Huei	Bǎi Huì	百會	Point near the crown of the head.
Pai Pu	Bǎi Bù	擺步	Pendulum step
Pai Suh	Bài Shì	敗式	*Tan Shan Suh* with the body rotated backwards.
Pai Ta Kung	Pāi Dǎ Gōng	拍打功	Energizing strikes on the body.
Paisu	Bàishī	拜師	Initiation ceremony where the student is accepted as indoor disciple.
Pakua Chang	Bāguà Zhǎng	八卦掌	Eight Trigram Palm. Martial Arts style.
Panma Suh	Bàn Mǎ Shì	半馬式	Half horse-riding stance.
Pao Fa Ching	Bào Fā Jìng	爆發勁	Explosive energy
Pao Piao	Bǎobiāo	保鏢	Bodyguard
Paoputzu	Bàopǔzǐ	抱樸子	*The book of the master who embraces simplicity*, treatise by Ke Hung.

Papu Kanchan	Bābù Gǎnchán	八步趕蟬	Eight steps to catch the cicada.
Papu Tanglang Chuan	Bābù Tángláng Quán	八步螳螂拳	Eight-step Praying Mantis, Martial Arts style.
Pei Yang	Běi Yáng Dà Xué	北洋大學	Present day Tianjin University.
Pek Mei	Bái Méi	白眉	White Eyebrow, Martial Arts style.
Peng Chuan	Bēng Quán	崩拳	Rebound fist
Pi	Pǐ	癖	*Pachi Chuan* master, disciple of the monk Lai.
Pi Pao	Pī Bào	劈抱	Chop and embrace
Pien Hua Chi Tzu	Biànhuà Qìzhì	變化氣質	Development of the energy and structure of the body.
Pikua Chuan	Pīguà Quán	劈掛拳	Chop-hanging fist, Martial Arts style.
Pimen Tanglang Chuan	Bìmén Tángláng Quán	秘門螳螂拳	Secret door Praying Mantis, Martial Arts style.
Pu Ting Pu Pa Suh	Bù Dīng Bù Bā Shì	不丁不八式	Neither "T" nor "Eight" stance.
Pu Tue Suh	Pū Tuǐ Shì	仆腿式	Low leg stance
Pu Yi	Pǔyí	溥儀	The last emperor of China.
Pusa	Púsà	菩薩	Bodhisattva, enlightened being.
Ren Mo	Rèn Mò	任脈	Directing Vessel, a meridian.
Rou Tanglang	Róu Tángláng	柔螳螂	Soft Praying Mantis
Ruhuan Suh	Rùhuán Shì	入環式	Close the Door stance
San Chin Kong	Sān qīng gōng	三青宮	Temple where Wang Lang taught Praying Mantis.
San Ta	Sǎndǎ	散打	Combat exhibition

San Tsai	Sān Cái	三才	The three treasures: Heaven, Earth and Mankind.
San Tsai Chi	Sān Cái Jù	三才聚	Union of spirit, energy and essence to reach a superior level.
San Tsai Chi Ching	Sān Cái Jù Jìng	三才聚勁	Projection of the energy of the Three Sages.
Shaolin	Shǎolín	少林	Name of a Chan Buddhist Temple where a homonymous Martial Arts style was born.
Shen	Shén	神	Spirit
Shen Chiang Li	Shén Qiāng Lǐ	神槍李	"Li, the spear wizard", nickname of Li Shu-Wen.
Shen Hsiao Tao Ren	Shēng Xiāo Dào Rén	升霄道人	A Taoist monk, disciple of Wang Lang.
Shen Long Tien Ti	Shén Lóng Tiāndì	神龍天地	Prehistoric martial activities.
Shen Tien Chi	Xiān Tiān Qì	先天氣	Natural energy of the body.
Shen Yen	Shén Yǎn	神眼	Eye of Saint
Shi Suh	Xū Shì	虛式	Emtpy stance
Shih Liu Suh	Sì Liù Shì	四六式	Four-Six Stance
Shuai Chiao	Shuāi Jiǎo	摔角	Form of wrestling that uses grappling and dislocations.
So Shen Fa	Suō Shēn Fǎ	縮身法	Surrender technique
Song Chu-Long	Sòng Jǔlóng	宋舉龍	*Meihua Tanglang Chuan* master, disciple of Liu Tzu-Yuan.
Song Jiang Zhen	Sòng Jiāngzhèn	宋江陣	Platoon weapon manouvres.
Su Yu-Chang	Sū Yùzhāng	蘇昱彰	Master of *Tanglang Chuan, Pachi Chuan, Pikua Chuan, Pakua Chang, Tai Chi Chuan* and *Hsing-I*.

Suaishou Tanglang Chuan	Shuāi shǒu Tángláng Quán	摔手螳螂	Whip Hand style Praying Mantis.
Suh Pachi	Sǐ Bājí	死八極	"Dead" Pachi. Initial version in which a *Pachi Chuan* form is practiced.
Suh Tzu Ching	Shí Zì Jìng	十字勁	Energy in form of cross.
Sun Tzu Ping Fa	Sūn Zǐ Bīng Fǎ	孫子兵法	*The Art of War*, classic Martial Arts book written by Sun Wu.
Sun Wu	Sūn Wǔ	孫武	Army general, author of the Sun Tzu Ping Fa.
Ta Chang	Tā Zhǎng	塌掌	Crushing hand
Ta Mo	Dá Mó	達摩	Bodhidharma
Ta Tsuei	Dà Zhuī	大椎	Point in the lower neck, below the prominence of the 7th cervical vertebra.
Tai Chi	Tàijí	太極	The Supreme Ultimate
Tai Chi Chuan	Tàijí Quán	太極拳	Supreme Ultimate Fist, Martial Arts style.
Tai She-Che	Dài Shìzhé	戴士哲	*Liohoe Tanglang Chuan* master, disciple of Chang Hsiang-Shan.
Taitzu Chang Chuan	Tàizǔ Cháng Quán	太祖長拳	Great Ancestor Long Fist, Martial Arts style.
Tan	Dàn	彈	Elastic energy
Tan Shan Suh/Pu	Dēng Shān Shì/Bù	登山式 / 步	Mountain-climbing stance/step.
Tan Tien	Dāntián	丹田	Focal point of energy
Tang Tung	Dān Tōng	單通	Army general, enemy of Wang Lang.
Tanglang Chuan	Tángláng Quán	螳螂拳	Praying Mantis Fist, Martial Arts style.
Tao	Dào	道	The way
Tao In Chi Kung	Dǎo Yǐn Qì Gōng	導引氣功	Exercises to channel energy through the meridians.

Tao Lu	Tào Lù	套路	Forms
Ti Kung	Dì Gōng	地功	Ground combat
Tie Chi	Tiě Chǐ	铁齿	Iron tooth
Tie Kuo Po	Tiě Gē Bó	鐵胳膊	Iron Arm
Tien Tzu	Tiānzǐ	天子	Master Liu Yun-Chiao's name as a secret agent.
Tientsin	Tiānjīn	天津	Important Chinese city
Tientsin Wusu	Tiānjīn Wǔshì Huì	天津武士會	Tientsin Kung Fu association.
Ting Ching	Tīng Jìng	聽勁	Listening energy
Ting Fa-Hsiang	Dīng Fāxiáng	丁發詳	*Pachi Chuan* master
Ting Hsin Chou	Dǐng Xīn Zhǒu	頂心肘	High elbow to the heart.
Ting Pu	Dīng Bù	丁步	"T" Step
Ting Tzu Pa Pu Suh	Dīng Zì Bā Bù Shì	丁字八步式	Eight Forms to generate Energy in a Triangle.
Ting Tzu-Cheng	Dīng Zìchéng	丁子成	Liohoe Tanglang Chuan Master.
To Liang Huan Tzu Pu	Tōu Liáng Huàn Zhù Bù	偷樑換柱步	Steps to secretly substitute the good spine by a bad one.
Toh Hua Ching	Tòu Huà Jìng	透化勁	Penetrating energy
Tong Chong-I	Tóng Zhōngyì	佟忠義	*Liohoe Chuan* and *Shuai Chiao* master.
Tong Pei Chuan	Tōng Bēi Quán	通背拳	Through the back Fist, Martial Arts style.
Tong Shan	Dōngshān Xiāng	東山鄉	Village where Master Su was born.
Tsang Zhou	Cāng Zhōu	滄州	Prefectural city, located in Hou Pei province.
Tsao Tsao	Cáo Cāo	曹操	Kuan Yu's staunch enemy.
Tsong Tan Tien	Zhōng Dāntián	中丹田	Middle Tan Tien, located at the level of the heart.
Tsun Ching	Cùn Jìng	寸勁	Transmission of energy with a short range strike (1 inch).

Tsun Na	Cùn Nà	寸那	Transmission of energy with a thrust (from contacting position).
Tsun Toh	Cùn Tòu	寸透	Transmission of energy that goes through the opponent.
Tu Li Suh	Dúlì Shì	獨立式	Stand in one leg stance.
Tu Mo	Dū Mò	督脈	Governing Vessel, a meridian.
Tung Chang	Tōng Chán	通禪大師	Shaolin monk who took Wang Lang to the Shaolin temple.
Tuo Chang	Tuō Zhǎng	托掌	Support palm
Tzuei Pai Hou Chuan	Zuì Bái Hóu Quán	醉白猴拳	Drunk White Monkey form.
Tzuei Tanglang Chuan	Zuì Tángláng Quán	醉螳螂拳	Drunk Praying Mantis form.
Tzui Chih-Ko	Cuī Zhìguó	崔治國	*Chihsing-Meihua Tanglang Chuan* master, adopted son of Li Kuen-Shan.
Tzuo You Pen Hua Pu	Zuǒ Yòu Biàn Huà Bù	左右变化步	Left-right changing steps.
Wang Chiu-Hsiung	Wáng Qiūxióng	王秋雄	*Papu Tanglang Chuan* master, disciple of Wei Hsiao-Tang.
Wang Chong-Chen	Wáng Zhōngqìng	王中慶	*Hsing-I* and *Pakua* master, co-founder of *Papu Tanglang Chuan*.
Wang Lang	Wáng Lǎng	王朗	Modern founder of the Praying Mantis style.
Wang Song-Ting	Wáng Sōngtián	王松田	Martial Arts master, specialized in weapons.
Wei Chi	Wèi Qì	衛氣	Circuit of energy
Wei Hsiao-Tang	Wèi Xiàotáng	衛笑堂	*Papu Tanglang Chuan* Master.
Wei San	Wèi Sān	魏三	*Liohoe Tanglang* master

Wei Shien	Wéi Xiàn	潍县	County of Shandong province, now called Weifang.
Wing Chun	Yǒng Chūn	永春	Eternal Springtime, Martial Arts style.
Wu Chia Tai Chi Chuan	Wújiā Tàijí Quán	吴家太極拳	Tai Chi Chuan of the Wu family.
Wu Chin Hsi	Wǔ Qín Xì	五禽戲	*Movements of Five Playing Animals*, book on health-oriented Chi Kung.
Wu Chung	Wú Zhōng	吴鐘	*Pachi Chuan* master, the first in the recorded history of the style.
Wu Rong	Wú Róng	吴榮	*Pachi Chuan* master; Wu Chung's daughter.
Wu Shing Chi	Wǔ Xíng Qì	五行氣	Energy of the Five Elements.
Wu Shing Chi Ching	Wǔ Xíng Qì Jìng	五行氣勁	Projection of energy of the Five Elements.
Wu Tang Shan	Wǔdāng Shān	武當山	Group of Taoist monasteries located in a homonymous mountain range.
Wu-I	Wǔyì	武藝	Superior Martial Art
Wukung	Wǔ Gōng	武功	Martial work
Wushu	Wǔ Shù	武術	Martial Art
Wutan Kuo-shu Tuikuang Chunghsin	wǔtán guóshù tuīguǎng zhōngxīn	武壇國術推廣中心	Wutan Martial Arts Development Center.
Yi Shing Huan Pu	Yí Xíng Huàn Bù	移形換步	Magic steps
Yin Yang Liang Pu Chie	Yīn Yáng Liǎng Bù Jiē	陰陽兩不接	Where Yin and Yang cannot be together.
Ying Chi	Yíng Qì	营氣	Circuit of energy
Ying Chua Chuan	Yīng Zhuǎ Quán	鷹爪拳	Eagle Claw Fist, Martial Arts style.
Yueh Fei	Yuè Fēi	岳飛	Army general, founder of *Pachi Chuan*.
Yuhuan Suh	Yùhuán Shì	玉環式	Jade Ring stance

Pachi Tanglang International Martial Arts Institute is a cultural association for the dissemination and teaching of the traditional aspects of Chinese culture, including philosophy, martial arts, acupuncture and meditation. Its founder and president is Master Su Yu-Chang. Its head office is in Taipei, Taiwan, with branches in several countries.
For more information, contact:

Taiwan Tatungshan Pachimen International Martial Arts Institute
5th Floor, No. 26, Section 4, Xinyi Road, Da'an District
Taipei City 106
Taiwan (R.O.C.)
www.pachimen.com
ycsu.master@msa.hinet.net
Tel: +886-2-27000787

EUROPE

The Netherlands
Pachi Tanglang Chuan Holland
Reeuwijk, The Netherlands
www.pachitanglang.nl
info@pachitanglang.nl

Norway
Pachi Tanglang Martial Arts Institute
Sørlandet, Norway
www.pachitanglangnorway.webs.com
marit@pachitanglang.com

Spain, Barcelona
Pachi Tanglang Chuen Barcelona
Barcelona, Spain
www.pachitanglangbarcelona.com
info@pachitanglangbarcelona.com

Spain, Mallorca
Asociación Europea Pachi Tanglang
    Chuen y Tao
Palma de Mallorca, Spain
www.centropachitanglang.com
info@centropachitanglang.com

United Kingdom
Pachi Tanglang Cambridge
Cambridge, UK
www.sites.google.com/site/pachicambridge
pachitanglangcambridge@gmail.com

THE AMERICAS

New York
Pachi Tanglang Martial Arts
    Institute U.S.A.
New York City, NY
www.pachitanglang.com
cary@pachitanglang.com

Venezuela
http://pachitanglangvenezuela.weebly.com
· **Caracas**
Pachi Tanglang Caracas
robertorozco21@gmail.com

· **Mérida**
Pachi Tanglang Mérida
pachitanglangmerida@gmail.com

ASIA

Japan
Pachi Tanglang Martial Arts
    Institute Japan
Tokyo, Japan
www.pachitanglang.jp
info@pachitanglang.jp

Taiwan, Kaohsiung
Pachi Tanglang International Taiwan
Kaohsiung, Taiwan
www.pachitanglang.org.tw
service@pachitanglang.org.tw

www.ingramcontent.com/pod-product-compliance
Lightning Source LLC
Chambersburg PA
CBHW081153020426
42333CB00020B/2494